SHAPED BY THE NUANCED CONSTITUTION

There is growing judicial, academic and political interest in the concept of common law constitutional rights. Concurrently, significant public law judgments, including *R (Miller) v The Prime Minister*, *R (Begum) v Special Immigration Appeals Commission* and *R (Privacy International) v Investigatory Powers Tribunal*, continue to sustain and enrich the academic debate on the nature of the UK constitution.

Bringing these two highly topical themes together, the book argues, firstly, that neither common law constitutionalism nor political constitutionalism adequately captures the nature of public law litigation because neither is fully able to account for the co-existence and interplay between parliamentary sovereignty and the rule of law. Advancing the idea of a 'nuanced' constitution instead, the book then provides an in-depth analysis of common law constitutional rights, looking at their history, conceptual foundations, contemporary characteristics, coverage and resilience.

In doing so, this book highlights and re-conceptualises the dynamics and mechanisms of constitutional law adjudication and provides the first comprehensive critique of common law constitutional rights jurisprudence. It is centred around extensive case law analysis which focuses predominantly on recent Supreme Court judgments.

Shaped by the Nuanced Constitution

A Critique of Common Law Constitutional Rights

Christina Lienen

•HART•
OXFORD • LONDON • NEW YORK • NEW DELHI • SYDNEY

HART PUBLISHING

Bloomsbury Publishing Plc

Kemp House, Chawley Park, Cumnor Hill, Oxford, OX2 9PH, UK

1385 Broadway, New York, NY 10018, USA

29 Earlsfort Terrace, Dublin 2, Ireland

HART PUBLISHING, the Hart/Stag logo, BLOOMSBURY and the Diana logo are trademarks of Bloomsbury Publishing Plc

First published in Great Britain 2023

A catalogue record for this book is available from the British Library.

Library of Congress Cataloging-in-Publication data

Names: Lienen, Christina, author.

Title: Shaped by the nuanced constitution : a critique of common law constitutional rights / Christina Lienen.

Description: Oxford ; New York : Hart, 2023. | Based on author's thesis (doctoral – University College London, 2020). | Includes bibliographical references and index. | Summary: "This book highlights and re-conceptualises the dynamics and mechanisms of constitutional law adjudication and provides the first comprehensive critique of common law constitutional rights jurisprudence. It is centered around extensive case law analysis which focuses predominantly on recent Supreme Court judgments. There is growing judicial, academic and political interest in the concept of common law constitutional rights. Concurrently, significant public law judgments, including R (Miller) v The Prime Minister, R (Begum) v Special Immigration Appeals Commission, and Privacy International v Investigatory Powers Tribunal continue to sustain and enrich the academic debate on the nature of the UK constitution. Bringing these two highly topical themes together, the book argues, firstly, that neither common law constitutionalism nor political constitutionalism adequately capture the nature of public law litigation because neither is fully able to account for the co-existence and interplay between parliamentary sovereignty and the rule of law. Advancing the idea of a 'nuanced' constitution instead, the book then provides an in-depth analysis of common law constitutional rights, looking at their history, conceptual foundations, contemporary characteristics, coverage, and resilience"— Provided by publisher.

Identifiers: LCCN 2022055725 (print) | LCCN 2022055726 (ebook) | ISBN 9781509948802 (hardback) | ISBN 9781509948840 (paperback) | ISBN 9781509948826 (pdf) | ISBN 9781509948819 (Epub)

Subjects: LCSH: Civil rights—Great Britain. | Constitutional law—Great Britain. | Common law—England.

Classification: LCC KD4080 .L54 2023 (print) | LCC KD4080 (ebook) | DDC 342.4108/5—dc23/eng/20230206

LC record available at https://lccn.loc.gov/2022055725

LC ebook record available at https://lccn.loc.gov/2022055726

ISBN: HB: 978-1-50994-880-2
ePDF: 978-1-50994-882-6
ePub: 978-1-50994-881-9

Typeset by Compuscript Ltd, Shannon

CONTENTS

Table of Cases..........ix
Table of Legislation..........xix

Introduction..........**1**
I. The Constitutional Context..........4
II. The Leading Two Theories on Public Power and an Alternative Reading of the Constitution..........5
III. The Nuanced Constitution..........6
IV. Common Law Constitutional Rights..........7
V. The Questions this Book Sets Out to Answer..........10
VI. The Structure, Style and Chapters of this Book..........11
A. Chapter One..........11
B. Chapter Two..........12
C. Chapter Three..........13
D. Chapter Four..........14
E. Chapter Five..........16

PART I
A THIRD ALTERNATIVE – THE NUANCED CONSTITUTION

1. An Introduction to the Nuanced Constitution..........**21**
I. The Two Competing Forms of Constitutionalism..........21
II. Not One or the Other, but Both: Thesis and Methodology..........25
III. Why the UK Constitution is not Political in Nature..........29
A. Parliamentary Sovereignty is not Uniformly Endorsed as the UK's Supreme Constitutional Principle..........30
B. Value-Driven Interpretation of Primary and Secondary Legislation, Including Through Common Law Constitutional Rights..........33
C. The Recognition of Constitutional Statutes..........39
IV. Why is the Nuanced Constitution not the Common Law Constitution?..........42
V. Taking Stock..........47

VI. How Did We Get Here? 48
A. European Law 48
B. The English Common Law 50
VII. A Closer Look at the Constitution and Common Law Constitutional Rights 53

2. A Closer Look at the Nuanced Constitution Through Four Case Studies 54
I. *R (Privacy International) v IPT* 55
A. The Facts 57
B. The Divisional Court Judgment 58
C. The Court of Appeal Judgment 59
D. *Privacy International* in the Supreme Court: Is Parliament Truly Sovereign? 60
II. *R (Miller) v Prime Minister* 63
A. The Facts 64
B. *Miller v Prime Minister* in the Court of Sessions and the Divisional Court 64
C. The Supreme Court's Unanimous, Ground-Breaking Decision 65
III. The Common Law Constitutionalist Side of the Spectrum: Themes, Characteristics and Vulnerabilities 69
IV. *R (Begum) v Special Immigration Appeals Commission* 74
A. The Facts 74
B. The Court of Appeal Decision 76
C. The Supreme Court Decision 77
V. *R (O (A Child)) v Secretary of State for the Home Department* 81
A. The Facts 82
B. The High Court's and Court of Appeal's Decisions 83
C. The Supreme Court's Decision: Limiting the Effect of *UNISON* by Creating a New Constitutional Principle 84
VI. Rights, Reasoning and Precedent on the Political Constitutionalist Side of the Spectrum 87

PART II
COMMON LAW CONSTITUTIONAL RIGHTS

3. A Short History of Common Law Constitutional Rights 95
I. Three Famous Antecedents: A Tale of Precedents, Mythmaking and Common Law Legacy 98

II. The First Modern Phase of Common Law Constitutional Rights Jurisprudence 104
A. Examples of Common Law Constitutional Rights and their Claim to Sufficiency During the First Phase 105
B. Enabling and Contributing Factors: Constitutional Trajectory and the European Mirror 107
III. Phase Two: In the Shadow of the Human Rights Act? 112
IV. Contemporary Common Law Constitutional Rights Jurisprudence in the Supreme Court: Putting the Common Law Back on the Map 116

4. The Nature and Characteristics of Common Law Constitutional Rights 123
I. The Positive and Negative Dimensions of Common Law Constitutional Rights 126
II. The Six Characteristics Stemming from Five Leading Cases: Approach, Summary and Facts 129
A. *R (Guardian News) v City of Westminster Magistrates' Court* 131
B. *Kennedy v Charity Commission* and *A v BBC* 132
C. *R (UNISON) v Lord Chancellor* 134
III. The First Characteristic: Rights Specific Conceptualisations of Jurisdiction to Develop Domestic Rights Jurisprudence 136
IV. The Second Characteristic: The Principle of Legality 139
V. The Third Characteristic: Turning to the Common Law First (but not Exclusively) 142
VI. The Fourth Characteristic: A Fluid Notion of Precedent and the Influence of Non-Legal Sources 147
VII. The Fifth Characteristic: Domestic Validation Through Legal Comparativism 154
VIII. The Sixth Characteristic: Proportionality Review 156
IX. Taking Stock 159

PART III
RIGHTS UNDER THE NUANCED CONSTITUTION

5. The Shortcomings of the Nuanced Constitution: Rights Protection, Unlimited Legislative Power and the English Common Law 163
I. The Uncertainties Underlying Common Law Constitutional Rights Jurisprudence: Theories, Sources and Values 164
II. The Trump Card: Parliamentary Sovereignty and Fundamental Rights 169

III. The English Common Law: Simultaneous Facilitator and Impediment 172
IV. Where We are at: A Snapshot of the Constitutional Rights Recognised under the Nuanced Constitution 175
V. The Constitutional Legacy of *UNISON* and *Privacy International* 182
VI. Where Does this Leave Us? Rights Protection, Unlimited Legislative Power and the Question of Legitimacy 185
VII. The Way Forward 186

Bibliography *193*
Index *203*

TABLE OF CASES

A Local Authority v DL [2012] EWCA Civ 253, [2013] Fam 1 137
A v B (Investigatory Powers Tribunal: Jurisdiction) [2009] UKSC 12, [2010] 2 AC 1 58
A v BBC [2014] UKSC 25, [2015] AC 588 ....15, 34, 49, 117, 119, 129, 131–34, 137–38, 141, 143, 148, 154, 166, 176, 183
A v Her Majesty's Treasury [2008] EWHC 869 (Admin), [2008] 3 All ER 361 176
A v Secretary of State for the Home Department [2005] UKHL 71, [2006] 2 AC 221 ....167–68, 177
Al Rawi v Security Service [2011] UKSC 34, [2012] 1 AC 531 176
Alam and Khan v United Kingdom App no 2991/66 (1967) 24 CD 116 104
Allister v Secretary of State for Northern Ireland, Peeples v Prime Minister [2022] NICA 15, [2022] 3 CMLR 8 82
Anisminic Ltd v Foreign Compensation Commission [1969] 2 AC 147 (HL) 53, 56, 61, 109
Armes v Nottinghamshire CC [2015] EWCA Civ 1139, [2016] QB 739 38
Armes v Nottinghamshire CC [2017] UKSC 60, [2018] AC 355 .... 38, 52
Associated Provincial Picture Houses Ltd v Wednesbury Corporation [1948] 1 KB 223 (CA) 107, 156
Association of British Civilian Internees Far East Region v Secretary of State for Defence [2002] EWHC 2119 (Admin), [2002] CLY 46 178
Attorney-General v BBC [2022] EWHC 826 (QB), [2022] 4 WLR 74 87
Attorney-General v Blake [2001] 1 AC 268 (HL), [2000] 3 WLR 625 176
Attorney-General v Observer Ltd (No 2) [1990] 1 AC 109 (HL) 106
B v Secretary of State for Justice [2011] EWCA Civ 1608, [2012] 1 WLR 2043 177
Bank Mellat v Her Majesty's Treasury (No 2) [2013] UKSC 39, [2014] AC 700 156
Beghal v DPP [2015] UKSC 49, [2016] AC 88 ....44–45, 47, 130, 142, 177, 181
Begum v Special Immigration Appeals Commission and Others [2020] EWCA Civ 918, [2020] 1 WLR 426 76–77
Bishopsgate Investment Management Ltd v Maxwell [1993] Ch 1 (CA) 181
Bremer Vulkan Schiffbau und Maschinenfabrik v South India Shipping Corporation Ltd [1981] AC 909, [1981] 2 WLR 141 ....137, 156, 176

Browne v The Parole Board of England & Wales [2018] EWCA Civ 2024 (unreported). 158
Campbell v Mirror Group Newspapers Ltd [2004] UKHL 22, [2004] 2 AC 457.... 174, 179
Capital & Counties Plc v Hampshire CC [1997] QB 1004 127
Carnduff v Rock [2001] EWCA Civ 680, [2001] 1 WLR 1786.... 80, 89
Case 222/84 Johnston v Chief Constable of the Royal Ulster Constabulary [1986] ECR 1651 111
Case 29/69 Stauder v City of Ulm [1969] ECR 419; *Case 11/70 Internationale Handelsgesellschaft mbH v Einfuhr- und Vorratsstelle fur Getreide und Futtermittel* [1970] ECR 1125....111
Chan Wing-Siu v The Queen [1985] 1 AC 168 (UKPC) 173
Cheshire West and Chester Council v P [2011] EWCA Civ 1257, [2012] PTSR 1447....28
Cheshire West and Chester Council v P [2011] EWHC 1330 (Fam)....28
Cheshire West and Chester Council v P and another [2014] UKSC 19, [2014] AC 896....28
Chester v Bateson [1920] 1 KB 829 (KB) 836.... 141, 176
Chesterfield Propertie de Walden Estates s Plc v Secretary of State for the Environment (1998) 76 P&CR 117, [1998] JPL 568....176
Chorlton v Lings (186869) LR 4 CP 374 (COCP) 383....174
Church of Scientology of California v Department of Health and Social Security [1979] 1 WLR 723 (CA) 138
Colonial Sugar Refining Company Ltd v Melbourne Harbour Trust Commissioners [1927] AC 343....125
Commissioner of Police of the Metropolis v DSD and another [2018] UKSC 11, [2019] AC 196.... 49, 127
Cooper v Wandsworth Board of Works [1863] 143 ER 414, (1863) 14 CB NS 180 (COCP) 144, 150, 168
Council of Civil Service Unions v Minister for the Civil Service [1985] AC 374, [1984] 3 WLR 1174 .... 63, 66
Cox v Ministry of Justice [2016] UKSC 10, [2016] AC 660 38
Derbyshire CC v Times Newspaper Ltd [1993] AC 534 (HL) 106–07, 118, 176
Douglas v Hello! Ltd (No 6) [2005] EWCA Civ 595, [2006] QB 125....176
Dover DC v Campaign to Protect Rural England [2017] UKSC 79, [2018] 1 WLR 108 51–52
Dr Bonham's Case 77 ER 638, (1608) 8 Co Rep 107.... 102–04
Entick v Carrington (1765) 2 Wilson, KB 275, 95 ER 807.... 57, 66, 98–100, 123
G and H v Upper Tribunal and SSHD [2016] EWHC 239 (Admin)....4
Ghaidan v Godin-Mendoza [2004] UKHL 30, [2004] 2 AC 557 .... 24, 114
Gillan v United Kingdom (2010) 50 EHRR 1105 45
GIO Personal Investment Services Ltd v Liverpool & London Steamship Protection and Indemnity Association Ltd [1999] 1 WLR 984 (CA)....138

Gorringe v Calderdale Metropolitan Borough Council [2004] UKHL 15, [2004] 1 WLR 1057 127
Gregson v Gilbert 99 ER 629 102
Her Majesty's Treasury v Mohammed Jabar Ahmed [2010] UKSC 1, [2010] 2 AC 697 186
Hirst v the United Kingdom (2006) 42 EHRR 41 120
HM Advocate v Montgomery (David Shields) (2000) JC 111 145
Hollins v Fowler (1874–75) LR 7 HL 757 96
Huang v Secretary of State for the Home Department [2007] UKHL 11, [2007] 2 AC 167 156
Hurtado v California (1884) 110 US 516 181–82
Hutchings' Application for Judicial Review [2019] UKSC 26, [2020] NI 801 41
In Re Racal Communications Ltd [1981] AC 374 (HL) 109–10
In Re S-C (Mental patient: habeas corpus) [1996] QB 599 (CA) 603 177
In the matter of D (A Child) [2017] EWCA Civ 1695, [2018] PTSR 1791 177
Iraqi Civilians v Ministry of Defence and another [2017] UKSC 1, [2017] AC 649 113
Irish Bank Resolution Corp Ltd (In Special Liquidation) v Revenue and Customs Commissioners [2020] EWCA Civ 1128, [2020] STC 1946 40
JK v Revenue and Customs Commissioners [2019] UKFTT 411 (TC), [2019] SFTD 1094 148
Joanna Cherry MP and others v the Advocate General [2019] CSIH 49 64–65
Joanna Cherry MP and others v the Advocate General [2019] CSOH 70 64
Kennedy v Charity Commission [2014] UKSC 20, [2015] AC 455 .... 15, 34, 49, 52, 116–18, 129, 131–34, 137–41, 143–48, 151, 158, 166, 176, 189
Kent v Griffiths (No 3) [2001] QB 36, [2000] 2 WLR 1158 127
Kruse v Johnson [1898] 2 QB 91 (QB) 177
Langley v North West Water Authority [1991] 1 WLR 697, [1991] 3 All ER 610 137
Lanphier v Phipos (1838) 8 C&P 475, 173 ER 581 127
Lee v Ashers Baking Co Ltd and others [2018] UKSC 49, [2018] 3 WLR 1294 179
Liversidge v Anderson [1942] AC 206 (HL) 107
London Historic Parks and Gardens Trust v Minister of State for Housing [2022] EWHC 829 (Admin) 82
Magyar Helsinki Bizottság v Hungary App no 18030/11 (ECtHR, 8 November 2016) 145
Manchester City Council v Pinnock [2010] UKSC 45, [2011] 2 AC 104 27
Marcel v Commissioner of Police of Metropolis [1992] Ch 225, [1991] 2 WLR 1118 106
McCartan Turkington Breen v Times Newspapers Ltd [2001] 2 AC 277 113

McDonald v McDonald [2016] UKSC 28, [2017] AC 273 28
Mellacher v Austria (1990) 12 EHRR 391 46
Metropolitan Asylum District Managers v Hill (1881) 6 AC 193 125
Michael and others (FC) v The Chief Constable of South Wales Police and another [2015] UKSC 2, [2015] AC 1732 127
Mohammed (Serdar) v Ministry of Defence [2017] UKSC 1, [2017] AC 649 67
Montgomery v Lanarkshire Health Board [2015] UKSC 11, [2015] AC 1430 .... 49, 176, 181
Moohan v Lord Advocate [2014] UKSC 67, [2015] AC 901 .... 41, 65, 73, 118, 121, 130, 147, 154, 173, 177, 180, 190
Morris v Beardmore [1981] AC 446 .... 106–07, 176
Muuse v Secretary of State for the Home Department [2010] EWCA Civ 453, [2010] CLY 77 72
Nicklinson v United Kingdom App nos 2478/15 and 1787/15 (16 July 2015) 43
O (A Child) v Rhodes [2015] UKSC 32, [2016] AC 219 9
O'Reilly v Mackman [1983] 2 AC 237 (HL) 57, 61
Padfield v Minister of Agriculture, Fisheries and Food [1968] AC 997, [1968] 2 WLR 924 .... 72, 108–09
Paula Gallagher & Mary McCarthy v Basildon District Council v Commission for Local Administration in England [2010] EWHC 2824 (Admin), [2011] PTSR 731 72
Peake v Automotive Products Ltd [1978] QB 233 (CA) 178
Petition of A v Secretary of State for the Home Department [2013] CSIH 43, 2013 SC 533 133
Pham v Secretary of State for the Home Department [2015] UKSC 19, [2015] 1 WLR 1591 157
PJS v News Group Newspapers Ltd [2016] UKSC 26, [2016] AC 1081 .... 118, 174, 176
Privacy International v SSFCA [2016] UKIP Trib 14_85-CH 57
QX v Secretary of State for the Home Department [2022] EWHC 836 (Admin), [2022] ACD 97 (appeal outstanding) 88
R (A, J, K, B and F) v Secretary of State for the Home Department [2022] EWHC 360 (Admin), [2022] ACD 65 40
R (Amin) v Secretary of State for the Home Department [2003] UKHL 51, [2004] 1 AC 653 .... 128, 153, 177, 179
R (Anufrijeva) v Secretary of State for the Home Department [2003] UKHL 36, [2004] 1 AC 604 113
R (BA) v Secretary of State for Health [2017] EWHC 2815 (Admin), [2018] 4 WLR 2 179
R (Bancoult) v Foreign Secretary (No 2) [2008] UKHL 61, [2009] 1 AC 453 90
R (Bancoult) v Secretary of State for Foreign and Commonwealth Affairs (No 2) [2001] QB 1067, [2001] 2 WLR 1219 126

R (Barclay and another) v Secretary of State for Justice and the Lord Chancellor and others [2014] UKSC 54, [2015] AC 276 176
R (Begum) v Secretary of State for the Home Department [2021] UKSC 7, [2021] AC 765 46
R (Bourgass and another) v Secretary of State for Justice [2015] UKSC 54, [2016] AC 384 176
R (Buckinghamshire CC) v Secretary of State for Transport [2014] UKSC 3, [2014] 1 WLR 324 .... 39, 114, 121
R (C) v Secretary of State for Justice [2016] UKSC 2, [2016] AC 1081, [2016] 1 WLR 444 .... 118, 148, 176
R (Carlile) v Secretary of State for the Home Department [2014] UKSC 60, [2015] AC 945 87
R (Cart) v Upper Tribunal [2011] UKSC 28, [2012] 1 AC 663 .... 4, 58, 61
R (Conway) v Secretary of State for Justice [2018] EWCA Civ 1431, [2020] QB 1 .... 177, 179
R (Coughlan) v Minister for the Cabinet Office [2022] UKSC 11, [2022] 1 WLR 2389 82
R (Daly) v Secretary of State for the Home Department [2001] UKHL 26, [2001] 2 AC 532 .... 36, 113, 183
R (Edwards) v Environment Agency [2010] UKSC 57, [2011] 1 WLR 79 166
R (Elgizouli) v Secretary of State for the Home Department [2020] UKSC 10, [2021] AC 937 .... 9, 118, 128, 130, 133, 144–45, 147, 151, 153, 168, 174, 179, 180
R (Evans) v Attorney-General [2015] UKSC 21, [2015] AC 1787 .... 30, 34, 39, 48, 71, 119, 121, 134, 171
R (Gallagher) v The Competition and Markets Authority [2018] UKSC 25, [2019] AC 96 168
R (Guardian News and Media Ltd) v City of Westminster Magistrates' Court [2012] EWCA Civ 420, [2013] QB 618 .... 15, 117–18, 129, 131, 134, 138, 143, 155, 166, 176
R (Gujra) v Crown Prosecution Service [2012] UKSC 52, [2013] 1 AC 484 176
R (H) v Secretary of State for Health and Social Care [2019] EWHC 2095 (Admin) (30 July 2019, unreported) 44
R (Halligen) v Secretary of State for the Home Department [2012] UKSC 20, [2012] 1 WLR 1604 [31] 177
R (Haworth) v Revenue and Customs Commissioners [2021] UKSC 25, [2021] 1 WLR 3521 36–38
R (Jackson) v Attorney General [2005] UKHL 56, [2006] 1 AC 262 .... 24, 33, 38, 121
R (JL) v Secretary of State for Defence [2012] EWHC 2216 (Admin), [2012] AC 121 27

R (Joint Council for the Welfare of Immigrants) v Secretary of State for the Home Department [2019] EWHC 452 (Admin), [2019] 4 All ER 527...........170
R (Joint Council for the Welfare of Immigrants) v Secretary of State for the Home Department [2020] EWCA Civ 542, [2021] 1 WLR 1151.....................170
R (Kambadzi) v Secretary of State for the Home Department [2011] UKSC 23, [2011] 1 WLR 1299 177
R (Keyu) v Secretary of State for Foreign and Commonwealth Affairs [2015] UKSC 69, [2016] AC 1355....................157
R (L) v Commissioner of Police of the Metropolis [2009] UKSC 3, [2010] 1 AC 410....................115
R (Lord Carlile of Berriew QC and others) v Secretary of State for the Home Department [2014] UKSC 60, [2015] AC 945.............................. 121, 170
R (Mighty) v Secretary of State for the Home Department [2011] UKSC 12, [2012] 1 AC 245....................177
R (Miller) v Prime Minister [2019] EWHC 2381 (QB), [2019] ACD 136 32
R (Miller) v Prime Minister; Cherry and others (Respondents) v Advocate General for Scotland [2019] UKSC 41, [2020] AC 373 .... 12, 32, 37, 54, 64, 66–69, 72–73, 100, 121
R (Miller) v Secretary of State for Exiting the European Union [2017] UKSC 5, [2018] AC 61 ....21, 30, 32, 63, 66–67, 72, 121
R (Miller) v Secretary of State for Exiting the European Union [2016] EWHC 2768 (Admin), [2017] 1 All ER 158....................31
R (Miller) v The Prime Minister [2019] EWHC 2381 (QB), [2019] ACD 136.......65
R (Mohamed) v Secretary of State for Foreign and Commonwealth Affairs (No 1) [2008] EWHC 2048 (Admin)....................177
R (National Council for Civil Liberties) v Secretary of State for the Home Department and another v National Union of Journalists [2019] EWHC 2057 (Admin), [2020] 1 WLR 243....................43
R (Newby) v Secretary of State for Justice [2019] EWHC 3118 (Admin) (19 November 2019, unreported) 44
R (Nicklinson) v Ministry of Justice [2013] EWCA Civ 961, [2014] 2 All ER 32 43
R (Nicklinson) v Ministry of Justice [2014] UKSC 38, [2015] AC 657...... 43, 47, 121
R (O (A Child) v Secretary of State for the Home Department [2021] EWCA Civ 193, [2021] 1 WLR 3049....................84
R (on the application of O (A Child)) v Secretary of State for the Home Department [2022] UKSC 3, [2022] 2 WLR 343 ...... 9, 12, 54, 37, 84–86
R (Osborn) v Parole Board [2013] UKSC 61, [2014] AC 1115.......8, 15, 34, 88, 117, 119–20, 127–29, 138, 131, 134, 138, 141, 143–44, 146–49, 155, 168, 176–77, 183, 189

R (Plan B Earth) v Prime Minister [2021] EWHC 3469 (Admin) (21 December 2021, unreported at the time of writing)....46
R (Pretty) v DPP [2001] UKHL 61, [2002] 1 AC 800....43
R (Privacy International) v Investigatory Powers Tribunal [2017] EWCA Civ 1868, [2018] 1 WLR 2572....60
R (Privacy International) v Investigatory Powers Tribunal [2019] UKSC 22, [2019] 2 WLR 1219....12, 54, 56, 69, 99, 109, 119, 121, 140, 182
R (Privacy International) v Investigatory Powers Tribunal [2021] EWHC 27 (Admin), [2021] QB 936....99–100, 139
R (Project for the Registration of Children as British Citizens and others) v Secretary of State for the Home Department [2019] EWHC 3536 (Admin), [2020] 1 WLR 1486....83–84, 90
R (Prudential Plc) v Special Commissioner of Income Tax [2013] UKSC 1, [2013] 2 AC 185....118, 176
R (Quintavalle) v Secretary of State for Health [2003] UKHL 13, [2003] 2 AC 687....47
R (SC) v Secretary of State for Work and Pensions [2021] UKSC 26, [2022] AC 223....46–47
R (Sky Broadcasting Ltd) v Central Criminal Court [2011] EWHC 3451 (Admin), [2011] EWHC 3451....176
R (Smith) v Parole Board for England and Wales [2005] UKHL 1, [2005] 1 WLR 350....144
R (Unison) v Lord Chancellor [2017] UKSC 51, [2020] AC 869....34, 36–37, 49, 52, 65, 68–69, 81, 95, 118–19
R (W (A Child)) v Secretary of State for the Home Department [2020] EWHC 1299 (Admin), [2020] 1 WLR 4420....140
R (Wagstaff) v Secretary of State for Health [2001] 1 WLR 292 (QB), [2000] HRLR 646....128
R (Wheeler) v Leicester City Council [1985] AC 1054 (HL)....123
R (Williams) v Secretary of State for the Home Department [2017] EWCA Civ 98, [2017] 1 WLR 3283....83–84
R (Wilson George) v Mayor of London [2003] EWHC 1257 Admin (8 April 2003, unreported)....103
R (X) v Chief Constable of the West Midlands Police [2004] EWCA Civ 1068, [2005] 1 WLR 65....115
R (Youssef) v Secretary of State for Foreign and Commonwealth Affairs [2016] UKSC 3, [2016] AC 1457....158, 177
R and W Paul Ltd v Wheat Commission [1937] AC 139, [1936] 2 All ER 1243....106
R v A (No 2) [2001] UKHL 25, [2002] 1 AC 45....114
R v Cambridge University, ex p Bentley 93 ER 698 (1724) 2 Ld Raym 1334....144, 168

R v Director of Public Prosecutions, ex p Kebilene [2000] 2 AC 326 29
R v Gough [1993] AC 646 (HL) 176
R v Hull University Visitor, ex p Page [1993] AC 682 (HL) 57
R v Jogee [2016] UKSC 8, [2017] AC 387 173
R v Local Government Board, ex p Arlidge [1915] AC 120, HL 107
R v Lord Chancellor, ex p Witham [1998] QB 575 (QB) 105–06, 176, 186
R v Metropolitan Police Commissioner, ex p Parker [1953] 1 WLR 1150..............107
R v Parole Board, ex p Bradley [1991] 1 WLR 134 (QB)..144
R v Parole Board, ex p Wilson [1992] QB 740 (CA) 144
R v Secretary of State for Social Security, ex p Joint Council for the Welfare of Immigrants [1997] 1 WLR 275... 84–85
R v Secretary of State for the Environment, ex p Nottinghamshire, County Council [1986] AC 240...67
R v Secretary of State for the Home Department, ex p Bugdaycay [1987] AC 514 (HL) 158
R v Secretary of State for the Home Department, ex p Doody [1994] 1 AC 531 (HL) 51, 144
R v Secretary of State for the Home Department, ex p Fire Brigades Union [1995] 2 AC 513.. 63, 66
R v Secretary of State for the Home Department, ex p Leech (No 2) [1994] QB 198, [1993] 3 WLR 1125 ....36, 106, 156, 183
R v Secretary of State for the Home Department, ex p Pierson [1998] AC 539 (HL) 107, 140
R v Secretary of State for the Home Department, ex p Robb [1995] Fam 127 (Fam) 176
R v Secretary of State for the Home Department, ex p Saleem [2001] 1 WLR 443, [2000] 4 All ER 814...186
R v Secretary of State for the Home Department, ex p Simms [1999] UKHL 33, [2000] 2 AC 115 ....8, 23, 35, 106
R v Secretary of State for Transport, ex p Factortame Ltd (No 2) [1991] 1 AC 603, [1990] 3 WLR 818 24
R v Shayler [2002] UKHL 11, [2003] 1 AC 247 ....112–13, 176
R v SSHD [2007] EWCA Civ 1363 (22 November 2007, unreported) 177
Raymond v Honey [1983] 1 AC 1 (HL)..106, 156, 176
Re E (SA) (A Minor) (Wardship) [1984] 1 WLR 156, [1984] 1 All ER 289 171
Re McKerr [2004] UKHL 12, [2004] 1 WLR 807 127
Re S (Minors) (Care Order: Implementation of Care Plan) [2002] UKHL 10, [2002] 2 AC 291 114
Reichhold Norway ASA and another v Goldman Sachs International (a firm) [2000] 1 WLR 173 137
Ridge v Baldwin [1964] AC 40 (HL) 108–09
Rushbridger v Attorney-General [2003] UKHL 38 176
Scott v Scott [1913] AC 417 (HL) 148–50, 154, 167

Secretary of State for the Home Department v P3 [2021] EWCA Civ 1642, [2022] 1 WLR 2869 87–88
Secretary of State for the Home Department v Rehman [2001] UKHL 47, [2003] 1 AC 153 .... 78, 87
Secretary of State for the Home Department, ex p Daly [2001] UKHL 26, [2001] 2 WLR 1622 125
Shindler and another v Chancellor of the Duchy of Lancaster and another [2016] EWCA Civ 469, [2017] QB 226 .... 147, 173
Sir W De Crespigny v Wellesley (1829) 5 Bingham 392, 130 ER 1112 96
Somerset v Stewart (1772) Lofft 1, 98 ER 499 .... 14, 100–03, 123, 174
Stephen Hoey and Others v Commissioners for Her Majesty's Revenue and Customs [2022] EWCA Civ 656, [2022] 1 WLR 4113 81
Stovin v Wise [1996] AC 923 (HL) 127
Summers v Fairclough Homes Ltd [2012] UKSC 26, [2012] 1 WLR 2004 137
Szabo v Hungary App no (37138/14), (2016) 63 EHRR 3 72
Tapling v Jones (1865) 11 HLC 290, (1865) 20 Common Bench Reports (New Series) 166 96
Tariq v Home Office [2011] UKSC 35, [2012] 1 AC 452 80
Thoburn v Sunderland City Council [2002] EWHC 195 (Admin), [2003] QB 151 39–40
Thynne v United Kingdom (1991) 13 EHRR 666 144
Ullah v Special Adjudicator [2004] UKHL 26, [2004] 2 AC 323 121
Vidal-Hall v Google Inc [2015] EWCA Civ 311, [2016] QB 1003 174
W (Algeria) v Secretary of State for the Home Department [2012] UKSC 8, [2012] 2 AC 115 176
Wainwright v Home Office [2003] UKHL 53, [2004] 2 AC 406 .... 174, 179
Watkins v Secretary of State for the Home Department [2006] UKHL 17, [2006] 2 AC 395 .... 9, 114, 177, 181
Western Counties Railway Co v Windsor and Annapolis Railway Co (1882) 7 App Cas 178 96
Wheeler v Leicester City Council [1985] AC 1054 106
Willis v Earl of Beauchamp (1886) 11 PD 59 137
Wilson v First County Trust Ltd (No 2) [2003] UKHL 40, [2004] 1 AC 816 29
Xavier v The Governor of HMP Whitemoor & Another [2021] EWHC 3060 (Admin), [2022] ACD 3 147
XXX v Camden LBC [2020] EWCA Civ 1468, [2020] 4 WLR 165 148

TABLE OF LEGISLATION

Act of Settlement 1700 8
Bill 117 2022–23 (as introduced) 1–2, 29, 119
Bill of Rights 1688 .... 8, 69, 152
Companies Act 2006 52
Council Directive 76/207/EEC of 9 February 1976 on the implementation of the principle of equal treatment for men and women as regards access to employment, vocational training and promotion, and working conditions [1976] OJ L39/40 111
County Courts Act 1984 137
Criminal Justice Act 1991 144
European Union (Withdrawal) Act 2018 40
Finance Act 2014 36
Human Rights Act 1998 .... 1–2, 9, 14, 17, 24, 26–29, 43–45, 49–50, 52, 75, 87, 97, 104–05, 112–16, 118–20, 130, 133, 140, 146, 155, 165, 174–175, 189, 192
Immigration Act 2014 .... 55, 74, 82, 86, 89, 170
Ireland Act 1800 40
Judicial Review and Courts Act 2022 .... 3, 61
Magna Carta 8, 34, 97, 100, 156
Petition of Right 1627 8
Rights Brought Home: The Human Rights Bill (Cm 3782, 1997) 29, 105
Senior Courts Act 1981 .... 4, 27, 137
SI 2013/1893 .... 34, 95
The Immigration Act 1971 .... 75, 79
Town and Country Planning (Development Management Procedure) (England) (Amendment) Order 2013 (SI 2013/1238) 51
United Kingdom Internal Market Act 2020 4

Introduction

This book was written during a time marked by significant constitutional change.

In December 2020, almost 50 years after joining, the UK ceased being a member of the European Union. 'Brexit' put an end to the supremacy and direct effect of EU law and the jurisdiction of the European Court of Justice over certain domestic matters, thereby abrogating various legal constraints on the executive as well as remedies previously available to individuals, including in the human rights sphere.

One year later, in December 2021, the Government set out to 'restore common sense'[1] as well as 'parliament's role as ultimate decision maker'[2] by replacing the Human Rights Act 1998 (HRA), the legislation transposing into UK law the vast majority of the rights protected by the European Convention on Human Rights (ECHR), with a new Bill of Rights. This announcement was published on the same date as the Independent Human Rights Act Review, which recommended various changes to the HRA, including an amendment of section 2 (the duty to take into account case law by the European Court of Human Rights) and an amendment to section 3 (the duty to interpret legislation in conformity with the ECHR). A consultation was launched, which closed in March 2022.

Fast forward to June 2022, after more than a decade of uncertainty as to whether the HRA would be repealed, the Johnson Government introduced a bill into Parliament that finally proposed to do just that, the Bill of Rights bill.[3] Much can be said about the bill, which introduced novel legal tests,[4] purportedly allowing domestic courts to adopt reasoning and make findings that violate the UK's international human rights obligations,[5] and which overall represented a significant reduction from the current level of human rights protection under the HRA. As for the latter, most notably perhaps, the bill set out to repeal section 3 of the

[1] Ministry of Justice, Open consultation, 'Human Rights Act Reform: A Modern Bill of Rights – consultation' (updated 12 July 2022), Foreword, retrievable at www.gov.uk/government/consultations/human-rights-act-reform-a-modern-bill-of-rights/human-rights-act-reform-a-modern-bill-of-rights-consultation.

[2] Ministry of Justice, 'Plan to Reform Human Rights Act' (Press release, 14 December 2021), retrievable at www.gov.uk/government/news/plan-to-reform-human-rights-act.

[3] Bill 117 2022–23 (as introduced).

[4] See, eg, *ibid*, section 3 (3)(a) which provides that 'a court determining a question which has arisen in connection with a Convention right may not adopt an interpretation of the right that expands the protection conferred by the right unless the court has no *reasonable doubt* that the European Court of Human Rights would adopt that interpretation if the case were before it' (emphasis added).

[5] *ibid*, section 24.

HRA, meaning courts would no longer be required to interpret domestic legislation 'so far as it is possible to do so' consistently with the rights protected under the Convention.[6] The bill also prevented courts from adopting, post-commencement, an interpretation of a Convention right that would require a public authority to comply with a positive obligation,[7] provided a Parliament-centric steer to declarations of incompatibility,[8] and introduced a permission stage for individuals wishing to rely on the rights protected by the ECHR.[9]

At the time of writing, the bill is understood to have been shelved by Prime Minister Truss, however no definitive announcement has been made, and the bill may well progress or be reintroduced in an amended version. In any event, the prospects of the replacement of the HRA or a substantive reform of human rights law in the UK brings the topic of this book into sharp relief. The bill put on statutory footing that a court determining a question arising in connection with a Convention right 'may have regard to' the development under the common law of any right that is similar to the Convention right.[10] In doing so, the relevant provision revealed the Government's ignorance about the well-established constitutional position in relation to common law constitutional rights, which is more prescriptive and robust than merely suggesting that a court 'may' have regard to them. Any future proposal may entail a similarly common law focused approach. More broadly, however, there is a risk that, if the bill or a similar bill is passed, we might witness at least a partial replication of the 1980s and 1990s. During that time, domestic courts effectively inflated the common law to make up for the lack of effective, Convention-based human rights protection. In the event of a legislative limitation on rights protection, it is likely that recourse to common law constitutional rights would, again, intensify, which may lead to some unintended constitutional consequences for the Government, seeing how potent a device common law constitutional rights have been moulded into by the Supreme Court.

Apart from these what one might call 'framework' changes, there have been other, more self-contained legal developments which are set to reconfigure public law principles, especially the relationship between the executive and the legislature. One example is the Overseas Operations (Service Personnel and Veterans) Act 2021, which applies to prosecutions relating to military operations outside the UK. The preceding bill's stated aim was to address vexatious claims ('addressing the problem of "Lawfare" (the judicialisation of armed conflict)'[11]). The passing of the Overseas Operations Act is a particularly worrying development given

[6] On some of the implications of this see M Elliott, 'The UK's (new) Bill of Rights' (*Public Law for Everyone Blog*, 22 June 2022), retrievable at https://publiclawforeveryone.com/2022/06/22/the-uks-new-bill-of-rights/.

[7] Bill 117 2022–23 (as introduced), section 5(1).

[8] *ibid*, section 7.

[9] *ibid*, section 15.

[10] *ibid*, section 3(3)(b).

[11] Bill 117 – EN 2019–21, March 2020, Explanatory Notes, Policy Background, para 6.

the 2020 conclusions by a prosecutor at the International Criminal Court that various forms of abuse were committed by members of the UK armed forces against Iraqi civilians between 2003 and 2009.[12] The Act, which applies to both private and Crown Prosecution Service prosecutions, stipulates that, once five years have passed, certain conditions must be met for prosecutions to be brought against the Ministry of Defence, the Secretary of State for Defence, or any individual member of the UK's military forces. In doing so, it creates a presumption against prosecution (which is in fact the title of Part 1 of the Act) by devising an 'exceptionality' test. It also establishes that a prosecution can only proceed if the Attorney General consents to it, and reduces the scope for judicial discretion for lengthening limitation periods to bring civil actions against the military. As Shiner and Chowdhury have said, this legislation is part of a wider, 'general attempt by the current government to re-configure British constitutionalism through expanding executive power at the expense of human rights, judicial and parliamentary oversight, and other accountability mechanisms …'.[13] Such expansion of executive power in the judicial sphere is troubling, especially in light of the continuing politicisation and degradation of the office of Attorney General, one of whose recent post holders has said the UK needs to 'restore' the balance of power between the executive, legislature and the courts.[14] Legislation like the Overseas Operations Act are a manifestation of the view promoted by key political figures that there is a problem which needs to be fixed. Complemented by section 14 of the Bill of Rights bill, the Act also feeds into a broader theme of successive Conservative governments seeking to limit or altogether avoid legal accountability, including in contexts marked by potentially severe human rights abuses.

Other examples of recently adopted legislative measures with constitutional implications include the Police, Crime, Sentencing and Courts Act 2022, which received Royal Assent on 28 April 2022. It increases the power of the state – principally the police and the Home Secretary – to regulate and restrict protest and activism. The Bar Council, the representative body for approximately 17,000 barristers in England and Wales, commented on the preceding bill that the latter 'gives expansive powers to the police, which encompass the arrest of one individual who is independently protesting' and that '[t]here are legitimate concerns that it would allow the Government to prevent protests with which it does not agree'.[15] Another example is the Judicial Review and Courts Act 2022, which makes two

[12] International Criminal Court, 'Situation in Iraq/UK Final Report' (9 December 2020), retrievable at www.icc-cpi.int/itemsDocuments/201209-otp-final-report-iraq-uk-eng.pdf.

[13] B Shiner and T Chowdhury, 'Ministry of Defence Impunity: The Overseas Operations (Service Personnel and Veterans) Act 2021 [2022] *PL* 289, 290–91.

[14] S Braverman, 'Judicial Review Trends and Forecasts 2021: Accountability and the Constitution' (Public Law Project Conference, 19 October 2021).

[15] The Bar Council, 'Police, Crime, Sentencing and Courts Bill 2021 Briefing for Peers – Bar Council Summary' (September 2021), retrievable at www.barcouncil.org.uk/uploads/assets/de532913-d53f-45f1-bd323836fd83cc02/Bar-Council-Summary-Police-Crime-Sentencing-and-Courts-Bill-Briefing-for-Peers-Sept-2021.pdf.

principal changes to judicial review. First, it introduces a new section 29A to the Senior Courts Act 1981, enabling judges to grant a prospective quashing order, or remove or limit any retrospective quashing effect. Second, it reverses the Supreme Court judgment in *R (Cart) v The Upper Tribunal*[16] by legislating an ouster clause which excludes, save in limited circumstances, the judicial review of Upper Tribunal permissions to appeal decisions. The latter is likely to disadvantage vulnerable litigants, including victims of trafficking.[17] Finally, it was only after the legal profession's collective outcry that the Government amended a bill which contained provisions that would break international law in a 'specific and limited way',[18] by allowing ministers to make regulations inconsistent with the UK's obligations under the Brexit Withdrawal Agreement.[19]

I. The Constitutional Context

These political trends and legislative developments operate in the context of a democratic constitution whose nature is often said to be uniquely amenable to change. Rather than having one codified constitutional document, the UK famously relies on a combination of legislation, judicial decisions, legal principles and conventions to inform its framework of public power and individual rights. As Foster puts it,

> The United Kingdom constitution often draws wide-eyed amazement from those who live under a written, formal and entrenched constitution, where governmental power and its limits are clearly identified, and breaches of the constitution are enforced, legally, by a constitutional court.[20]

There is no such formal, comprehensive entrenchment in the UK constitution although, as this book explains, some level of entrenchment has been given to different components of the constitution.

It is also worth highlighting that the UK, albeit placing a strong emphasis on democratic representation and accountability, in fact functions on the basis of an equally unique system in which, for instance, one of the two houses of Parliament, the House of Lords, is not democratically elected, but relies on a system of appointments that is coming under increasing scrutiny.[21]

[16] *R (Cart) v The Upper Tribunal* [2011] UKSC 28, [2012] 1 AC 663.

[17] For an example of a successful 'Cart-style' judicial review, see *G and H v Upper Tribunal and SSHD* [2016] EWHC 239 (Admin).

[18] This quote is taken from a statement made by the then Secretary for Northern Ireland to the House of Commons on 8 September 2020.

[19] This is the Internal Market Bill, which was passed into law as the United Kingdom Internal Market Act 2020 in December 2020.

[20] S Foster, 'The Rule of Law in Modern Times: Not a Priti Sight' (2021) 26(2) *Coventry Law Journal* 1.

[21] Several recent appointments have been highlighted in public discourse, including that of Zack Goldsmith who was defeated at the 2019 general election by almost 8,000 votes but was then awarded with a life peerage by then Prime Minister Boris Johnson, allowing Goldsmith to retain his ministerial position despite his democratic defeat.

While it is true that the House of Lords, which is believed to be the world's second biggest assembly outside of China, can technically be outvoted in the democratically elected House of Commons, in practice they often are not.[22] Thus, a key feature of the constitutional system in which we operate is an unelected, unaccountable chamber – some of whose members are still there today due to having inherited their place from their fathers – of significant size with a strong influence on policy and law-making. Apart from this, there are other peculiarities inherent in the legal-political system, including the first-past-the-post electoral system, which can deliver significant majorities to parties who attract less than 50 per cent of the electoral vote and a constitutional set-up which, via the convention of the monarch's consent, allows the monarch to lobby ministers in a way that can influence UK laws. It is also notable that the country's last three Prime Ministers (including the present one at the time of writing) were, initially, not elected in a public election but, instead, voted into office by less than one per cent of the electorate.

II. The Leading Two Theories on Public Power and an Alternative Reading of the Constitution

In the absence of a single constitutional document, various theories have emerged about the constitution's nature, its key constitutional principles, and the appropriate roles and power of the three branches of state. Writings on the nature of the constitution and the relationship between the judiciary on the one hand, and the executive and legislature on the other, are typically grounded in one of two competing theories. One of them is common law constitutionalism, a unique domestic variant of the theory of legal constitutionalism, which understands itself as being based on substantive notions of the rule of law and legal principles of justice and fairness (as they arise from the case law). The alternative proposition is political constitutionalism, which understands itself as being based on the concept of parliamentary sovereignty.

The first part of this book argues that neither of these theories adequately captures the nature of constitutional law litigation in this country because neither is able fully to account for the complex interplay between parliamentary sovereignty and the rule of law. A proper understanding of that interaction leads us to see that, in fact, the reality of constitutional law is much less theoretically sound and principled than is conveyed. Looking at recent case law in the constitutional sphere, I call the sum of the dynamics I discern not the *political* or the *common law* constitution, but the *nuanced* constitution.

[22] The Constitution Unit (UCL) runs a tracker of the Government's defeats in the House of Lords at www.ucl.ac.uk/constitution-unit/research/parliament/changing-role-house-lords/government-defeats-house-lords.

The second part of this book delves into the history of rights which are endemic to the UK legal system, ie those rights that are embedded in the common law: common law constitutional rights. It also describes the nature and contemporary characteristics of these rights.

The third part of this book explores the impact the nature of the nuanced constitution has on the protection of common law constitutional rights. I argue that the nuanced constitution is normatively deficient because it does not adequately protect constitutional rights from political will, because of the unprincipled way in which constitutional rights have historically developed, and because of the barriers to the development of a comprehensive contemporary rights system.

III. The Nuanced Constitution

Neither of the two mainstream theories accurately captures what the case law suggests about public power and rights. Looking at the case law from a fresh perspective, one can readily see that constitutional law jurisprudence is marked by a combination of the core tenets of the two competing theories, parliamentary sovereignty and the rule of law. It is not 'one or the other', but both. In other words, we cannot detect a principled, uniform constitutional philosophy guiding judicial decision-making. What we find instead is jurisprudence marked by the irreconcilable tenets of political and legal constitutionalism, which demonstrates a lack of clarity and uniform understanding around the justification for political and judicial power.

The more accurate depiction of our constitutional law reality, what I call the nuanced constitution, can be conceptualised by viewing constitutional law adjudication as operating on a spectrum. We can picture parliamentary sovereignty, the key tenet of political constitutionalism, at one end of the spectrum, and common law constitutionalism at the other. In some cases, elements of the political constitution will be more prominent. In others, aspects of the common law constitution will dominate. Rather than being firmly placed on one side of the spectrum or the other and, therefore, rather than being conceptually coherent, judicial reasoning will arrive at a particular spot, figuratively speaking, somewhere along the spectrum.

Typically, the courts view public law cases through the prism of parliamentary sovereignty unless such an approach would result in an infringement of one or more fundamental values. When that point is reached, a case is pulled closer towards the legal constitutionalism side of the spectrum, and the courts consider if any applicable legislative wording is general enough to allow for a 'value-compatible' interpretation. *Sometimes*, if a value is deemed sufficiently important, it will overcome the limit that has been put in place by the relevant legislation, albeit this will not always be openly recognised. Rather, an interpretation of the legislation in question is adopted that accommodates the protection of the value in question. One can readily see that this is a somewhat cumbersome exercise which involves a degree of discrepancy between what is *said* to be done, and what can be *seen* to be done. Indeed, this book says that the constitution is marked by inconsistencies and competing philosophical assumptions, pulling in different directions on a spectrum of ideas, and a gap between judicial rhetoric and reality, including as far as the legal rights protected by the common law are concerned.

Some might interject at this point and say that constitutions are by their very nature nuanced. Does not every democratic legal order comparable to the UK's contain both precise rules and broad principles, and does not every constitutional adjudication necessarily entail normative reasoning, thereby creating room for nuance? Perhaps. However, first, due to the UK's distinct, flexible constitutional set up and legal sources, the continuous reshaping of public power is a process that is arguably more pronounced than in other jurisdictions. The basic tenets of public law jurisprudence are more readily developed and changed than one can expect to be the case in comparable polities. Second, public law scholarship largely operates on the basis of the rule of law/parliamentary sovereignty dichotomy. The contribution this book seeks to propose – based on critical engagement with the case law – is that we need to recognise that the reality is less black and white, and that the nuanced constitutional dynamics we find have a significant impact on the protection of individuals' rights.

The contention that the UK has a nuanced constitution might be met by objections on the basis that it would be neater to offer a more 'definite' or 'demarcated' reading of the case law. However, we should not trade simplicity for accuracy. Recognising the inherently nuanced, ill-defined character of constitutional law adjudication offers a more accurate analysis. Moving away from the established dichotomy allows us to see more clearly, in general terms, the actual nature of constitutional reasoning, and it also enables us to see, in part, why domestic constitutional rights protection is in such a fragile state. Put differently, it is only by re-thinking how we understand the nature of the constitution, which is neither a common law constitution, nor a positivist constitution, but instead *nuanced* in character, that we can fully understand the development, strength and potential reach of common law constitutional rights. It is to this topic that I turn next.

IV. Common Law Constitutional Rights

The UK constitution, contrary to what is stipulated by Hart's rule of recognition, offers no 'single supreme criterion of what constitutes law'.[23] Equally, there is no clear, definite ranking of the different sources of law. In the absence of a single supreme criterion, and due to the presence of substantive values within the

[23] NW Barber, 'Sovereignty Re-Examined: The Courts, Parliament & Statutes' (2000) 20(1) *OJLS* 131, 136.

UK's nuanced constitution, a space has been carved out for the phenomenon of common law constitutional rights.

Common law constitutional rights are increasingly conceptualised as a free-standing source of law, which means they are classified expressly as rights rather than being indirectly protected through, for instance, criminal law or tort law. That said, they are not a comprehensive jurisprudential block, and cannot 'fruitfully be understood or interrogated as an undifferentiated mass'.[24] Rather, they can be characterised as a *range* of substantive and procedural rights which are protected not through legislation (eg a codified constitution or bill of rights) or international treaties, but through the English common law itself. Examples include the right to be heard where a public authority makes a determination regarding an individual, the right to open justice and the right of access to justice.

Common law constitutional rights are normally utilised by the courts to protect values which judges consider have historically been shown to have significant constitutional importance in the absence of a codified constitution and without a comprehensive bill of rights.[25] The narrative accompanying the recognition of these rights emphasises the longevity of rights protection in this jurisdiction. Domestic rights are perceived as indigenous to the legal system, and present a natural facet of the English common law. In particular, any dependence or inferiority to European human rights protection is – both politically and judicially – rejected. Thus, recent case law proclaims that 'the protection of human rights is not a distinct area of the law, based on the case law of the European Court of Human Rights, but permeates our legal system'.[26] As this book and the other main publication[27] on this jurisprudential development suggest, closer academic scrutiny of the phenomenon of common law constitutional rights in fact shows that these rights are not on par with the scale, scope and level of protection offered by, for example, the rights protected by the ECHR. It is true that common law constitutional rights can command considerable influence and force, having been characterised by senior judges as 'principles of constitutionality little different from those that exist in countries where the power of the legislature is expressly limited by a constitutional document'.[28] However, they can also be comparatively weak, or indeed non-existent, compared to their international counterparts as we will see in the example of the right to vote and the right not to be subjected to torture.

[24] M Elliott and K Hughes (eds), *Common Law Constitutional Rights* (Hart Publishing, 2020) 7.

[25] I do not consider the Magna Carta, the Petition of Right 1627, the Act of Settlement 1700 or the Bill of Rights 1688 to be bills of rights in the modern sense of the word, ie, a legally enforceable instrument that lists individuals' rights against the state in a comprehensive way.

[26] *R (Osborn) v Parole Board* [2013] UKSC 61, [2014] AC 1115 [55].

[27] Elliot and Hughes (n 24).

[28] *R v Secretary of State for the Home Department, ex p Simms* [2000] 2 AC 115 (HL) 131 (per Lord Hoffmann).

This book uses the term common law 'constitutional' rights, terminology adopted by authoritative judges and academics, including in the leading edited volume on the subject.[29] An alternative term commentators sometimes employ is common law 'fundamental' rights.[30] The term 'constitutional' may be more ambiguous,[31] in particular in the UK, where there is no single authoritative document providing guidance, and where there is academic disagreement as to how the word 'constitutional' should be understood. However, it is also more fitting as it openly acknowledges the constitutional dimension of these rights, notably their judicial enforcement against the state and the protection the state offers individuals in the context of their private dealings.[32] Their constitutional dimension further springs from the fact that these rights impact on the relationship and hierarchy of different legal sources and their respective interpretation in this jurisdiction. Finally, some of the leading cases have adopted the phrase 'common law constitutional rights'.[33] Thus, while 'fundamental' and 'constitutional' are interchangeable,[34] this book prefers the term common law constitutional rights.

What then is the link between the nuanced constitution and common law constitutional rights? This book proposes that common law constitutional rights are a manifestation of the nuanced constitution whilst at the same time being an important driver of the nuanced constitution. Put differently, their reach and resilience are a product of the qualities of our constitutional law more broadly speaking; they are what they are because the nuanced constitution is what it is. At the same time, they contribute to the nuanced character of the constitution, also because of the sometimes flexible understanding of legal values, principles and judicial reasoning they entail, which in turn has an impact outside the sphere of common law constitutional rights, as this book shows.

[29] M Elliott, 'Beyond the European Convention: Human Rights and the Common Law' (2015) 68(1) *Current Legal Problems* 85; Lady Hale, 'UK Constitutionalism on the March?' (Constitutional and Administrative Law Bar Association Conference, 12 July 2014); Elliott and Hughes (n 24).

[30] Sir P Sales, 'Rights and Fundamental Rights in English Law' (2016) 75(1) *Cambridge Law Journal* 86; TRS Allan, *The Sovereignty of Law: Freedom, Constitution and Common Law* (Oxford University Press, 2013). Note that Allan used the term 'constitutional rights' in 'Constitutional Rights and Common Law' in *Law, Liberty, and Justice: The Legal Foundations of British Constitutionalism* (Oxford University Press, 1994) Ch 6.

[31] But see Elliott's discussion of the term 'fundamental' in Ch 9 of Elliott and Hughes (n 24).

[32] The majority of common law constitutional rights operate against the state. This is not to say the English common law does not enforce some rights with constitutional dimensions in horizontal relationships, see, eg, *O (A Child) v Rhodes* [2015] UKSC 32, [2016] AC 219, in which the Supreme Court reinforced the Appellant's right to freedom of speech against another private individual.

[33] See, eg, *R (UNISON) v Lord Chancellor* [2017] UKSC 51, [2017] 3 WLR 409 [65]; *R (Elgizouli) v Secretary of State for the Home Department* [2020] UKSC 10, [2021] AC 937 [175].

[34] The Supreme Court has implied that the two terms are synonymous: *R (O (A Child)) v Secretary of State for the Home Department* [2022] UKSC 3, [2022] 2 WLR 343 [33]: 'this appeal is not concerned with common law rights which have been recognised as fundamental or constitutional nor is it asserted that any Convention rights under the Human Rights Act 1998 are engaged'. The remainder of the judgment uses both terms interchangeably. See also J Beatson and others, *Human Rights: Judicial Protection in the United Kingdom* (Sweet & Maxwell, 2008) 8 citing *Watkins v Home Office* [2006] UKHL 17, [2006] 2 AC 395.

V. The Questions this Book Sets Out to Answer

What are the key characteristics of common law constitutional rights? What is their normative reach and have new rights developed over time? How resilient are they in the face of legislation? What function and importance do they hold within the wider public law landscape? What is their foundational origin, and how do judges legitimise the enforcement and development of these rights? Are common law constitutional rights a positive development, or do they under-deliver? Can they be reconciled with the philosophy traditionally associated with the UK constitution, ie, political constitutionalism, or do they point towards the UK having adopted a common law constitution based on legal constitutionalism and the rule of law?

This book sets out to contribute to answering these complex questions about this remerging line of jurisprudence through a combination of doctrinal, conceptual and normative analyses. Centring around extensive case law analysis focusing predominantly on recent Supreme Court jurisprudence, it:

- highlights and conceptualises the dynamics and mechanisms of rights-based constitutional law reasoning;
- challenges commonly held perceptions about what such reasoning represents;
- criticises the incoherence and normative deficiencies of contemporary common law constitutional rights jurisprudence; and
- identifies the concept of parliamentary sovereignty and the workings of the English common law as the key impediments to the development of a principled model for constitutional rights adjudication.

In doing so, the book provides the first comprehensive critique of common law constitutional rights jurisprudence.

The key criticism developed throughout this book is that the nuanced constitution offers a fragile foundation for principled domestic constitutional rights protection. Due to the tension inherent in constitutional reasoning, the range and scope of common law constitutional rights remains unclear, and their legitimacy contested. Furthermore, given the continued role and force of the concept of parliamentary sovereignty despite having been qualified overall, common law constitutional rights are at constant risk of being abrogated by clear statutory language. Impacted by the ambiguities underlying the wider constitutional framework, there is no properly articulated foundation for common law constitutional rights. This means that the practical development and application of these rights has been incoherent. That being the case, the book concludes that the contemporary judicial treatment of common law constitutional rights is problematic as it lacks both principle and effectiveness.

VI. The Structure, Style and Chapters of this Book

This book discusses the nature of common law constitutional rights in a comprehensive manner rather than on a right by right basis. In doing so, it makes for a complementary companion to the recently published, insightful *Common Law Constitutional Rights*.[35] In offering a connection between constitutional rights jurisprudence and the nature of the constitution itself, including its conceptual and normative shortcomings, the book covers a broad theme, combining legal theory and practice in a way that is, I hope, accessible and relevant to readers from both academic and legal practice backgrounds as well as members of the judiciary.

A. Chapter One

Chapter one introduces the idea of the nuanced constitution. It argues that it is time to recognise that our constitution cannot be explained by reference to political or common law constitutionalism. We cannot sensibly shoehorn the rich variety of constitutional cases into the tenets of either school of thought. In reality, we can observe a combination of the two positions in judgments which have constitutional implications.

The chapter first shows that parliamentary sovereignty is not the domineering constitutional principle political constitutionalists say it is. It is not consistently raised above other important constitutional principles such as the rule of law and the separation of powers. There is ample evidence that parliamentary sovereignty is among the most fundamental constitutional principles. However, notably, in none of the leading constitutional cases decided by the Supreme Court is the principle endorsed as the supreme one. This is unsurprising in light of how constitutional law adjudication has developed.

Having demonstrated the absence of an unequivocal, consistent endorsement of parliamentary sovereignty as the pinnacle of the constitutional order at the highest judicial level, the chapter then argues that while institutional legitimacy concerns continue to play a central role in a large share of public law adjudication, attention is also regularly paid – and significant weight is given to – substantive values. These contextualise, particularise, develop and, sometimes, depart from what is, on the face of it, prescribed by Parliament. Additionally, both common law constitutional rights and constitutional statutes introduce an element of hierarchy into constitutional analyses, focusing on values that are deemed so fundamental that special measures are required for them to be overridden. In doing so, they qualify the notion of unlimited law-making power.

[35] Elliott and Hughes (n 24).

Despite these findings, looking at constitutional practice in the round, we cannot say that the constitution is therefore best characterised as a common law constitution. Making this claim would, for example, ignore the fact that the judiciary has abstained from quashing an Act of Parliament, that there is no explicit, let alone consistent judicial endorsement of the common law constitution, and that in many, if not in the majority of public law cases, law enacted by Parliament takes centre-stage, and common law rules and principles play a minor role. I highlight some of the recent case law which reveals a commitment to the tenets associated with political constitutionalism and further suggest that we must also recognise that the way in which practitioners approach legal disputes is not commensurate with common law constitutionalism's understanding.

Chapter one concludes that, viewed in their aggregate, the cases presented strongly suggest that the UK has neither a political nor a legal (or common law) constitution. A more nuanced picture presents itself. Before delving into the boundaries of the nuanced constitution in more detail in the following chapter, the final section of chapter one explores some of the reasons behind the gradual qualification of parliamentary sovereignty, focusing on two enabling factors, namely European and international law and the properties of the English common law itself.

B. Chapter Two

In chapter two I delve deeper into the constitutive elements and the boundaries of the nuanced constitution on the basis of four judgments: *R (Privacy International) v Investigatory Powers Tribunal,*[36] *R (Miller) v Prime Minister*[37] *R (Begum) v Special Immigration Appeals Commission*[38] and *R (O (A Child)) v Secretary of State for the Home Department.*[39]

I set out the reasoning employed in each of them in detail, including by courts other than the Supreme Court. It is hoped that seeing the trajectory and reading a detailed summary of the judicial analyses in each set of proceedings will convey to readers important aspects of the current state of the UK constitution. This is then complemented by analysis in which I highlight and critique certain aspects of each decision, while also establishing commonalities and differences between them. The broader aim is to convey, through these case studies, a better understanding of what the nuanced constitution entails, which is essential to understand – and provide a meaningful critique of – common law constitutional rights, the second key theme of this book.

The key characteristics underlying the nuanced constitution are the following. First, our constitution is marked by significant disagreement between the country's

[36] *R (Privacy International) v Investigatory Powers Tribunal* [2019] UKSC 22, [2019] 2 WLR 1219.

[37] *R (Miller) v Prime Minister; Cherry and others (Respondents) v Advocate General for Scotland* [2019] UKSC 41, [2020] AC 373.

[38] *R (Begum) v Special Immigration Appeals Commission* [2021] UKSC 7, [2021] 2 WLR 556.

[39] *R (O (A Child)) v Secretary of State* (n 34).

most senior courts and judges as to the meaning and application of constitutional fundamentals. Beneath the surface of a case we can often observe both schools of thought, ie political and legal constitutionalism. Second, the nuanced constitution allows judges to openly question the (continued) acceptance of absolute legislative competency. Third, however, the nuanced constitution is often marked by judicial reasoning which attempts the impossible by trying to reconcile what is in essence common law constitutionalist reasoning with the orthodox Diceyan position of unlimited legislative law-making powers, resulting in logically and conceptually vulnerable judicial reasoning. Fourth, the cases analysed show that the Supreme Court is willing to explore and enforce newly and creatively argued dimensions of the principle of parliamentary sovereignty that in fact strengthen the common law constitutional components of the nuanced constitution.

Fifth, depending on the value in question, the Supreme Court is willing to break new ground in judgments on the basis of what can be a very loose application of previously established legal principles. In some cases, we see an arguably revolutionary level of abstract reasoning and an arguably equally unprecedented transformation of constitutional values into legally enforceable rules. Sixth, we can, however, also detect a theme of judicial deference to executive decisions, including in the field of national security, and what one might think is an uncharacteristic downplaying of the importance and status of procedural rights, which are normally among the most cherished rights of the English common law. In certain contexts, what is considered 'institutional legitimacy' will easily trump legal rights. Seventh, recent case law re-emphasises the need to ascertain the meaning of the words used by Parliament, a process which is said to involve an objective assessment of the meaning which a reasonable legislature would be seeking to convey in using the statutory words adopted. Eighth, there appears to be a hierarchy of rights which, counterintuitively perhaps, suggests that common law constitutional rights are more important than statutory rights.

Ninth, the constitution offers comparatively little legal protection to rights that are most important to the functioning of our democracy. Tenth, certain rights which are ordinarily cast as beacons of our constitutional rights protection may in certain circumstances not be instrumental to a decision's reasoning, let alone its outcome. Eleventh, the Supreme Court may in some cases base its reasoning on little more than one sentence in a previous, relatively unrelated judgment, but will in others easily dismiss the relevance of previous judicial reasoning. Twelfth, we can observe a blurring of the lines between legal principles, values, presumptions and other 'mechanisms', which results in uncertainty as to the correct approach to legal reasoning in public law cases.

C. Chapter Three

Having explored the constitutional foundation on which domestic rights jurisprudence is developed, beginning with chapter three the book focuses on common law constitutional rights. In this first of two chapters homing in on this jurisprudential development, the book presents a short history of constitutional rights protection in the UK. It takes a chronological approach, setting out a summary of how common law constitutional rights have developed, focusing in particular on the last few decades.

I highlight that homegrown rights protection often mixes historical reality with a level of mythmaking, hyperbole and selection bias, which is, increasingly perhaps, also leveraged by politicians. One of the examples substantiating this point is the way in which the decision in *Somerset v Stewart*,[40] one the three famous antecedents discussed in chapter three, has been romanticised. More broadly speaking, the judgments analysed share a special affinity with powerful language and imagery, and their combined legacy is the perception that the English common law is a source of justice and reason.

The brief historical discussion is followed by an analysis of what I divide into three phases of more contemporary common law constitutional rights development. These are placed into the wider legal and political context of their time, showing that common law constitutional rights have been significantly influenced and driven by external factors. In short, the first modern phase of common law constitutional rights developed in the context of the UK's obligations under the ECHR, mainly in the 1980 and 1990s, in which domestic courts stressed the comparative strength and sufficiency of the common law's rights framework. The second phase is marked by the co-existence of the common law with the then newly implanted legal obligations under the HRA. During this phase, which is roughly captured by the period between 2000 and 2010, the courts' focus increasingly began to shift towards the HRA, often at the expense of considering what the common law had to offer. That said, suggestions that the HRA completely overshadowed domestic rights protection during this time are not tenable on closer analysis. It is more accurate to say that the Act became increasingly dominant to the point that, in the third phase, the Supreme Court felt the need to reiterate the common law's continued relevance. The final section of chapter three then discusses the contemporary common law constitutional rights phase, which I argue is more powerful than the first phase.

I conclude that the UK courts' renewed interest in the constitutional properties of the English common law raises a plethora of questions about legitimacy. Specifically, it brings to the fore debates around the separation of powers, the boundaries of judicial reasoning, the relationship between domestic and international human rights protection and the conceptualisation of the rule of law.

D. Chapter Four

Having set out the development of common law constitutional rights in a broad chronological order, chapter four intends to set out the nature and key

[40] *Somerset v Stewart* (1772) Lofft 1, 98 ER 499.

characteristics of these rights. First, I show that contemporary common law constitutional rights cannot accurately be described as having an exclusively negative or gap-filling character, in contrast to the traditional conceptualisation of civil liberties. Rather, they are an independent source of law with heightened legal status. The notion of a right, as conceptualised in contemporary UK jurisprudence, implies either that government action cannot interfere or that special justification is needed for government or legislative action to override the right in question. Second, I explain that common law constitutional rights can be both positive and negative in nature. *R (Osborn) v Parole Board*,[41] one of the main cases analysed in this book, is a prime example of a common law constitutional right having been held to vest positive obligations (to hold an oral hearing) in a state institution.

Having set out these two overarching observations, the chapter then establishes six characteristics that can be extrapolated from the case law, focusing in particular on *R (Guardian News) v City of Westminster Magistrates' Court*,[42] *R (Osborn) v Parole Board*,[43] *Kennedy v Charity Commission*,[44] *A v BBC*[45] and *R (UNISON) v Lord Chancellor*.[46] I stress that it is not possible to treat the vast variety of common law constitutional rights as one homogenous mass or standardised jurisprudential concept, which is reflected in the six characteristics I flesh out. Put succinctly, the six characteristics establish that there is, first, no established conceptual basis for the courts' jurisdiction to develop common law constitutional rights. Second, common law constitutional rights are principally enforced through the principle of legality, which is, however, not always applied uniformly. Third, the jurisprudence signifies an attempted redefinition of the relationship between the common law and the ECHR, in which the former is accorded primacy, however it can be shown that, in fact, common law constitutional rights and rights protected under the Convention are strongly intertwined. Fourth, contemporary rights enforcement often relies on a broad conceptualisation of domestic precedent. Fifth, we can see, depending on how established the right in question is, extensive reliance on judicial reasoning from other common law jurisdictions. Sixth, common law constitutional rights in general trigger proportionality review, however even here we find a level of discrepancy in the case law.

The chapter concludes that while common law constitutional rights incorporate many other public law principles and reasoning techniques, the quest to characterise them as one uniform model or concept proves, despite their likeness

[41] *R (Osborn) v Parole Board* (n 26).
[42] *R (Guardian News and Media Ltd) v City of Westminster Magistrates' Court* [2012] EWCA Civ 420, [2013] QB 618.
[43] *R (Osborn) v Parole Board* (n 26).
[44] *Kennedy v Charity Commission* [2014] UKSC 20, [2015] AC 455.
[45] *A v BBC* [2014] UKSC 25, [2015] AC 588.
[46] *R (UNISON) v Lord Chancellor* (n 33).

in nature, very challenging. The fragility, uncertainty and insularity that can be associated with this jurisprudential development is reflective of the wider inconsistencies and shortcomings underlying the nuanced constitution.

E. Chapter Five

Chapter five evaluates the ramifications of the findings in chapters one to four, and elaborates on the shortcomings of the nuanced constitution as far as constitutional rights protection through the common law is concerned. It highlights that there is no standardised understanding of how we ought to interpret public law cases where competing important legal values and principles are at play. Meanwhile, on a substantive level, given the strong pull towards the political constitutionalist side of the spectrum, which often operates as the lens through which a case is approached, the substantive constitutional values we theoretically adhere to are at constant risk of being undermined and also, in any event, likely to be shaped or significantly influenced by institutional rather than substantive considerations. Both of these factors have hampered the principled development of a comprehensive rights regime anchored in a firm foundation. Adding to this the way in which the English common law develops, we can see that public law adjudication, including in cases concerning constitutional rights, can be highly ambiguous, and with uncertain outcomes.

The chapter then proceeds to elaborate on these points further by discussing the uncertainties underlying common law constitutional rights jurisprudence, which are in large part prompted by the facets of the nuanced constitution. I highlight, first, that common law constitutional rights jurisprudence suggests that anything that is part of the English common law is for judges to determine. Second, I argue that it is not established what values judges can draw on to develop domestic rights. Third, I suggest that there is uncertainty around the types of sources that can shape, and indeed create, a common law constitutional right, noting that there is a wide range of sources that have historically triggered legal protection, ranging from religious references to judicial opinions (not in the legal sense of the term). Additionally, I argue that there is uncertainty around what exactly makes a value legally enforceable, and that the concept of legal precedent, and the perceived need thereof, may vary from case to case. Next, I home in on one major factor that may prevent the enforcement of rights which are said to be of a constitutional nature, namely parliamentary sovereignty. I show that despite having been qualified as a matter of constitutional practice, its core idea continues to shape judicial reasoning. Indeed, in some ways, it can be said to frame the spectrum of the nuanced constitution. Also, it typically acts as a trump card where legislative wording is considered sufficiently precise, no matter how well-established the right in question. Finally, I discuss the nature of the common law itself, which I explain has contributed to the unprincipled development of common law constitutional rights, highlighting in particular its strong affiliation with the past and legal tradition.

Having argued that the nuanced constitution has led to an underdeveloped constitutional rights framework, the second part of this final chapter provides an overview of some of the common law constitutional rights that have been recognised under the nuanced constitution. Taking a closer look at these rights, which are presented in a non-exhaustive list, reinforces the concerns raised. For example, rights with stronger domestic roots are typically better protected compared to more 'contemporary' rights, such as the right to equality, which is arguably indispensable in a democracy. We can also see that some rights that are commonly protected in international treaties or domestic constitutions, such as the right to freedom of religion, are noticeably absent at common law whereas some rights have been expressly confirmed not to have attracted the protection of the common law. Others, such as the right not to be subjected to torture, are in fact much more restricted than the name of the right suggests. Yet other rights, including the right to vote, appear to exist only in a very basic form, and thus would feature on this 'list', but in practice their content is too restricted or underdeveloped. In consequence, they would not carry any meaningful practical benefits for litigants, especially in the face of statutory occupation of the field. Furthermore, the scope of many of the rights listed, including their actual practical legal force beyond their general recognition, is unclear.

The book concludes that, under the nuanced constitution, despite the judiciary's express recognition that certain common law rights are 'important', 'fundamental', 'basic', 'near to absolute' and 'inherent to democratic civilised society', their violation may not carry any legal consequences. This being the case, the remainder of chapter five looks at how the state of domestic human rights protection could be improved, arguing that it is unlikely that common law constitutional rights protection will be sufficiently strengthened by being placed on firmer conceptual ground in the near future. This being the case, it becomes even more important to correct the popular narrative that domestic constitutional rights protection is comparable to the protection offered by the HRA, or that it is, in any event, sufficiently effective and conceptually sound.

PART I

A Third Alternative – The Nuanced Constitution

1

An Introduction to the Nuanced Constitution

In *R (Miller) v Secretary of State for Exiting the European Union*, the Supreme Court held that the Government did not have the power, under the Crown's prerogative, to give notice pursuant to article 59(2) of the Treaty on European Union, which would have set in motion the process of the UK withdrawing from the European Union (EU). The Court held that such a step required an Act of Parliament. As part of the Court's judgment, no less than eight Justices of the Supreme Court endorsed the proposition that,

> The United Kingdom does not have a constitution in the sense of a single coherent code of fundamental law which prevails over all other sources of law. Our constitutional arrangements have developed over time in a pragmatic as much as in a principled way, through a combination of statutes, events, conventions, academic writings and judicial decisions.[1]

Most legal commentators, practitioners and judges would endorse this description, however some of the most fundamental aspects of this characterisation are heavily debated. Specifically, there is significant disagreement as to the boundaries of different public bodies' responsibility and power, and the hierarchy between some of the sources mentioned. Indeed, 'contestability' has been suggested to be inherent in the nature of the UK constitution.[2]

I. The Two Competing Forms of Constitutionalism

A helpful entry point to the discussion on the competing claims to the nature of the UK constitution is Lord Steyn's explanation that constitutionalism 'is neither a rule [n]or a principle of law. It is a political theory as to the type of institutional

[1] *R (Miller) v Secretary of State for Exiting the European Union* [2017] UKSC 5, [2018] AC 61 [40] (judgment for the majority by Lord Neuberger, who was the president of the Supreme Court at the time).

[2] RB Taylor, 'The Contested Constitution: An Analysis of the Competing Models of British Constitutionalism' [2018] *PL* 500, 522.

arrangements that are necessary in order to support the democratic ideal'.[3] When we speak of the contest between legal and political constitutionalism, we are looking at two different assessments as to what our constitutional arrangements *are*, and two different ideas as to what our constitutional arrangements *ought to be* in order to safeguard and support the system theorists from both schools of thought agree is the political reality and the normative aim of our society: democracy. As Latham-Gambi puts it, the two forms of constitutionalism exemplify contrasting ways of imagining the political world.[4]

Legal constitutionalism, the younger of the two philosophies (in the European context, that is), advocates a system of restrained government in which the judiciary upholds the rule of law by imposing certain standards, including principles of fairness and human rights, on the elected branches of state. It takes a multi-faceted view of legitimacy, proposing that 'the democratic legitimacy of laws stems from a complex constellation of requirements and conditions that no longer involves popular sovereignty alone, but also basic rights and liberties …'.[5] Political power wielded by the executive and the legislature is subject to what is referred to as 'the sovereignty of law'.[6] In the context of the UK's political-legal system, where there is no single constitutional document, legal constitutionalism takes the form of common law constitutionalism; the principles of the English common law (which is how parliamentary sovereignty, for example, is understood) dictate the legality of public acts and omissions.

Conversely, political constitutionalism, which has been firmly embedded in UK constitutional theory at least since the writings of Dicey, ascribes unlimited authority to the state's main political institution, the Westminster Parliament. It views judge-made law and human rights adjudication with suspicion due to the 'judicial activism' these invite, which is criticised on the basis of legitimacy concerns. Parliamentary sovereignty, which is, as Elliott puts it, 'as extravagant as it is simple'[7] – is the 'absolute omnipotence of Parliament'.[8] As Jennings, one of the theory's early main proponents put it, 'The Supremacy of Parliament *is* the Constitution'.[9]

[3] Lord Steyn, 'The Weakest and Least Dangerous Department of Government' [1997] *PL* 84.

[4] A Latham-Gambi, 'Political Constitutionalism and Legal Constitutionalism – an Imaginary Opposition?' (2020) 40(4) *OJLS* 737.

[5] JEK Murkens, 'Democracy as the Legitimating Condition in the UK Constitution' (2018) 38(1) *Legal Studies* 42, 58.

[6] A phrase which has been shaped by the writing of TRS Allan, see, eg, TRS Allan, *The Sovereignty of Law: Freedom, Constitution, and Common Law* (Oxford University Press, 2013).

[7] M Elliott, '1000 words, Parliamentary Sovereignty' (Public Law for Everyone, 15 October 2014).

[8] AV Dicey, *England's Case against Home Rule* (Murray, 1886) 168. As others have shown, behind the purported simplicity lies considerable complexity, see, eg, A Greene, 'Parliamentary Sovereignty and the Locus of Constituent Power in the United Kingdom' (2020) 18(4) *International Journal of Constitutional Law* 1166.

[9] WI Jennings, *The Law and the Constitution*, 5th edn (London University Press, 1959) 314 (emphasis added).

Parliamentary sovereignty (or the synonymously but less commonly used parliamentary 'supremacy')[10] establishes a hierarchy under which primary legislation is the superior source of legal authority, rendering the validity and effect of all other sources of law conditional upon there being no conflicting parliamentary intention. Parliament has the unlimited authority to enact, amend and repeal any law save binding their successors (positive dimension) and no other institution or person can override or set aside such law (negative dimension).[11] In the words of Dicey,

> Parliament thus defined has, under the English constitution, the right to make or unmake any law whatever; and, further, that no person or body is recognised by the law of England as having a right to override or set aside the legislation of Parliament. A law may, for our present purposes, be defined as 'any rule which will be enforced by the Courts.' The principle then of Parliamentary sovereignty may, looked at from its positive side, be thus described; any Act of Parliament, or any part of an Act of Parliament, which makes a new law, or repeals or modifies an existing law, will be obeyed by the Courts. The same principle, looked at from its negative side, may be thus stated; there is no person or body of persons who can, under the English constitution, make rules which override or derogate from an Act of Parliament, or which (to express the same thing in other words) will be enforced by the Courts in contravention of an Act of Parliament.[12]

Under this theory, law, including human rights, is ultimately a matter of majority will. As Lord Hoffmann famously put it in *R v Secretary of State for the Home Department, ex p Simms*, 'Parliamentary sovereignty means that Parliament can, if it chooses, legislate contrary to fundamental principles of human rights.'[13] The only serious limit to political power is that posed by 'the possibility of popular resistance.'[14]

Once largely unchallenged, doubt has begun to grow as to whether the traditional view of the nature of the constitution, political constitutionalism, can indeed accurately describe the practical workings of the UK constitution.[15] Particularly during the time of the UK's membership of the European Union the idea that Parliament was indeed (still) fully sovereign was questioned. The 'European pressures' on the concept of parliamentary sovereignty were brought into sharp focus

[10] See, eg, TRS Allan, 'Legislative Supremacy and the Rule of Law: Democracy and Constitutionalism' (1985) 44(1) *CLJ* 111.

[11] AV Dicey, *Introduction to the Study of the Law of the Constitution*, 8th edn (Palgrave MacMillan, 1915) 3–4. For some, this extends to the international sphere as well; see, eg, J Goldsworthy who has said that 'it is the business of the government and Parliament, not the courts, to decide whether or not Britain should abide by its treaty commitments' in J Goldsworthy (ed), *Parliamentary Sovereignty: Contemporary Debates* (Cambridge University Press, 2010) 287.

[12] Dicey, *ibid* 37–38.

[13] *R v Secretary of State for the Home Department, ex p Simms* [1999] UKHL 33, [2000] 2 AC 115 [131].

[14] Dicey (n 11) 76.

[15] See also A Tucker, 'Uncertainty in the Rule of Recognition and in the Doctrine of Parliamentary Sovereignty' (2011) 31(1) *OJLS* 61, 61.

when, in 1990, the House of Lords disapplied an Act of Parliament, the Merchant Shipping Act 1995.[16] Applying the latter would have frustrated the exercise of European Union law rights (in that case, the rights of Spanish fishermen to trawl in UK waters). Those rights, the House of Lords held, enjoyed supremacy over national law, which had to give way. However, beyond the EU context, which is no longer a live concern, purely domestic pressures have themselves put into question the ability of political constitutionalism realistically to capture constitutional practice as manifested by judicial approaches to adjudication. For example, the narrative that Parliament's power is legally unlimited was questioned directly by the House of Lords in 2004, in *R (Jackson) v Attorney General* (*Jackson*).[17] Several of the Law Lords pondered what were to happen if Parliament legislated the 'unthinkable': the abolition of judicial review or the ending of the ordinary role of the courts. Stating that this would be unacceptable, Lord Hope suggested – in obiter – that '... parliamentary sovereignty is no longer, if it ever was, absolute ... step, by step, gradually but surely, the English principle of the absolute sovereignty of Parliament which Dicey derived from Coke and Blackstone is being qualified'.[18]

Other examples commonly cited as prompting a shift away from the political constitution are devolution and international law. An example of the latter is the European Convention on Human Rights (ECHR), which was transposed into domestic law by the Human Rights Act 1998 (HRA) more than 20 years ago. As canvassed in this book's introduction, the HRA is one of the most controversial pieces of legislation in contemporary British political-legal debate. Academics and influential right-wing think tanks have long criticised its impact on parliamentary sovereignty, and have argued for its repeal. For example, Policy Exchange has said that 'Parliament should never have enacted the HRA'.[19] Key to the critics' objections is section 3 of the HRA (though sections 2 and 4 are also viewed negatively), which requires the courts, so far as it is possible to do so, to read and give effect to domestic primary legislation and subordinate legislation in a way which is compatible with Convention rights, a requirement which was interpreted broadly by the House of Lords in cases such as *Ghaidan v Godin-Mendoza*.[20]

[16] *R v Secretary of State for Transport, ex p Factortame Ltd (No.2)* [1991] 1 AC 603, [1990] 3 WLR 818. A selection of the vast commentary on this seminal decision includes J McEldowney, 'The Factortame Litigation: Sovereignty in Question' in S Juss and M Sunkin (eds), *Landmark Cases in Public Law* (Hart Publishing, 2017); W Wade, 'Sovereignty: Revolution or Evolution' (1996) 112 *LQR* 568 and NW Barber, 'The Afterlife of Parliamentary Sovereignty' (2011) 9(1) *International Journal of Constitutional Law* 144.

[17] *R (Jackson) v Attorney General* [2005] UKHL 56, [2006] 1 AC 262.

[18] *ibid* [104]. Both Coke and Blackstone have in their writings expressed views that contradict the notion of absolute Parliamentary Sovereignty, which is why the accuracy of the second part of the sentence is questionable.

[19] See R Ekins and G Gee, 'Submission to the Joint Committee on Human Rights, 20 years of the Human Rights Act' (Policy Exchange, 18 September 2018).

[20] *Ghaidan v Godin-Mendoza* [2004] UKHL 30, [2004] 2 AC 557.

In light of these and other developments, the argument is made that the UK no longer functions on the basis of a political constitution.[21] That said, many proponents of common law constitutionalism make a more timeless and what one might term 'contemporary development-independent' claim as to the nature of the constitution. They say it has *always* been based on legality (as defined by the common law).[22]

II. Not One or the Other, but Both: Thesis and Methodology

A significant share of UK public law debate has busied itself with the question of whether the nature of the constitution is (still) political, or whether it is (and always has been) legal. This book argues that rather than seeking, through theoretical or historical analyses, to firmly place the UK constitution in the political constitutional or legal constitutional camp, the time has come to recognise that we are being too generous in our assumption that our constitutional practice is embedded in a coherent overarching framework. It is not. We cannot sensibly shoehorn the rich variety of constitutional cases into the tenets of either of the aforementioned schools of thought. In reality, we can observe a combination of the two schools of thought in public law judgments. Put differently, our legal system is irreconcilable with both of these normative positions; neither 'of the competing models provide a complete and accurate picture of the contemporary British constitution'.[23]

In this first chapter I develop the idea of an alternative reading of the UK's constitutional dynamics, which I term the nuanced constitution. This is followed by chapter two, in which I delve deeper into the constitutive elements and the boundaries of the nuanced constitution. Taken together, the first two chapters provide the basis on which we can then proceed to assess the development and state of domestic rights protection under the nuanced UK constitution before looking at the nuanced constitution and common law constitutional rights in the round in the final part of this book.

My analysis is principally grounded in case law that speaks to constitutional dynamics and principles, the principal basis for this being Supreme Court jurisprudence. I recognise at the outset that I do not provide a strict empirical analysis of the UK's public law jurisprudence. No doubt, if there was a machine one could

[21] See, eg, A McHarg, 'Reforming the United Kingdom Constitution: Law, Convention, Soft Law' (2008) 71 *MLR* 853, 853.

[22] One of the theory's key contemporary proponents argues that Dicey's influential writings themselves can be read as offering support for some of common law constitutionalism's key tenets: see MD Walters, *AV Dicey and the Common Law Constitutional Tradition: A Legal Turn of Mind* (Cambridge University Press, 2020).

[23] Taylor (n 2) 501.

feed all public law decisions over the past 500 years for analysis, a more accurate picture would emerge. Happily though, my thesis is less demanding in this regard than the competing theses of common law constitutionalism and political constitutionalism. I do not need to accommodate all relevant case law authorities, nor does the thesis suffer if one decision emerges that goes contrary to what I am suggesting because my theory itself suggests that the case law pulls us in different directions.

In carrying out this analysis, I adopt a wide definition of 'constitution' and 'constitutional', using the terms essentially synonymously with the amalgamation of judicial manifestations of public law. There is a simple reason for this. Looking at the sources that are generally recognised as forming part of the UK constitution – as set out in the *Miller v Secretary of State for Exiting the European Union* quote at the beginning of this chapter – one can readily appreciate that those sources are applied in a wide range of public law contexts and court procedures.[24]

The most obvious category of cases lending themselves to discerning how public power and individual rights are shaped by the courts is judicial review, a type of court proceeding in which the High Court of England and Wales reviews the lawfulness of a decision, action, or omission by a public body (and other entities exercising 'public functions') against an established set of legal requirements. As the leading practitioner's text on judicial review highlights, judicial review itself can no longer sensibly be viewed as being purely about – or set within the framework of – administrative law. The lines have been blurred due to the increasing review (and/or interpretation) of things other than 'administrative action', including the review of high-level policy decisions, local authority byelaws, and delegated legislation, and indeed primary legislation due to sections 3 and 4 of the HRA.[25]

Judicial review is the most high-profile, and often a very effective way in which individuals can challenge public bodies. It is regarded as being able to 'disrupt government action and to cause political embarrassment'.[26] However, the scope of judicial review is famously limited both in what it can achieve, and in its availability. As for what it can achieve, the courts cannot, in theory, enquire into the

[24] I do not, for the purposes of this analysis, distinguish, nor do I think one can clearly distinguish, between constitutional law and administrative law because 'The constitution shapes administrative law and in turn is shaped by it': Lord Woolf et al, *De Smith's Judicial Review*, 8th edn (Sweet & Maxwell, 2018) 'The Constitutional Context of Judicial Review', 'The Purpose of Judicial Review', 1-015. Constitutional law and administrative law can be viewed as (often indistinguishable) sub-sets of public law, which is the law applicable to relationships and dealings between public bodies or public bodies and individuals.

[25] Lord Woolf et al, *ibid* 1-013.

[26] M Sunkin and AP Le Sueur, 'Can Government Control Judicial Review?' (1991) 44 *Current Legal Problems* 161; see also S James, 'The Political and Administrative Consequences of Judicial Review' (1996) 74 *Public Administration* 613, 619, both of which are referenced in the more recent BC Jones, 'Judicial Review and Embarrassment' [2022] *PL* 179, 179.

merits of the decision under scrutiny; they merely conduct a review of the process by which the decision was reached. As for availability, the claim form must be filed 'promptly' and in any event not later than three months after the grounds to make the claim first arose.[27] The High Court will scrutinise any reasons for delay (including within the three-month period) very closely, and a lack of promptness can have add-on effects on the availability of relief.[28] These and other factors, including funding, mean that individuals aggrieved by measures by public bodies may not (be able to) resort to judicial review, but may instead attempt to hold public authorities accountable via alternative litigation avenues, or via litigation already underway outside the High Court.

This being the case, while judicial review is arguably the most important and statistically relevant type of proceedings that pronounces on public law matters in a way that suggests something about the nature of the constitution, it is not the only type. Beyond judicial review, individuals across the country regularly instigate proceedings in the County Court, suing local authorities, central government departments or both for damages and declaratory relief under legislation including the HRA and the Equality Act 2010 (Equality Act). Conversely, individuals may be pursued in public law claims, such as in the context of anti-social behaviour measures. These types of claims can raise important questions of a public law nature, and the determination of some of them, depending on how the cases are pleaded, may say something about the nature of the constitution. While County Court judgments are of course not precedent setting, appeals from the County Court to the senior courts result in binding judicial decisions on the obligations of public bodies towards individuals, including in the sphere of human and constitutional rights.

The prime example of a case that started as a County Court possession claim which resulted in the leading case on the application of proportionality review in possession proceedings is *Manchester City Council v Pinnock*.[29] A demotion order had been made against Mr Pinnock in respect of his secure council tenancy following serious anti-social behaviour allegations against his partner and children. The local authority then commenced possession proceedings on the basis of alleged further anti-social behaviour. Mr Pinnock had defended the claim on the basis that a possession order would violate his rights under article 8 ECHR. Both the County Court and the Court of Appeal considered that the order granting possession should be made, reasoning that the courts' role did not extend to considering whether article 8 ECHR had been complied with. While Mr Pinnock did not succeed on the facts, the Supreme Court disagreed with the

[27] CPR 54.5(1).

[28] Under s 31(6) of the Senior Courts Act 1981.

[29] *Manchester City Council v Pinnock* [2010] UKSC 45, [2011] 2 AC 104 [45]; *R (JL) v Secretary of State for Defence* [2012] EWHC 2216 (Admin), [2012] AC 121 [59].

legal position adopted by the Court of Appeal. It held that he could avail himself of a public law defence under article 8 ECHR, even at the County Court level, by arguing that possession would be disproportionate.[30]

Another example is the field of social care and mental health law, a growing area of law, which is significantly impacted by human rights considerations. Perhaps the most famous precedent in this area is a case in point. *Cheshire West and Chester Council v P and another*[31] started its life as a Court of Protection case, not as judicial review proceedings. An individual with cerebral palsy and Down's syndrome who lacked the mental capacity to make decisions as to his care was authorised by the Court of Protection to be moved to housing association accommodation close to his family home when his family was no longer able to look after him. He shared his accommodation with two other residents and one or two members of staff. Due to occasional aggressive behaviour, the restrictions in his care plan included physical restraint in addition to the forcible removal of certain items from him. Staff dressed him in an all-in-one body suit to prevent him from accessing those items. The Court of Protection held that it was lawful and in the individual's best interests for him to continue to reside where he had been placed, in accordance with the restrictions set out in the care plan, finding that the care plan involved a deprivation of the individual's liberty for the purposes of article 5 ECHR.[32] The Court of Appeal allowed the local authority's appeal against the judge's declaration that the care plan engaged article 5 ECHR, taking into account the 'benevolent purpose' of the restrictions imposed.[33] The Supreme Court allowed the appeal, devising what is known as the acid test for a deprivation of liberty imputable to the state, ie whether the individual is under continuous supervision and control, and not free to leave, regardless of whether the purpose is benevolent or beneficial, and regardless of whether or not the person objects.[34]

Given, amongst other things, their implications for public authority liability under the HRA, the courts' role in devising and applying tests under the relevant Convention articles, and/or the principles they establish concerning the courts' review powers, both *Cheshire West* and *Pinnock* have, despite not being judicial review proceedings, constitutional implications. This is why cases of this nature are, where relevant, referred to throughout this book in addition to judicial review decisions.

[30] Compare private tenancies, where this defence is not available: *McDonald v McDonald* [2016] UKSC 28, [2017] AC 273.

[31] *Cheshire West and Chester Council v P and another* [2014] UKSC 19, [2014] AC 896.

[32] *Cheshire West and Chester Council v P* [2011] EWHC 1330 (Fam).

[33] *Cheshire West and Chester Council v P* [2011] EWCA Civ 1257, [2012] PTSR 1447.

[34] *Cheshire West and Chester Council v P and another* (n 31). See in particular [48]–[50].

III. Why the UK Constitution is not Political in Nature

First, I argue that, whilst of course occupying an important place in UK constitutional theory and practice, parliamentary sovereignty is not the domineering constitutional principle political constitutionalists say it is. It is a concept too simple and exclusive to capture the rich character of the UK constitution. Taking a close look at the constitutional dynamics in this jurisdiction, it can be shown that the UK constitution cannot convincingly be described as one that is political in nature.

The argument that the UK constitution is not political in nature is developed throughout this book. In this chapter, I begin constructing my argument. I do this on the basis of three contentions. First, this jurisdiction's senior judiciary has not expressly and consistently endorsed parliamentary sovereignty as the most important, overarching or primary constitutional principle. Second, even if that was the case, ie, if we found consistent judicial statements as to parliamentary sovereignty being the key tenet of our constitution, the jurisprudence shows that there is ample evidence of value-driven judicial interpretation of legislation and phenomena which conflict with how parliamentary sovereignty is conceptualised. Third, the recognition of constitutional statutes, as do common law constitutional rights, show that there is some *nuance* when it comes to constitutional importance and hierarchy, and a level of entrenchment which cannot be explained by reference to the political constitution either.

Much has been said about the potential of the HRA limiting or indeed abolishing the concept of parliamentary sovereignty.[35] In engaging with the claims put forward, one must first remember that the HRA was deliberately designed to maintain a certain version of the latter.[36] I would tentatively argue that the HRA's mechanisms and resulting dynamics support my claim that the UK constitution is *nuanced* in nature as opposed to being political or legal.[37] However, while referring to the HRA intermittently in this chapter and throughout this book, I do not rely on it as a freestanding argument in this section. Thus, the thesis put forward retains its force even if the Bill of Rights bill,[38] or a different bill abolishing or replacing the HRA, is passed into law.

[35] For a comprehensive overview of this topic, see AL Young, *Parliamentary Sovereignty and the Human Rights Act* (Hart Publishing, 2009); A Kavanagh, *Constitutional Review under the UK Human Rights Act* (Cambridge University Press, 2009); A Tucker, 'Parliamentary Sovereignty and the Ingenuity of the Human Rights Act' (2012) 3(1) *Jurisprudence* 307.

[36] 'Rights Brought Home: The Human Rights Bill' (Cm 3782, 1997) 10, retrievable at https://assets.publishing.service.gov.uk/government/uploads/system/uploads/attachment_data/file/263526/rights.pdf. See also judgments to this effect: *R v Director of Public Prosecutions, Ex p Kebilene* [2000] 2 AC 326, 367; *Wilson v First County Trust Ltd (No 2)* [2003] UKHL 40, [2004] 1 AC 816 [120].

[37] Particularly given the HRA, s 3. See also A Kavanagh, 'The Role of Parliamentary Intention in Adjudication under the Human Rights Act 1998' (2006) 26(1) *OJLS* 179.

[38] Bill 117 2022–23 (as introduced).

A. Parliamentary Sovereignty is not Uniformly Endorsed as the UK's Supreme Constitutional Principle

Forsyth, a key proponent of the political constitution, states 'Parliament is sovereign', explaining that 'this does not flow from an attachment to the doctrine of sovereignty on [his] part' or from 'any particular fondness for the doctrine; it flows, in the first place, from the pronouncements of the courts'.[39] Given especially the Supreme Court's constitutional, but also its practical role in shaping the constitution, as a matter of principle, I agree that what the courts say about our constitutional dynamics is a highly important aspect when seeking to determine the nature of the constitution. I also accept Forsyth's contention that parliamentary sovereignty is regularly recognised and endorsed by the judiciary. However, as I hope to show in this section, the case law paints a very nuanced picture in the sense that parliamentary sovereignty is *not consistently raised above* other important constitutional principles such as the rule of law and the separation of powers. Thus, whilst there is ample evidence that parliamentary sovereignty is *among* the most fundamental constitutional principles, in none of the leading constitutional cases decided by the Supreme Court do the Justices endorse it as the *supreme* one. It is one of several fundamental constitutional principles rather than master of them all.

In *Miller v Secretary of State for Exiting the European Union*, the case that famously determined that an Act of Parliament was needed to trigger article 50 in the Brexit process, it was said that parliamentary sovereignty is '*a* fundamental principle of the UK constitution',[40] and that it is 'fundamental to the United Kingdom's constitutional arrangements'.[41]

I accept that Lord Wilson in *Miller v Secretary of State* twice calls it '*the* fundamental principle' of the legal framework.[42] However, this should come as no surprise. Lord Wilson is known to lean towards the political constitutionalist side of the spectrum, as is for example evident from his judgment in *R (Evans) v Attorney-General*.[43] *Evans* concerned the question whether the Attorney-General's certificate issued under s 53 of the Freedom of Information Act 2000 to override an Upper Tribunal decision that communications between the then Prince of Wales and government departments should be disclosed was lawful. The Supreme Court held, Lord Wilson and Lord Hughes dissenting, that the Attorney-General had not been entitled to issue the certificate under s 53 of the Act in the way he had done, principally because the starting point was that a binding court decision could be

[39] C Forsyth, 'Privacy International Symposium – Ouster Clauses and Sovereignty' (*Administrative Law in the Common Law World Blog*, 21 November 2018).

[40] *Miller v Secretary of State* (n 1) [43] (emphasis added).

[41] *ibid* [67]; see also [27].

[42] *ibid* [163] (emphasis added).

[43] *R (Evans) v Attorney-General* [2015] UKSC 21, [2015] AC 1787 [168].

ignored or set aside by anyone, including the executive, and because it could not be said that the grounds put forward were 'reasonable', as required by s 53 of the Act, where, as here, there had been a detailed judicial decision; the Attorney-General had simply disagreed with the judicial conclusions, on the same material. Lord Wilson's dissenting opinion, which criticised the majority for having 're-written' s 53 of the Act, referred to parliamentary sovereignty being 'the most precious' constitutional principle, 'emblematic of our democracy'.[44]

One can find other individual judgments in which parliamentary sovereignty is viewed as the pinnacle of the constitutional order. For example, in the Divisional Court's judgment in *Miller v Secretary of State*, Sales LJ (as he then was) said,

> It is common ground that the *most fundamental rule* of UK constitutional law is that the Crown in Parliament is sovereign and that legislation enacted by the Crown with the consent of both Houses of Parliament is supreme … Parliament can, by enactment of primary legislation, change the law of the land in any way it chooses. There is no superior form of law than primary legislation, save only where Parliament has itself made provision to allow that to happen.[45]

However, these occurrences do not undermine my argument. First of all, they do not take away from the fact that leading constitutional law cases such as *Miller v Secretary of State* do not boast *unanimous support* for parliamentary sovereignty as the supreme constitutional principle. Indeed, more broadly speaking, the fact that not all senior judges, let alone Justices of the Supreme Court, ascribe to it having an overarching, unmatched legal status, is sufficient to show that there is no uniform consistent express judicial endorsement of parliamentary sovereignty in the strict sense of what the concept promotes and requires.

Furthermore – a point which should not be overlooked – we must not underestimate the significance of the *context* in which remarks such as Lord Sales' were made. *Miller v Secretary of State* concerned the relationship and allocation of power between the legislature and the executive. Failing to endorse parliamentary sovereignty in this instance would have resulted in a judicial endorsement of the loss of significant rights by individuals at the hands of the executive. The case did not in a notable way touch upon the relationship between the judiciary and Parliament. When academics write about parliamentary sovereignty, they principally rely on the principle to argue against what they consider to be democratic debilitation through 'judicial activism'. However, *Miller v Secretary of State* is not concerned with this dimension. It merely addresses the separation of powers as far as the legislature and the executive are concerned. Therefore, even if the judgment *had* entailed a unanimous unequivocal commitment to ultimate legislative power, *Miller v Secretary of State* would have to be viewed in light of that context.

[44] *ibid* [168].

[45] *R (Miller) v Secretary of State for Exiting the European Union* [2016] EWHC 2768 (Admin), [2017] 1 All ER 158 [20] (emphasis added).

In other words, context is key. As the judgment in *R (Privacy International) v Investigatory Powers Tribunal*,[46] discussed in detail in chapter two, shows, the Supreme Court has been much more reluctant to enforce parliamentary sovereignty as far as the relationship between Parliament and the courts is concerned. If the courts were to declare that parliamentary sovereignty is the supreme principle of the UK constitution in a case like *Miller v Secretary of State*, which focused on the relationship between the political branches of state, this would not allow us to reach conclusions on the constitution more broadly. It would tell us rather little, for example, about the power the courts consider themselves to have to scrutinise primary legislation that is detrimental to human rights, an area highly relevant to both political and legal constitutionalists. *R (Miller) v Prime Minister*,[47] also discussed at length in chapter two, points in the same direction. For present purposes, in *Miller v Prime Minister* the Supreme Court had to determine whether the Prime Minister's advice to Queen Elizabeth II to prorogue Parliament for five weeks was unlawful. Giving a unanimous judgment, the Court held that the prorogation frustrated the constitutional principles of parliamentary sovereignty and parliamentary accountability. Given the absence of a clear, reasonable justification for the prorogation, the latter was declared unlawful, 'null and of no effect'.[48] The Court had no difficulty, as the unanimous, comparatively short judgment demonstrates, to strengthen Parliament in the face of an overreach by the executive. Relevantly for our present discussion, both the High Court (which had dismissed Mrs Miller's challenge) and the Supreme Court used more nuanced terminology as far as parliamentary sovereignty is concerned. For example, the High Court said,

> In the first place, *alongside* the principle of Parliamentary Sovereignty, the separation of powers, reflecting the different constitutional areas of responsibility of the courts, the Executive and Parliament, is also *a* fundamental principle of our unwritten constitution.[49]

Meanwhile, the Supreme Court refers to parliamentary sovereignty as the 'foundational principle of our constitution'[50] whilst also referring to it as *one out of* 'Two fundamental principles of our constitutional law',[51] the second being 'parliamentary accountability' (the accountability of ministers to Parliament for the conduct of government), which, as the Supreme Court in *Miller v Prime Minister* said, was described by Lord Carnwath in his judgment in *Miller v Secretary of State* as being 'no less fundamental to our constitution' than parliamentary sovereignty.[52]

[46] *R (Privacy International) v Investigatory Powers Tribunal* [2019] UKSC 22, [2020] AC 491.
[47] *R (Miller) v Prime Minister* [2019] UKSC 41, [2020] AC 373.
[48] *ibid* [69] (per Lady Hale with whom all Justices agreed).
[49] *R (Miller) v Prime Minister* [2019] EWHC 2381 (QB), [2019] ACD 136 [60] (per Lord Burnett of Maldon CJ with whom Sir Terence Etherton MR and Dame Victoria Sharp P agreed) (emphasis added).
[50] *R (Miller) v Prime Minister* (n 47) [42].
[51] *ibid* [41].
[52] *ibid* [46] referencing *Miller v Secretary of State for Exiting the European Union* (n 1) [249].

It is unclear whether there is a contradiction here, or whether the Supreme Court deemed parliamentary sovereignty to be the 'founding' principle whereas, today, it is seen as one of many fundamental constitutional principles.

Finally, there are of course the (in)famous dicta in *Jackson v Attorney General*, in which Lord Hope said,

> But Parliamentary sovereignty is no longer, if it ever was, absolute. It is not uncontrolled in the sense referred to by *Lord Birkenhead LC in McCawley v The King* … It is no longer right to say that its freedom to legislate admits of no qualification whatever.[53]

In summary, this section argued that one argument in favour of the claim that the UK constitution is nuanced in nature is the express language used by senior courts. We do not find at the highest judicial level an unequivocal, consistent linguistic endorsement of parliamentary sovereignty as the pinnacle of the constitutional order. This is unsurprising. In light of the development of UK constitutional law, in which the rule of law is playing an increasingly central role, it would indeed be very difficult for a judge to accord parliamentary sovereignty complete dominance over and above all other constitutional principles.

In addition to what we find when we look at the express language used, there is of course the perhaps more subtle reality of how cases are decided and what principles are, in practice, irrespective of theoretical utterances about constitutional principles, given more weight. This is what the next section focuses on.

B. Value-Driven Interpretation of Primary and Secondary Legislation, Including Through Common Law Constitutional Rights

Parliamentary sovereignty is *a*, not *the most* fundamental constitutional principle. Conceptually, this has significant consequences. Parliamentary sovereignty does not allow any co-equals. As soon as we say that the rule of law (understood as it is by the courts not simply to mean that everyone is subject to law but, rather, that there are substantive legally enforceable values and principles which moderate and shape legal outcomes) is as important as parliamentary sovereignty, whatever rules are prescribed by Parliament are necessarily amended because parliamentary intention becomes, to some degree, conditional.

As I hope to show in this section, while institutional legitimacy concerns – which is effectively what the concept of parliamentary sovereignty encapsulates – continue to play a central role in a large share of public law adjudication, attention is also regularly paid, and significant weight is given to, substantive values. UK courts, when interpreting primary and secondary legislation, employ reasoning which – sometimes directly, and other times indirectly – endorses the view that

[53] *R (Jackson) v Attorney General* (n 17) [104].

our democracy includes the protection of rights and legal principles whose origin is not Parliament. In applying these non-legislative principles, the courts regularly contextualise, particularise, develop and, sometimes, depart from what is, on the face of it, prescribed by Parliament. The strongest examples of the latter scenario to date are arguably the Supreme Court judgments in *Privacy International*,[54] *Miller v Prime Minister* and *R (Evans) v Attorney-General*,[55] the first two of which chapter two in particular discusses in detail. In this chapter, I merely introduce the idea of nuanced reasoning under our constitution, ie, reasoning which balances parliamentary dictate with common law principles and rights, potentially leading to the modification and partial or complete qualification of the former.

R (UNISON) v Lord Chancellor,[56] the strongest manifestation of the strength of common law constitutional rights to date, is a good starting point to explore the constitutional richness and nuance of statutory interpretation in the twenty-first century. The trade union UNISON brought judicial review proceedings, contending that the making of the Employment Tribunals and the Employment Appeal Tribunal Fees Order 2013[57] was an unlawful exercise of the Lord Chancellor's statutory powers seeing as, amongst other things, the prescribed fees (£390 and £1,200 respectively) interfered unjustifiably with the right of access to justice under both the common law and EU law. Lord Reed, one of the contemporary judicial architects of common law constitutional rights jurisprudence,[58] reasoned in his lead, unanimous judgment, that 'the constitutional principles which underlie the text, and the principles of statutory interpretation which give effect to those principles'[59] were crucial to determine whether the relevant legislation was unlawful. The Supreme Court declared the fees order void *ab initio*, and quashed it, on the basis that it had the effect of preventing access to justice, a common law constitutional right.

In saying that 'the right of access to justice is not an idea recently imported from the continent of Europe, but has long been deeply embedded in our constitutional law',[60] *UNISON* echoes the jurisprudence on common law constitutional rights that had previously been powerfully shaped by other Supreme Court judgments, notably *R (Osborn) v Parole Board*,[61] *A v BBC*[62] and *Kennedy v Charity Commission*.[63] Similarly to those cases, *UNISON* displays an emphasis on the historical foundation of the constitutional right in question. It references Magna Carta, influential historical writings such as Sir Coke's *Institutes of the Laws of*

[54] *R (Privacy International) v Investigatory Powers Tribunal* (n 46).
[55] *R (Evans) v Attorney-General* (n 43).
[56] *R (UNISON) v Lord Chancellor* [2017] UKSC 51, [2020] AC 869.
[57] SI 2013/1893.
[58] Lord Reed also gave the single majority judgment in *R (Osborn) v Parole Board* [2013] UKSC 61, [2014] AC 1115.
[59] *R (UNISON) v Lord Chancellor* (n 56) [65].
[60] *ibid* [64].
[61] *R (Osborn) v Parole Board* (n 58).
[62] *A v BBC* [2014] UKSC 25, [2015] AC 588.
[63] *Kennedy v Charity Commission* [2014] UKSC 20, [2015] AC 455.

England as well as case law from the first peak of common law constitutional rights in the 1980s and 1990s, which I discuss more extensively in chapter three.

As I argue throughout this book, *UNISON* represents a 'new high-water mark'.[64] For example, Lord Reed seems to expand the notion of the concept of legality, the key principle for statutory interpretation in human rights cases, which was authoritatively defined by the House of Lords in *Simms*.[65] In *Simms*, the House of Lords held that the prohibition on journalists to visit prisoners (with a view to investigate and report whether there had been any miscarriages of justice) was unlawful. Mr Simms, who was serving a life sentence for murder but maintained his innocence, had sought assistance from an investigative journalist to challenge his conviction. The legal challenge arose in response to the Home Secretary's introduction of a blanket requirement that journalists visiting prisoners sign an undertaking confirming that none of the information obtained during their visits would be used in a professional capacity, which the journalist visiting Mr Simms refused to comply with, such that the visits ceased. The House of Lords held that the Secretary of State's policy amounted to an unjustifiable curtailment of the right to freedom of expression, establishing that any general powers of decision-making conferred by statute were presumed to have been enacted subject to fundamental civil liberties.

The 'Simmsean' principle of legality avails to the courts the following interpretative mechanism. Fundamental rights cannot be overridden by general or ambiguous words. Accordingly, where express language is said to be lacking, or where wording is thought to be ambiguous, the courts presume that the wording adopted was intended to be subject to the basic rights of the individual, and will uphold these by interpreting the statute in question accordingly. In the famous words of Lord Hoffmann,

> Parliamentary sovereignty means that Parliament can, if it chooses, legislate contrary to fundamental principles of human rights … The constraints upon its exercise by Parliament are ultimately political, not legal. But the principle of legality means that Parliament must squarely confront what it is doing and accept the political cost. Fundamental rights cannot be overridden by general or ambiguous words. This is because there is too great a risk that the full implications of their unqualified meaning may have passed unnoticed in the democratic process. In the absence of express language or necessary implication to the contrary, the courts therefore presume that even the most general words were intended to be subject to the basic rights of the individual. In this way the courts of the United Kingdom, though acknowledging the sovereignty of Parliament, apply principles of constitutionality little different from those which exist in countries where the power of the legislature is expressly limited by a constitutional document.[66]

[64] See also R Rawlings, 'The UNISON Case: A New High-Water Mark' (2018) 29(3) *Public Law Review* 190.
[65] *R v Secretary of State for the Home Department, ex p Simms* (n 13).
[66] *ibid* 131 E-G.

UNISON goes further than *Simms* in that it explores a dimension of the principle of legality the courts do not typically entertain. Citing *R v Secretary of State for the Home Department, ex p Leech (No.2)*[67] and *R (Daly) v Secretary of State for the Home Department*,[68] Lord Reed says that 'even where primary legislation authorises the imposition of an intrusion on the right of access to justice, it is presumed to be subject to an implied limitation'.[69] This could be read to suggest that even in the face of *explicit* statutory constitutional rights curtailment,[70] ie even if a primary statute was to openly acknowledge its abrogating effect on a particular right, such a statute would still be read down to secure the right in question. This is only one step away from suggesting that no statute could ever oust judicial review, a notion I explore in later chapters.

UNISON has had a significant impact on public law litigation and the canons of statutory construction, indeed including beyond what would typically be considered the constitutional law realm. Thus, in *R (Haworth) v Revenue and Customs Commissioners*,[71] the Supreme Court applied *UNISON* to the interpretation of section 204 of the Finance Act 2014. That section applies where a taxpayer has completed their tax return claiming they are entitled to a tax advantage, such as avoidance of a tax charge, because of certain arrangements they have entered into. HMRC may then form the view that the taxpayer is not entitled to that tax advantage because a court or tribunal has decided that arrangements of the kind submitted are not effective, or are unlawful. If certain conditions are met, HMRC may then serve a notice, informing the taxpayer of the amount that needs to be paid. The taxpayer who receives such a notice can opt to respond by taking the 'corrective action', ie pay the tax they had initially sought to avoid. Conversely, if the taxpayer maintains they are entitled to the advantage claimed, but then ultimately lose his or her case before the tribunal, he or she will have to pay the tax as well as a substantial penalty. Section 205 of the Act provides that a previous judicial ruling is 'relevant' to tax arrangements if '… the principles laid down, or reasoning given, in the ruling *would*, if applied to the chosen arrangements, deny the asserted advantage or a part of that advantage …'.[72]

HMRC argued that the provisions of Part 4 of the Finance Act 2014 were different from the fees order challenged in *UNISON*, and that a taxpayer who receives a notice could still assert his or her right to the tax advantage in the tribunal; they were merely discouraged from doing so by the threat of the penalty.

[67] *R v Secretary of State for the Home Department, ex p Leech (No.2)* [1994] QB 198, [1993] 3 WLR 1125.

[68] *R (Daly) v Secretary of State for the Home Department* [2001] UKHL 26, [2001] 2 AC 532.

[69] *R (UNISON) v Lord Chancellor* (n 56) [88].

[70] Compare J Varuhas who distinguishes between what he calls the 'augmented principle of legality' and the 'proactive principle of legality' in 'Conceptualising the Principle(s) of Legality' (2018) 29(3) *Public Law Review* 196.

[71] *R (Haworth) v Revenue and Customs Commissioners* [2021] UKSC 25, [2021] 1 WLR 3521.

[72] Finance Act 2014, s 205 (emphasis added).

Lady Rose concluded, not accepting that her interpretation put a gloss on the wording of the section in question, nor that it imposed a non-statutory threshold,

> There can be no doubt that the threat of the substantial penalty is intended firmly to discourage a taxpayer from pursuing his appeal. As Lord Reed JSC said at para 80 of *UNISON*, where a statutory power authorises an intrusion upon the right of access to the courts, it must be interpreted as authorising only such a degree of intrusion as is reasonably necessary to fulfil the objective of the provision in question. Applying that principle, the use of the word 'would' in the provision requires that HMRC must form the opinion that there is no scope for a reasonable person to disagree that the earlier ruling denies the taxpayer the advantage. Only then can they be said to have formed the opinion that the relevant ruling 'would' deny the advantage. An opinion merely that is likely to do so is not sufficient.[73]

This is a remarkable application of the reasoning in *UNISON* in a context that is very different from that in *UNISON*,[74] signifying the flexibility and the potential of common law rights and principle-based reasoning.

Equally remarkable perhaps is the fact that *UNISON* provided a key part of the template for *Miller v Prime Minister*.[75] Answering the question 'what is the legal limit upon the power to prorogue which makes it compatible with the ability of Parliament to carry out its constitutional functions?',[76] the Supreme Court said one must look at how the exercise of a power 'was liable to affect the operation of a constitutional principle' and that 'the courts have set a limit to the lawful exercise' of power 'by holding that the extent to which the measure impedes or frustrates the operation of the relevant principle must have a reasonable justification'.[77] This approach is directly derived from *UNISON*.[78]

What we can observe in these cases is how a constitutional right is much more than just a legal entitlement in a specific set of circumstances. Rather, constitutional rights open the door to a highly nuanced system of interpretation which is transferable to various contexts across the public law spectrum, affecting the relationship between the branches of state, entities and individuals, beyond the specific dispute before the court. Whilst offering, at this point, no opinion as to the normative validity of the concern expressed by Goldsworthy, it must be right as a matter of simple analysis that,

> if judges interpret legislation according to common law rights that they themselves have developed, regardless of Parliament's intentions, they become co-authors of the law that results from their interpretations. This is to subordinate Parliament's chosen means of communicating its intentions and purposes to moral values chosen by the judges.

[73] *R (Haworth) v Revenue and Customs Commissioners* (n 71) [61].

[74] Conversely, see the judgment in *R (on the application of O (A Child)) v Secretary of State for the Home Department* [2022] UKSC 3, [2022] 2 WLR 343, in which the Supreme Court said *UNISON* was inapplicable.

[75] *R (Miller) v Prime Minister* (n 47).

[76] *ibid* [48].

[77] *ibid* [49].

[78] *R (UNISON) v Lord Chancellor* (n 56) [80]–[82] and [88]–[89].

> Parliament is no longer the sole author of the statute it enacts; no matter what words it uses, their meaning will be determined partly by values preferred by the judges. This is applauded by opponents of legislative supremacy, who say that the meaning of any statute is 'the joint responsibility of Parliament and the courts' [TRS Allan, 'Legislative Supremacy and Legislative Intention: Interpretation, Meaning, and Authority' (2004) *Cambridge Law Journal* 685, 689, fn 13] and is therefore a collaborative enterprise.[79]

UNISON, *Miller v Prime Minister* and *Haworth* are an exemplification of how the Supreme Court, in the words of Lord Hope in *Jackson* 'step, by step, gradually but surely' qualifies the sovereignty of Parliament. There are many other Supreme Court decisions which adopt what we might call an 'expansive', ultimately Parliament-independent approach to statutory interpretation outside the sphere of a recognised common law constitutional right. I will briefly discuss one example, *Armes v Nottinghamshire CC*,[80] in which the Supreme Court held that local authorities can be vicariously liable for torts committed by foster parents against children local authorities place in their care.

The appellant, Ms Armes, had been committed into the care of Nottinghamshire County Council at the age of seven by a care order made under section 1 of the Children and Young Persons Act 1969. She was subsequently placed with two foster families, suffering emotional, physical and sexual abuse at the hands of both. Applying the requirements of the doctrine of vicarious liability established in *Cox v Ministry of Justice*,[81] Lord Reed reasoned that vicarious liability could be imposed beyond traditional employer/employee relationships where the tortfeasor was acting as an 'integral part' of somebody else's business, and for the latter's benefit. Lord Reed disagreed with the Court of Appeal, which had dismissed the claim on the basis that the relevant activity the foster parents were engaged in was providing daily family life.[82] The activity could not, the Court of Appeal said, be characterised as an integral part of the business of the council for the operation of its benefit. Adopting the wider, alternative interpretation, Lord Reed read the statutory framework in a way that imposed liability on a public body, and allowed Ms Armes to successfully sue the council, which was in a financial position to satisfy an award of damages.

In *Armes*, the notions of justice, fairness and reasonableness, inherent in the common law concept of vicarious liability, influenced statutory interpretation in such a way that it led to the recognition of positive duties vested in the state for the protection of those within its care. The judgment demonstrates how public power and obligations can be (re)defined in a field populated by both statute and the common law, with constitutional implications as far as the (financial) liability of local authorities is concerned.

[79] J Goldsworthy, 'Losing Faith in Democracy: Why Judicial Supremacy is Rising and What to Do About it' (9 March 2015), available at https://judicialpowerproject.org.uk/jeffrey-goldsworthy-losing-faith-in-democracy-why-judicial-supremacy-is-rising-and-what-to-do-about-it/.

[80] *Armes v Nottinghamshire CC* [2017] UKSC 60, [2018] AC 355.

[81] *Cox v Ministry of Justice* [2016] UKSC 10, [2016] AC 660.

[82] *Armes v Nottinghamshire CC* [2015] EWCA Civ 1139, [2016] QB 739.

Other examples of cases which do not accord Parliament the level of authority that is required to be accorded to it under the basic, commonly accepted definition of parliamentary sovereignty include, of course, *Evans*[83] and *Privacy International*,[84] the latter of which is discussed at length in chapter two.

C. The Recognition of Constitutional Statutes

The political constitution presumes the legitimacy of majoritarian decision-making[85] as well as the equal status of the output of primary legislative decision-making. All primary legislation is passed by a simple majority, and all laws can be abolished through the same mechanism. Thus, every Act of Parliament is of equal value, there can be no entrenchment. The abandonment of this long-standing assumption, which is implicit in the recognition of the concept of constitutional statutes, is further evidence of a more gradual, nuanced constitution.[86]

Constitutional statutes are judge-made constructs of the common law. Commentators have defined them as statutes

> at least a part of which (1) creates or regulates a state institution and (2) is among the most important elements of our government arrangements, in terms of (a) the influence it has on what state institutions can and may do, given our other governing norms, and (b) the influence it has on what state institutions can and may do through the difference it makes to our other norms. Put simply, a constitutional statute is a statute that is about state institutions and which substantially influences, directly or indirectly, what those institutions can and may do.[87]

The concept of constitutional statutes has been judicially affirmed in many judgments at the highest level. One of the most recent high profile cases endorsing the concept is *Miller v Secretary of State*, in which the Supreme Court said that the European Communities Act 1972 had a constitutional character, echoing the analysis in *Thoburn v Sunderland City Council*,[88] which Psygkas characterises as causing 'The first judicial cracks in the Diceyan orthodoxy'.[89] In *Thoburn*, the High Court made the following comments, obiter dicta:

> Ordinary statutes may be impliedly repealed. Constitutional statutes may not. For the repeal of a constitutional Act or the abrogation of a fundamental right to be

[83] *R (Evans) v Attorney-General* (n 43).

[84] *R (Privacy International) v Investigatory Powers Tribunal* (n 46).

[85] Murkens (n 5) 42.

[86] In one of the leading academic papers on the subject, the judicial recognition of constitutional statutes was referred to as 'the death of an orthodoxy': F Ahmed and A Perry, 'Constitutional Statutes' (2017) 37(2) *OJLS* 461, 461.

[87] *ibid* 471.

[88] *Thoburn v Sunderland City Council* [2002] EWHC 195 (Admin), [2003] QB 151. A more recent Supreme Court case dealing with constitutional statutes is *R (Buckinghamshire CC) v Secretary of State for Transport* [2014] UKSC 3, [2014] 1 WLR 324.

[89] A Psygkas, 'The United Kingdom's Statutory Constitution' (2020) 40(3) *OJLS* 449, 454.

> effected by statute, the court would apply this test: is it shown that the legislature's actual – not imputed, constructive or presumed – intention was to effect the repeal or abrogation? … the test could only be met by express words in the later statute, or by words so specific that the inference of an actual determination to effect the result contended for was irresistible. The ordinary rule of implied repeal does not satisfy this test. Accordingly, it has no application to constitutional statutes. … A constitutional statute can only be repealed, or amended in a way which significantly affects its provisions touching fundamental rights or otherwise the relation between citizen and State, by unambiguous words on the face of the later statute.[90]

Beyond *Miller v Secretary of State*, as was noted by the Northern Ireland Court of Appeal in *Peeples v Prime Minister*, which includes a detailed analysis of the concept of constitutional statutes, 'Whilst some commentators have expressed doubts about the validity of the classification of constitutional legislation we do not detect any substantial retreat from the principles expressed in *Thoburn* in these cases'.[91] The way in which the concept of constitutional statutes has been referenced and analysed in subsequent cases, including *R (A, J, K, B and F) v Secretary of State for the Home Department)*,[92] *Irish Bank Resolution Corp Ltd (In Special Liquidation) v Revenue and Customs Commissioners*[93] and *Privacy International*[94] suggests that there is, indeed, no ambiguity about the existence and basic characteristics of constitutional statutes at the judicial level.

Constitutional statutes, as developed by the senior judiciary, have, as the term suggests, implications for the constitution. They are 'systematically set apart and above the non-constitutional'[95] and accorded higher value, thereby breaking with long-accepted 'constitutional truths' and shaping a constitutional reality in which parliamentary sovereignty does not reign supreme. As Lady Hale puts it extra-judicially, 'The notion that our constitution is hierarchical is a profound change from the Diceyan view … that the Act of Union with Scotland had equal status to the Dentists Act'.[96]

[90] *Thoburn v Sunderland City Council* (n 88) [63].

[91] *Peeples v Prime Minister* [2022] NICA 15, [2022] 3 CMLR 8. This is an example of a case in which the two statutes in question, the European Union (Withdrawal) Act 2018 and the Ireland Act 1800 were both deemed constitutional, meaning no question of hierarchy and implied repeal arose, see [186], [191]–[195], [392]–[397]. For an overview of some of the cases that followed *Thoburn*, see also J McGarry and S Spence, 'Constitutional Statutes – Roots and Recognition' (2020) 41(3) *Statute Law Review* 378.

[92] *R (A, J, K, B and F) v Secretary of State for the Home Department* [2022] EWHC 360 (Admin) (18 February 2022, [2022] ACD 65 [10], [43].

[93] *Irish Bank Resolution Corp Ltd (In Special Liquidation) v Revenue and Customs Commissioners* [2020] EWCA Civ 1128, [2020] STC 1946 [57].

[94] *R (Privacy International) v Investigatory Powers Tribunal* (n 46).

[95] Ahmed and Perry (n 86) 464; see also M Elliott, 'Constitutional Legislation, European Union Law and the Nature of the United Kingdom's Contemporary Constitution' (2014) 10(3) *European Constitutional Law Review* 379.

[96] Lady Hale, 'The Changing Legal Landscape' (2019) 19(4) *Legal Information Management* 217, 219.

How does this impact on the Diceyan notion of parliamentary sovereignty? As Craig explains,

> the rule of recognition has been modified such that Parliament's power to repeal or amend any law either expressly or impliedly, is now subject to an exception not only in relation to EU law, but also in relation to constitutional instruments, such that implied repeal or amendment will only be recognised where it is irresistible.[97]

Put differently, Parliament may, unwittingly, in legislating constitutional statutes without designating them as such, make it more cumbersome for future parliaments to change the law. Apart from this, constitutional statutes are, as I said above, a common law construct in the constitutional sphere. While Psygkas has proposed an alternative way of identifying constitutional statutes, arguing that '… a statute should not become constitutional just because a court has held so',[98] that is presently how they are legally brought into existence. Both these facts chip away at parliamentary sovereignty's armour. Finally, constitutional statutes present the courts with yet another interpretative mechanism through which fundamental values can flourish, thereby increasingly limiting Parliament's legislative freedom, and Parliament's intention can be open to modification. This is because, similarly to ouster clauses, the question that arises is whether Parliament has made itself 'sufficiently clear' to effect repeal of a conflicting constitutional statute.

In this way, the judicial recognition and enforcement of constitutional statutes is similar to that of common law constitutional rights, which also – in theory and practice – qualify the notion of unlimited law-making power. Like constitutional statutes, they introduce an element of hierarchy into constitutional analyses, focusing on values that are deemed so fundamental that special measures are required for them to be overridden. Indeed, there is even authority to suggest that they could eventually be the basis for the courts not to accept a piece of primary legislation. In *Moohan v Lord Advocate*,[99] the applicants argued that not including prisoners in the franchise for the Scottish independence referendum was contrary to the ECHR or the common law. Having concluded that neither the ECHR nor domestic law extended the right to vote to referenda, the Supreme Court stated in obiter dicta that it could

> not exclude the possibility that in the very unlikely event that a parliamentary majority abusively sought to entrench its power by a curtailment of the franchise or similar device, the common law, informed by principles of democracy and the rule of law and international norms, would be able to declare such legislation unlawful.[100]

[97] P Craig, 'Constitutionalising Constitutional Law: HS2' [2014] *PL* 373, 392–93.

[98] Psygkas (n 89) 456.

[99] *Moohan v Lord Advocate* [2014] UKSC 67, [2015] AC 901.

[100] *ibid* [35] (per Lord Hodge). For similar reasoning as to the limits of a common law right in the context of the right to a fair trial and the right to trial by jury, see *In the matter of an application by Hutchings' Application for Judicial Review* [2019] UKSC 26, [2020] NI 801 [55].

Both common law constitutional rights and constitutional statutes are accorded special treatment. In the context of constitutional statutes, this is evident in the doctrine of modified implied repeal and their superiority over ordinary statutes. In the context of common law constitutional rights, it is evident in the protection the latter offer against 'unjust' secondary legislation as well as through the highly context-sensitive and purposive interpretation of primary legislation. Ahmed and Perry justify the higher value accorded to constitutional statutes by reference to legislative intent. Their analysis is well put, but it seems more realistic to suggest that, as with common law constitutional rights, judges are 'entrenching' law they deem, for one reason or another, more normatively important than others, irrespective of Parliament's views on the matter.

IV. Why is the Nuanced Constitution not the Common Law Constitution?

This chapter has started to build the argument that the contemporary UK constitution cannot be accurately characterised as reflecting political constitutionalism. Constitutional principles and practices and a value-driven approach to legal reasoning in which legislative intent is but one factor, shape an environment which cannot easily be reconciled with the political constitution. Some instances of these phenomena, such as constitutional statutes, appear to align with the common law constitutionalist understanding most closely associated with the writings of Allan. His theory can be summarised by reference to three key claims. First, Parliament's power is legitimised by and derived from law. Second, it does (therefore) not have unlimited legal power but is restrained by fundamental legal values which are conceptualised as a higher rule. Third, this higher rule is typically captured by the rule of law in tandem with the principle of legality, both of which are considered creatures of the common law. Taken together, these points mean that in the judicial process

> Authoritative sources are identified, interpreted, and (when necessary) moderated on the basis of reasoned argument. Moral deliberation comes to the fore as the defining characteristic of a system of law grounded on defensible principles of justice or fairness ...[101]

However, despite what we can observe in the themes and cases highlighted so far, looking at constitutional practice *in the round*, we cannot say that that the constitution is therefore best characterised as a common law constitution. Making this claim would ignore a number of facts. For example, despite a growing body of obiter dicta, the judiciary has abstained from quashing an Act of Parliament,

[101] TRS Allan, 'Law, Democracy, and Constitutionalism: Reflections on *Evans v Attorney General*' (2016) 75(1) *CLJ* 38, 39.

bearing in mind also the corollary that Parliament has the power to reverse judgments by legislation. Constitutional review in which primary legislation is quashed continues to be unprecedented in this jurisdiction.[102] Furthermore, there is no explicit let alone consistent judicial endorsement of the common law constitution. The closest we come to an *indirect* express endorsement of the theory is Lord Carnwath's judgment in *Privacy International*,[103] which is discussed in detail in chapter two.

Finally, the argument in focus in this section, in many if not the majority of public law cases, law enacted by Parliament takes centre-stage, and common law rules and principles play a minor role. Senior UK courts regularly deliver judgments in which the statutory framework prevails over individual rights and other common law principles even where there are possible legal avenues to protect the latter. One example of this phenomenon is the decision in *R (Nicklinson) v Ministry of Justice*.[104] The case concerned a challenge to the domestic criminalisation of assisted suicide under the Suicide Act 1961 on the basis of articles 2 ECHR (the right to life) and 8 ECHR (the right to respect for private and family life).[105] The claimants were facing the prospect of living for many years with serious medical conditions, in complete dependence on others, which they experienced as demeaning. They were physically incapable of ending their own lives, requiring the assistance of others, and sought declarations on the basis of both the common law and the ECHR that those assisting them to commit suicide ought not to be criminally prosecuted. The combined actions sought different outcomes: the appellants in the first action appealed against the Court of Appeal's decision[106] that the ban on assisted suicide did not infringe the ECHR, whereas the appellant in the other one, the Director of Public Prosecutions, appealed against a decision requiring her to amend the relevant policy on prosecutions.

A starkly divided Supreme Court held that the UK's prohibition of assisted suicide, imposed by section 2 of the Suicide Act 1961, was within the state's margin of appreciation[107] and that it could in principle adjudicate on the matter, but decided that it would not be constitutionally appropriate for it to rule on the compatibility of the law in question before Parliament was given the opportunity to reform that law. Among the nine Supreme Court Justices, five said the Court in principle had authority to issue a declaration under section 4 of the HRA

[102] The closest mechanism the courts have to constitutional review as it is generally understood is the power to declare primary legislation to be incompatible with the ECHR, which the case law has said 'is in substance a kind of constitutional review of primary legislation' albeit with the 'important limit' that the offending piece of legislation retains its effect: *R (National Council for Civil Liberties) v Secretary of State for the Home Department and another v National Union of Journalists* [2019] EWHC 2057 (Admin), [2020] 1 WLR 243 [88].

[103] *R (Privacy International) v Investigatory Powers Tribunal* (n 46).

[104] *R (Nicklinson) v Ministry of Justice* [2014] UKSC 38, [2015] AC 657.

[105] Prior to *Nicklinson*, the key authority on this issue was *R (Pretty) v DPP* [2001] UKHL 61, [2002] 1 AC 800.

[106] *R (Nicklinson) v Ministry of Justice* [2013] EWCA Civ 961, [2014] 2 All ER 32.

[107] This was subsequently confirmed by the European Court of Human Rights in Mr Nicklinson's subsequent challenge, see Application Nos 2478/15 and 1787/15.

that section 2 of the Suicide Act 1961 was incompatible with article 8 ECHR. However, Lord Neuberger, Lord Wilson and Lord Mance held that the ban was proportionate; only Lady Hale and the late Lord Kerr said that a declaration should be issued.

The approach and outcome in *Nicklinson* has, despite the internal disagreement, sent a clear signal which, in subsequent cases, led to the resounding rejection of individual claimants' attempts to challenge the legality of the Suicide Act 1961 in this regard. For example, in *R (Newby) v Secretary of State for Justice*[108] the Divisional Court, applying *Nicklinson*, held that the courts were not an appropriate forum for the discussion of the 'sanctity of life',[109] echoing Foster's verdict of *Nicklinson* that it was 'the fact that the case raises moral, social and ethical issues … that has led the courts to back down and show judicial deference'.[110] In the end, institutional legitimacy concerns determined the outcome of this case.[111] In doing so, the majority of the Supreme Court fettered 'what is otherwise a relatively broad discretionary power under s 4 of the HRA'.[112]

Second, there is *Beghal v DWP*,[113] a case which concerns the appeal of a criminal conviction, which is discussed again in later chapters. Mrs Beghal had been questioned at the East Midlands Airport under Schedule 7 of the Terrorism Act 2000 upon returning from France where her husband had been in custody on terrorism charges. Upon refusing to answer any questions, Mrs Beghal was convicted of the offence created by paragraph 18 of Schedule 7. The Supreme Court held that the power found in Schedule 7 to the Terrorism Act 2000, which allows detention for up to six hours to question and search individuals at ports and borders who 'appeared' to be concerned in the commission, preparation or instigation of terrorism, irrespective of whether the examining officer had grounds for suspecting that the individual was so concerned, was not incompatible with article 8 ECHR. The Court also held that the power in Schedule 7 did not violate article 5 ECHR, that the common law privilege against self-incrimination did not apply due to having been abrogated by necessary inference by the Terrorism Act 2000, and that the privilege against self-incrimination embedded in article 6 ECHR did not apply since Mrs Beghal had not been 'charged'.

[108] *R (Newby) v Secretary of State for Justice* [2019] EWHC 3118 (Admin) (19 November 2019, unreported).

[109] See also *R (H) v Secretary of State for Health and Social Care* [2019] EWHC 2095 (Admin) (30 July 2019, unreported) where the High Court highlighted that the issue of whether a genetic father should be named on a birth certificate in place of the surrogate's husband had been raised but ultimately withdrawn in Parliament during the passage of the relevant Act, and that it was therefore appropriate to give a wide discretion to Parliament in the setting of the statutory provisions.

[110] S Foster, 'Back to You: Judicial Deference, Parliament and the Right to Die' (2019) 24(2) *Coventry Law Journal* 105, 109.

[111] For a case study that criticises the judgment's effect on domestic human rights protection, see E Wicks, 'The Supreme Court Judgment in Nicklinson: One Step Forward on Assisted Dying; Two Steps Back on Human Rights' (2015) 23(1) *Medical Law Review* 144.

[112] S Martin, 'Declaratory Misgivings: Assisted Suicide in a Post-Nicklinson Context' [2018] *PL* 209, 222–23.

[113] *Beghal v DPP* [2015] UKSC 49, [2016] AC 88.

Two points are worth highlighting for our present discussion. The first is the restrictive interpretative approach taken by the majority in *Beghal* when looking at the common law privilege against self-incrimination part of the challenge. Lord Hughes (with whom Lord Hodge agreed)[114] reasoned that the appellant could not avail herself of the common law privilege against self-incrimination when questioned under Schedule 7 as the privilege was inapplicable because it was by 'necessary inference' abrogated by the statute in question.[115] Thus, *Beghal* demonstrates that very little weight may be given to a common law constitutional right and other fundamental common law concepts even if rights have not been abrogated expressly. The second point concerns the legality requirement, and the way in which the Court approached the question whether the power was 'in accordance with the law'. There are some serious question marks around the majority's conclusions concerning legality, especially in light of the Strasbourg jurisprudence in *Gillan v United Kingdom*, in which the European Court of Human Rights held that s 44 of the Terrorism Act 2000, which conferred power on a senior police officer to designate an area for no more than 28 days within which police officers could stop and search any person for articles which may be used for terrorist purposes.[116] As several legal commentators have shown, the late Lord Kerr's carefully reasoned dissenting opinion is more aligned with established public law jurisprudence,[117] including the majority's 'distinctly case-specific approach' to the question of legality.[118]

Why did the Supreme Court adopt Parliament or executive-centric stances in these cases? It would be too simple to suggest that *Beghal* is more geared towards recognising the centrality and or/dominance of statutory law as the law in question was an Act of Parliament as opposed to, for example, the fees order at stake in *UNISON*. *Evans* shows that things are not that black and white. In *Evans*, the Upper Tribunal's order to disclose Prince Charles' memos to government ministers was upheld by the Supreme Court even though Parliament had explicitly given the Attorney-General the statutory power to veto disclosure on 'reasonable grounds'. The 'fundamental composite principle' that a decision of a judicial body should be final and binding, and that it should not be capable of being overturned by a member of the executive, paved the way for a highly contextual interpretation of what was, on the face of it, clear primary statutory language. Thus, the type of legislation in question need not necessarily steer judicial reasoning one way or the other. More subtle factors are at play, such as the issue in question, the importance

[114] Lord Neuberger and Lord Dyson concurred.

[115] The reasoning was also in part based on the belief that there would be no sufficient risk that the answers would be used in subsequent criminal proceedings.

[116] *Gillan v United Kingdom* (2010) 50 EHRR 1105 [77].

[117] See, eg, J Rogers, 'Beghal v DPP: Some Unresolved Issues' (2016) 1 *Archbold Review* 4; H Wong and M Law, 'Powers to Search, Question and Detain under Schedule 7 of the Terrorism Act 2000: Beghal v Director of Public Prosecutions' (2015) 5 *European Human Rights Law Review* 512.

[118] S Wilson Stark, 'Facing Facts: Judicial Approaches to Section 4 of the Human Rights Act 1998' (2017) 133 *LQR* 631, 642.

attached to non-statutory legal principles, and the exact wording of the relevant statutory language.

Other recent Supreme Court decisions reveal a commitment to the tenets associated with political constitutionalism too. Among them is *R (Begum) v Secretary of State for the Home Department*,[119] which concerned appeals to the Special Immigration Appeals Commission and considered the question of effective participation in those appeals. The Supreme Court strongly disagreed with the Court of Appeal's decision that any national security concerns stemming from permitting the respondent to return to the jurisdiction for the purpose of pursing her appeal against being rendered stateless, were outweighed by the interests of fairness and justice, and could be addressed and managed on Ms Begum's return. The Supreme Court criticised the Court of Appeal Court for having 'overlooked the limitations to its competence, both institutional and constitutional, to decide questions of national security'.

Another instructive case is *R (SC) v Secretary of State for Work and Pensions*[120] in which the Supreme Court held that the two-child limit applicable under ss 9(3A) and 9(3B) of the Tax Credits Act 2002 for the payment of the individual element of child tax credit was compatible with the ECHR. The judgment contains a relatively lengthy discussion on the separation of powers, highlighting the different ways in which Parliament and the courts 'resolve disputes'[121] and that the courts are slow to interfere with decisions concerning social and economic policy in the field of welfare benefits. The executive's judgment would be respected, unless it was 'manifestly without reasonable foundation', which it had not been.[122] Lord Reed explained that 'it remains the position that a low intensity of review is generally appropriate, other things being equal, in cases concerned with judgments of social and economic policy in the field of welfare benefits and pensions'.[123] In *R (Plan B Earth) v Prime Minister* the High Court said the manifestly without reasonable foundation approach 'respects the constitutional separation between the Courts, Parliament and the executive. It also reflects the fact that the Court is not well equipped to form its own views on the matters in question'.[124]

That said, *SC* arguably also pulls towards common law constitutionalist maxims, in saying the following:

> the degree of respect which the courts should show to primary legislation in this context *will depend on the circumstances*. Among the relevant factors may be the subject-matter of the legislation, and whether it is relatively recent or dates from an age with different values from the present time. Another factor which may be relevant is whether Parliament can be taken to have made its own judgment of the issues which are relevant

[119] *R (Begum) v Secretary of State for the Home Department* [2021] UKSC 7, [2021] AC 765.
[120] *R (SC) v Secretary of State for Work and Pensions* [2021] UKSC 26, [2022] AC 223.
[121] *ibid* [169].
[122] This test/review mechanism is derived from *Mellacher v Austria* (1990) 12 EHRR 391 [45].
[123] *R (SC) v Secretary of State for Work and Pensions* (n 120) [158].
[124] *R (Plan B Earth) v Prime Minister* [2021] EWHC 3469 (Admin) (21 December 2021, unreported at the time of writing) [51].

> to the court's assessment. If so, the court will be *more inclined to accept* Parliament's decision, out of respect for democratic decision-making on questions of political controversy.[125]

Apart from the case law examples discussed in this chapter, we must also recognise that the way in which practitioners approach legal disputes is not commensurate with common law constitutionalism's understanding. In any given dispute, where primary legislation speaks to the matter in hand, the first port of call for any practitioner is the plain wording of the Act in question, which has been referred to as the 'cardinal rule', and which also goes by different names, including '"natural", "ordinary", "literal", "grammatical", "popular" and "primary"'.[126] Lawyers know that the starting point for the courts in interpreting a statute is that words are given their ordinary and natural meaning. That rule may then in certain circumstances be departed from, however the starting point of any prudent practitioner's legal research and submissions remains a close analysis of what the democratically elected branch of state has prescribed. Courts will continue to, as the starting point, seek to 'ascertain the intention of Parliament as expressed in the words it has chosen'.[127]

V. Taking Stock

Viewed in their aggregate, the cases presented in this chapter suggest strongly that the UK has neither a political nor a legal (or common law) constitution. A more nuanced picture presents itself. For example, while the courts' interpretative principles are based on the common law and in the process of constantly being developed, a fact recognised by parliamentary counsel,[128] the starting point of those principles is to accord respect to parliamentary intention. There are also numerous examples where moral deliberation, or the supposed striving of the common law towards justice and liberty, for example, does not come to the fore as the defining characteristic. Indeed, as *Nicklinson*[129] shows, the law may well be deemed to require judicial adaptation, yet the courts may still let institutional legitimacy concerns prevail. Meanwhile, in *Beghal*[130] the courts chose not to interpret draconian legislation under which individuals could be detained for a maximum of six hours without reasonable suspicion in a way that also respects a number of rights enshrined by statute or protected under the common law.

[125] *R (SC) v Secretary of State for Work and Pensions* (n 120) [180] (per Lord Reed).

[126] D Greenberg, *Craies on Legislation*, 12th edn (Sweet & Maxwell, 2020) 17.1.1.

[127] *R (Quintavalle) v Secretary of State for Health* [2003] UKHL 13, [2003] 2 AC 687 [38] (per Lord Millett). The court acts under the 'banner of loyalty to the will of Parliament' and needs to 'give effect to the true meaning of what Parliament has said': [8] (per Lord Bingham of Cornhill).

[128] D Bailey, 'Bridging the Gap: Legislative Drafting Practice and Statutory Interpretation' [2020] *PL* 220, 221.

[129] *R (Nicklinson) v Ministry of Justice* (n 104).

[130] *Beghal v DPP* (n 113).

Many other cases can be found in which the elements of legal constitutionalism, of which common law constitutionalism is a uniquely British variant, are almost entirely eclipsed. Indeed, typically it is parliamentary sovereignty rather than common law constitutionalist notions which provides 'a presuppositional frame that shapes perception, understanding and, in turn, practical reason'.[131] Still, we must recognise and embed in our reading of the constitution cases such as *Evans*[132] and *Privacy International*,[133] in which parliamentary intention played second fiddle.

The sum of these parts of the constitution is *nuance*. This nuance is created by judges engaging with substantive arguments about values and interests which are given legal status at the same time as according a fundamental status, and often primacy, to legislation. The majority of public law cases will have a combination of elements associated with the political constitution as well as legal constitutionalism. However, there are also cases which sit relatively firmly in one camp or the other. As I explain further in later chapters, the case law can be viewed as operating on a spectrum, and exactly where on the spectrum individual cases fall is determined by a range of factors. Looking at that spectrum, we can see a new understanding emerging, which cannot reasonably be said to represent, exclusively or predominantly, political or legal constitutionalist features.

VI. How Did We Get Here?

This chapter purports that the essential character of the UK constitution is nuance – judicial adherence to political or legal constitutionalism is not absolute in constitutional practice. Before delving into the boundaries of the nuanced constitution in more detail in chapter two, the remainder of this chapter explores some of the reasons behind the gradual qualification of parliamentary sovereignty. I focus on two enabling factors, one external and one internal: European law, by which I mean both the ECHR and EU law, and the properties of the English common law itself.

A. European Law

As I show in chapter three and chapter four, European law has had a strong influence on legal thinking in this jurisdiction.[134] One example is the way in which

[131] N Walker, 'Sovereignty Frames and Sovereignty Claims' in R Rawlings, P Layland and AL Young, *Sovereignty and the Law: Domestic, European and International Perspectives* (Oxford University Press, 2013) 21.

[132] *R (Evans) v Attorney-General* (n 43).

[133] *R (Privacy International) v Investigatory Powers Tribunal* (n 46).

[134] Compare R Cooke, 'The Road Ahead for the Common Law' (2004) 53(2) *ICLQ* 273, who says that the English common law is becoming 'less English'.

the principle of proportionality has influenced the development of the standard of review in public law cases. For instance, common law constitutional rights are, post-*Kennedy*,[135] applied by reference to proportionality review. One of the differences in the application of proportionality review and irrationality or Wednesbury unreasonableness review is that proportionality review allows the courts to *openly* balance competing interests whereas traditional common law review mechanisms strike this balance more covertly. The way in which proportionality review operates as a methodological tool that requires an open weighing of constitutional rights and the justification for their limitation is likely to have had an impact on the collective judicial mindset in this jurisdiction.

More broadly, although we cannot definitively measure the extent to which it has influenced legal reasoning in domestic adjudication, it also seems likely that an accustomisation with human rights thinking through the engagement with European human rights jurisprudence has led to a partial change in legal reasoning. It has become more natural for lawyers and judges to look at a legal problem from a rights-based angle to the extent that one could say English administrative law 'has undergone a "rights'-based" expansion'[136] because of, among other factors, the passing of the HRA. Indeed, under the stimulus of the latter, 'the courts have become increasingly conscious of the extent to which the common law reflects fundamental values'.[137]

As I explain further in chapter two, this comparing and contrasting between European and domestic legal sources has triggered a judicial reassertion of the virtue and strength of the English common law. Thus, as previously stated, in *UNISON*,[138] Lord Reed said that 'the right of access to justice is not an idea recently imported from the continent of Europe, but has long been deeply embedded in our constitutional law'.[139] Meanwhile, in *A v BBC*, Lord Reed identified the roots of the constitutional principle of open justice as being old enough to have been covered by 'the constitutional legislation enacted following the accession of William and Mary' in the Court of Session Act 1693.[140] In other cases, the Supreme Court refused to adapt the common law in view of the stronger rights protection offered by the ECHR. For example, *Commissioner of Police of the Metropolis v DSD and another*[141] saw two victims of sexual offences bring proceedings against the police, alleging failure to conduct effective investigations into these crimes after they had raised them with the authorities. The Supreme Court held that article 3 ECHR imposed a positive obligation on

[135] *Kennedy v Charity Commission* (n 63).

[136] JNE Varuhas, 'The Reformation of English Administrative Law? "Rights", Rhetoric and Reality' (2013) 72(2) *CLJ* 369.

[137] *Montgomery v Lankashire Health Board* [2015] UKSC 11, [2015] AC 1430 [80] (per Lord Kerr and Lord Reed).

[138] *R (UNISON) v Lord Chancellor* (n 56).

[139] *ibid* [64].

[140] *A v BBC* (n 62) [24].

[141] *Commissioner of Police of the Metropolis v DSD and another* [2018] UKSC 11, [2019] AC 196.

states to effectively investigate reported crimes perpetrated by private individuals, and that this obligation had been breached. Reasoning that the two bases of liability – the common law and the ECHR – were different, Lord Kerr said that the two regimes should not be aligned. In other words, in *DSD*, the non-convergence of the two legal sources in question allowed the Supreme Court to impose a positive obligation on the police even though no liability could be established under English tort law. The 'weaknesses' of the common law from a rights perspective presented no hindrance to the ultimate protection of the right in question. Thus, even in cases where the common law is not bolstered through the direct contrast with the European-based regime under the HRA, rights awareness is further shaped, and rights-based thinking is rehearsed. The rights under the Convention being predominantly leveraged against the state,[142] and there being a statutory duty to read legislation as far as possible compatibly with the rights protected by the HRA,[143] the courts are incentivised to take a nuanced approach to interpreting statutes. This has spilled over into common law constitutional rights case law and domestic jurisprudence more broadly.

B. The English Common Law

The qualification, in some cases, of the concept of parliamentary sovereignty has also been enabled by the way in which the English common law works. Indeed, it is arguably the combined effect of the partial 'Europeanisation' of UK law and the common law's inbuilt qualities which has made the UK constitution increasingly nuanced.

The English[144] common law approaches statutes in much the same way as it approaches common law rules in the sense that its interpretative mechanisms are a constant process of both reliance on the past concurrent with development and refinement. Most cases balance the two parameters of legal certainty, which is achieved, for example, by interpreting statutory language in a way that is loyal to the wording (and consistently across different cases), and some notion of *justice* or *fairness*, which is achieved through, for example, the application of substantive, value-driven legal principles or mechanisms such as rationality review. Summarised by Pound's 'the law must be stable, but it cannot stand still',[145] one of the hallmark of our legal system is

> its capacity to allow for change and innovation in an overall process that emphasizes the importance of continuity and stability. Indeed, the legal community insists that a

[142] On horizontal effect, see G Phillipson and A Williams, 'Horizontal Effect and the Constitutional Constraint' (2011) 74(6) *MLR* 878.

[143] HRA, s 3.

[144] Originally, the common law was not – strictly speaking – English but 'a species of continental feudal law developed into an English system by kings and justices of continental extraction', see RC Van Caenegem, *The Birth of the English Common Law* (Cambridge University Press, 1988) 110.

[145] R Pound, *Interpretations of Legal History* (Cambridge University Press, 1967) 1.

large part of adjudicative activity involves reliance on the legal past, whether by way of substantive results or argumentative consistency, to resolve present problems and to influence future results.[146]

Within this approach to legal reasoning, several specific characteristics can be made out that have shaped the nuanced constitution. First, one traditional aspect of the common law that has helped shape a more nuanced constitution is its *gap-filling character. Dover DC v Campaign to Protect Rural England*,[147] which recognised this quality specifically, is a case that gives us an insight into how this *gap-filling* function influences nuanced statutory interpretation. Developers had applied to Dover District Council for planning permission for an extensive residential development on two connected sites involving more than 500 dwellings. The development was categorised as one to which the Town and Country Planning Regulations 2011 applied, so the planning application was accompanied by an environmental impact statement. Objections had been received, including those by the claimant. The planning committee resolved to grant planning permission, but, contrary to what the planning officer had recommended, did not reduce the density and scale of the development. The Court held that regulation 24(1)(c) of the Town and Country Planning (Environmental Impact Assessment) (England and Wales) Regulations 1999 required the Council to publish a statement containing the main reasons and consideration on which the decision was based, a legal duty the Council had failed to discharge.

Making obiter dicta comments (the legal wrong had been committed on the basis of the EIA Regulations), Lord Carnwath nonetheless discussed the position at common law, and said that the common law could supplement statutory rules, and that fairness may in some circumstances require the giving of reasons even in a statutory context in which no express duty is imposed.[148] He made this statement despite there having been an abrogation of the duty to give reasons,[149] highlighting that the explanatory memorandum to the said abrogation stated that it should not 'detract from the general principle of transparency'.[150] Thus, *Dover DC* exemplifies both the common law's capacity to fill statutory gaps and its self-proclaimed affinity with fairness. Relying on *R v Secretary of State for the Home Department, ex p Doody*,[151] Lord Carnwath reasoned that the proper interpretation of the statute was underpinned by the principle of fairness, and specifically 'fairness as between the state and an individual citizen'.[152] He continued to say that a further common law principle was in play, namely the common

[146] AC Hutchinson, *Evolution and the Common Law* (Cambridge University Press, 2005) 1.
[147] *Dover DC v Campaign to Protect Rural England* [2017] UKSC 79, [2018] 1 WLR 108.
[148] *ibid* [54].
[149] By the Town and Country Planning (Development Management Procedure) (England) (Amendment) Order 2013 (SI 2013/1238), article 7.
[150] *Dover DC v Campaign to Protect Rural England* (n 147) [56].
[151] *R v Secretary of State for the Home Department, ex p Doody* [1994] 1 AC 531 (HL).
[152] *Dover DC v Campaign to Protect Rural England* (n 147) [54]–[55].

law principle 'that justice should not only be done, but also be seen to be done.[153] This makes *Dover* a primary example of how value-driven common law principles and rights cut across different areas of (public) law to shape the constitutional atmosphere within which individual cases operate.

Meanwhile, *Armes*[154] demonstrates how fairness can implicitly influence statutory interpretation through the development of the law on vicarious liability. In this case, Lord Reed moved away from a control-centric definition, traditionally a key element of employer/employee relationships. As public bodies who are responsible for decision-making in relation to children may find it

> advantageous to place them in foster care notwithstanding the inherent risk that some children may be abused, it may be considered *fair* that they should compensate the unfortunate children for whom that risk materialises, particularly bearing in mind that the children are under the protection of the local authority and have no control over the decision regarding their placement.[155]

The normative character of the statutory interpretation in *Armes* is further supported by Lord Reed's powerful dismissal of the argument that holding the council liable would open the floodgates, and that the imposition of vicarious liability would have major financial consequences. If this was the case, Lord Reed reasoned, this would mean that there had been such a widespread problem of child abuse by foster parents that there would indeed be 'every reason why the law should expose how this has occurred'.[156]

It is unsurprising that in a legal system that is principally made up of two legal sources, judge-made law and statutory law, the workings and principles of one legal source will influence the other. Under the nuanced constitution, statutory law alters the common law, and the common law shapes the way in which statutory law is interpreted. For example, rights protected by the common law will be enforced through the constitutional principle of legality when interpreting a statute which risks abrogating those rights. Equally, secondary legislation and other statutory instruments can be quashed if they violate aspects of the rule of law.[157] In turn, statutes can restate and replace parts of the common law.[158]

The nuanced constitution has been shaped incrementally and was perhaps always in existence. Contrary to what Bogdanor has suggested,[159] it is a reality that has not been solely brought about by our EU membership or the advent of the HRA. For example, the Supreme Court's heavy reliance in *Privacy International*[160]

[153] *Ibid* [55]. He then referred to *Kennedy v Charity Commission* (n 63), one of the main common law constitutional rights authorities discussed throughout this book.
[154] *Armes v Nottinghamshire CC* (n 80).
[155] *ibid* [61] (emphasis added).
[156] *ibid* [69].
[157] As was the case in *R (UNISON) v Lord Chancellor* (n 56).
[158] For example, the Companies Act 2006 did this for directors' duties.
[159] V Bogdanor, *The New British Constitution* (Hart Publishing, 2009).
[160] *R (Privacy International) v Investigatory Powers Tribunal* (n 46).

on *Anisminic Ltd v Foreign Compensation Commission*,[161] a case from the 1960s, demonstrates that this cannot be so. Just as Parliament acquired its status and power progressively, the courts have evolved in their constitutional role. The UK's uncodified constitution has facilitated this evolution. Inherently flexible, it has increasingly moved towards a model of democracy and adjudication that embodies a multiplicity of legal sources and principles of competing value, rather than complete deference to majority rule through Parliament alone.

VII. A Closer Look at the Constitution and Common Law Constitutional Rights

Having argued that the UK constitution is best described as a nuanced constitution – which is an alternative third model – in the next chapter I will take a closer look at the boundaries of the nuanced constitution through an in-depth analysis of four recent significant cases.

[161] *Anisminic Ltd v Foreign Compensation Commission* [1969] 2 AC 147 (HL).

2

A Closer Look at the Nuanced Constitution Through Four Case Studies

There has been no shortage of remarkable constitutional law cases over the last five years. Two judgments in particular stand out: *R (Privacy) International v Investigatory Powers Tribunal*[1] and *(R) Miller v Prime Minister; Cherry and others v Advocate General for Scotland*.[2] In *Privacy International* the key issue the Supreme Court had to determine was whether section 67(8) of the Regulation of Investigatory Powers Act 2000 (RIPA), which contains an ouster clause, prevents judicial review of a decision of the Investigatory Powers Tribunal (IPT). The Supreme Court held it does not, and Privacy International went on to win the case on substance. Meanwhile, in *Miller v Prime Minister* the Supreme Court was tasked with deciding whether the Prime Minister's advice to the late Queen in August 2019 to prorogue Parliament for five weeks almost immediately before the planned date for the UK's withdrawal from the EU was unlawful. The Supreme Court held that it was, having determined the preliminary question as to whether that question of lawfulness was justiciable in the first place in the affirmative.

Looking at those two cases, we can see that contemporary constitutional jurisprudence has spun a web of legal values and interpretative techniques that cannot be reconciled with the tenets of the political constitution. Rather, the constitution is in its essence nuanced, containing both political constitutionalist and common law constitutionalist facets. Having introduced the idea of the nuanced constitution in chapter one, the first part of this chapter provides case studies of *Privacy International* and *Miller/Cherry v Prime* Minster, drawing out common themes with a view to exploring the characteristics of the nuanced constitution on the common law constitutional side of the constitutional spectrum.

This analysis is followed by a discussion of two recent Supreme Court cases which sit on the opposite side of the spectrum, *R (Begum) v Special Immigration Appeals Commission*[3] and *R (O (A Child)) v Secretary of State for the Home Department*.[4] In *Begum* the Supreme Court was tasked with answering a number

[1] *R (Privacy International) v Investigatory Powers Tribunal* [2019] UKSC 22, [2019] 2 WLR 1219.

[2] *R (Miller) v Prime Minister; Cherry and others (Respondents) v Advocate General for Scotland* [2019] UKSC 41, [2020] AC 373.

[3] *R (Begum) v Special Immigration Appeals Commission* [2021] UKSC 7, [2021] 2 WLR 556.

[4] *R (O (A Child)) v Secretary of State for the Home Department* [2022] UKSC 3, [2022] 2 WLR 343.

of mainly technical questions relating to Ms Begum's challenge to her deprivation of citizenship and the decision not to grant her leave to return to the UK from Syria to pursue that challenge. The Supreme Court determined appeals in three separate sets of proceedings initiated by Ms Begum, which are difficult to summarise given the vast ground they cover. For present purposes, Ms Begum lost on all grounds, resulting in her not being allowed to return to the UK to pursue her appeal, which was, effectively, stayed indefinitely. The Supreme Court re-emphasised the traditional view that national security questions are for politicians, not the courts to decide. Meanwhile, in *O (A Child)*, the question was whether the Immigration and Nationality (Fees) Regulations 2018 were ultra vires the Immigration Act 2014. The appellant argued that the Secretary of State did not have the power to set the fee to apply for registration as British citizens at £973 (at the time), because the fee, due to it being unaffordable to many, trivialised the statutory right to become a British citizen. The Supreme Court, dismissing the appeal, emphasised the importance of parliamentary intention and held that the appropriateness of imposing a fee on children was a question of policy for political determination, not a matter for the courts.

These four cases highlight some of the key aspects of the nuanced constitution. In particular, they allow us to begin to appreciate the characteristics of the nuanced constitution, both as far as its political constitutionalist and its legal constitutionalist/common law constitutionalist components are concerned. I set out the reasoning employed in each of them in detail, including by courts other than the Supreme Court. The reason for this is that seeing the trajectory and reading a detailed summary of the judicial analyses in each set of proceedings will convey to readers important aspects of the current state of the UK constitution. To some extent, the cases speak for themselves, and it is hoped that readers will, in the first instance, benefit from the detailed summaries provided. This is then complemented by my own analysis, in which I highlight and critique certain aspects of each decision, while also establishing commonalities and differences between them. The broader aim is to bring out, through these case studies, some of the key characteristics of the nuanced constitution, which is essential to understand – and provide a meaningful critique of – common law constitutional rights, the second key theme of this book.

I. *R (Privacy International) v IPT*

The Supreme Court's judgment in *Privacy International* is remarkable, principally because of how far it pushes the Court's reasoning into the common law constitutionalist camp. The judgment has been recognised by academics[5]

[5] See, eg, BJ Ong, 'The Ouster of Parliamentary Sovereignty?' [2020] *PL* 41, who, at 49, believes one aspect of the judgment to be 'truly revolutionary', and E Bjorge, who says the decision 'concerned the

as carrying tremendous constitutional importance. As for politics, the Supreme Court's judgment in *Privacy International* was arguably, perhaps alongside the two *Miller* judgments, one of the propellers for the previous Government's constitutional law reform agenda.[6] To understand *Privacy International* it is helpful to understand the constitutional significance of ouster clauses. Ouster clauses are statutory provisions which aim to prevent the courts from considering a question or from reviewing a decision. As the case law shows, even an apparently clear legislative prohibition on the courts reviewing certain decisions will generally be insufficient for the clause to have any meaningful legal effect. One could say that ouster clause cases demonstrate the outer boundaries of statutory interpretation. What looks – on the face of it – like unambiguous statutory wording is interpreted in a nuanced way, taking into account constitutional principles. Thus, ouster clauses speak directly to the constitutional authority of – and the power dynamic between – the two branches of state. Indeed, as the way in which 'statutes are interpreted is crucial to the implementation of the doctrine of parliamentary sovereignty',[7] we can say that the judicial interpretation of ouster clauses exemplifies the softening of 'the potentially hard edges of legislative sovereignty'.[8]

The main authority relied on in *Privacy International* is *Anisminic Ltd v Foreign Compensation Commission*.[9] The appellants in *Anisminic* had had some of their property seized by the Egyptian Government in the aftermath of the UK's invasion of Egypt in 1956, which made them apply for compensation under the Foreign Compensation Act 1950. The body authorised by an Order in Council made under that Act to deal with such claims, the Foreign Compensation Commission, decided that the appellants were not eligible for compensation. This was due to their successor in title – an Egyptian owned organisation Anisminic Ltd had sold its mining properties to – not being British, as required by subordinate legislation. This prompted Anisminic Ltd to initiate judicial review proceedings seeking declarations that the Commission's determinations had been erroneous in law. Section 4(4) of the Foreign Compensation Act provided 'the determination by the Commission of any application made to them under this Act shall not be called in question in any court of law'.

very soul of the English constitution' in 'Legislation Purporting to Oust the High Court's Jurisdiction: Privacy International' (2020) 136 *LQR* 12, 17.

[6] See, eg, the Government's Response to the Judicial Review Reform Consultation (CP 477, July 2021), which explains at paras 50 and 51 that Parliament, in response to *Anisminic Ltd v Foreign Compensation Commission* [1969] 2 AC 147 (HL) 'passed wider ouster clauses which appeared to oust Judicial Review even for jurisdictional errors. This is what Parliament did in the provision at issue in *Privacy International v Investigatory Powers Tribunal* [2019] UKSC 22. However, this still led to interpretative difficulties'.

[7] J Goldsworthy, *Parliamentary Sovereignty: Contemporary Debates* (Cambridge University Press, 2010) 225.

[8] A Tucker, 'Parliamentary Intention, Anisminic, and the Privacy International Case (Part One)' (*UK Constitutional Law Association Blog*, 18 December 2018).

[9] *Anisminic Ltd v Foreign Compensation Commission* (n 6).

Nonetheless, the House of Lords found that the Commission had rejected the appellants' claim on a ground they had no authority to consider. It would only have been within its power to consider the issue of succession in title where 'the claimant was successor in title to an original claimant who no longer existed'.[10] As this had not been the case, the Commission had had no right to consider the matter. Accordingly, their determination was a nullity, or merely a 'purported determination'. This being the case, the jurisdiction of the courts had not been ousted, as there was never a determination in the first place.[11] As Daly has argued, what at first glance looks like formalistic reasoning (mainly the distinction between 'determinations' and 'purported determinations') has a strong *substantive* underpinning: the protection of fundamental and (now) well-settled constitutional principles.[12] It is this relationship between the rich substantive underpinning and the influence these constitutional principles have on the construction of statutory language that we also see at play in *Privacy International*.

A. The Facts

As stated above, the question in *Privacy International* was whether section 67(8) RIPA prevents judicial review of a decision made by the IPT. The IPT was also established under RIPA to examine, among other things, the conduct of the UK's intelligence services. Privacy International, a UK-based non-governmental organisation, suspected that it had been subjected to computer hacking by the Government Communications Headquarters under a 'thematic warrant' – a warrant authorising a broad class of possible hacking activity for a broad class of possible property. Privacy International challenged the legality of thematic warrants by MI5, MI6 and GCHQ before the IPT, arguing that section 5 of the Intelligence Services Act 1994, which authorises the Secretary of State to issue warrants on an application made by security services, needs to be construed against the background of the long-established aversion of the common law to general warrants.[13]

The IPT held that the UK security and intelligence services' collection of bulk personal datasets was lawful,[14] which prompted Privacy International to apply for judicial review.[15] In those proceedings, the IPT argued that there could

[10] D Feldman, '*Anisminic Ltd v Foreign Compensation Commission* [1968]: In Perspective' in S Juss and M Sunkin (eds), *Landmark Cases in Public Law* (Hart Publishing, 2017) 82.

[11] See also *O'Reilly v Mackman* [1983] 2 AC 237 (HL) 278 (per Lord Diplock). One of the main legacies of *Anisminic* is that it was subsequently considered to have rendered obsolete the distinction between errors going to the jurisdiction of the tribunal and other errors of law: *R v Hull University Visitor, ex p Page* [1993] AC 682 (HL) 701 (per Lord Browne-Wilkinson).

[12] P Daly, 'Three Aspects of Anisminic' (*Admin Law Blog*, 27 November 2018).

[13] As initially cemented in *Entick v Carrington* (1765) 2 Wilson, KB 275, 95 ER 807.

[14] *Privacy International v SSFCA* [2016] UKIP Trib 14_85-CH.

[15] It was only after the commencement of the proceedings that a statutory right to appeal to the Court of Appeal or Court of Sessions on points of law was introduced against certain decisions made by the IPT. This appellate route did not apply retrospectively, and was therefore not material to the proceedings.

be no judicial review as the jurisdiction of the High Court had been ousted by section 67(8) of the Act, which provides,

> Except to such extent as the Secretary of State may by order otherwise provide, determinations, awards, orders and other decisions of the [IPT] (including decisions as to whether they have jurisdiction) shall not be subject to appeal or be liable to be questioned in any court.

Concisely, the Divisional Court held that section 67(8) of the Act ousts the jurisdiction of the High Court.[16] Sir Brian Leveson, then President of the Queen's Bench Division, gave the longer of the two judgments. Leggatt J concurred with him albeit with strong reservations. The Court of Appeal subsequently dismissed Privacy International's appeal in a unanimous judgment by Sales LJ[17] (Floyd LJ and Flaux LJ agreeing). Finally, the Supreme Court allowed Privacy International's appeal on a narrow majority of four, finding that section 67(8) does not oust the jurisdiction of the High Court. Lord Carnwath (with whom Lord Kerr and Lady Hale agreed) gave the lead judgment, with which Lord Lloyd-Jones concurred. Lord Sumption (with whom Lord Reed agreed) and Lord Wilson gave dissenting judgments.

B. The Divisional Court Judgment

The Divisional Court held in favour of the IPT. Taking as the starting point that Parliament could generally oust the supervisory jurisdiction of the Court provided it did so clearly, Sir Brian reasoned that while there was, post-*Anisminic*, a presumption against ouster clauses, in this case there were several reasons why the ouster was effective. Among them was the fact that the IPT performed a similar function to that performed by the High Court in judicial review proceedings, being required to apply the same principles under the Act. Also, this case had to be distinguished from authorities in which the Court's jurisdiction had not been ousted, such as *R (Cart) v Upper Tribunal.*[18] The IPT was exercising a supervisory jurisdiction over public authorities whereas institutions such as the Upper Tribunal or, as in *Anisminic*, the Foreign Compensation Commission adjudicated on the enforcement of individual rights. He also noted that section 67 provided a potential appeal mechanism for appealing against IPT decisions, the key reason that had led to the Supreme Court accepting that section 67(8) operated as an ouster clause in *A v B (Investigatory Powers Tribunal: Jurisdiction).*[19] He noted that the Secretary of State had not authorised an appeal yet, however, surprisingly, this

[16] *R (Privacy International) v Investigatory Powers Tribunal* [2017] EWHC 114 (Admin), [2017] 3 All ER 1127.

[17] Sir Philip Sales was subsequently appointed as Justice of the Supreme Court.

[18] *R (Cart) v Upper Tribunal* [2011] UKSC 28, [2012] 1 AC 663.

[19] *A v B (Investigatory Powers Tribunal: Jurisdiction)* [2009] UKSC 12, [2010] 2 AC 1.

did not seem to impact on his reasoning. Thus, Sir Brian concluded, 'the provision achieves *the aim that Parliament clearly intended of restricting the means by which decisions of the IPT may be challenged* in the courts to the system of appeals for which the Act itself provides'.[20]

Leggatt J concurred albeit with strong reservations, which essentially amount to challenging the points made by Sir Brian. Indeed, he openly acknowledged that he was inclined to find that section 67(8) of the Act does not exclude the possibility of judicial review. Conversely to the then president's elaboration, he noted that despite the duty vested in the Secretary of State under section 67(9) of the Act to secure a route to appeal for decisions of the IPT, no such order had in fact been made despite the legislation having been in force for 16 years. Specifically, he said that while he would, 'readily accept that, once … there will be an adequate system of appeals from decisions of the IPT … it will not be appropriate for the High Court to entertain claims for judicial review'.[21] Recognising more explicitly the constitutional dimensions of this case, his judgment continued with a strong emphasis on the rule of law, arguing that judicial review serves the latter by providing a means of correcting legal error as well as saying that 'the integrity of the legal system would be undermined if a statutory tribunal operated as a legal island without any means by which its decisions on significant questions of law can reach the higher courts'.[22] However, 'having read the judgment of the [then] President', Leggatt J said he saw 'the cogency of the contrary opinion', and 'in circumstances where this court at least is not the final arbiter of the law that it applies, nothing would be served by causing the issue to be re-argued before a different constitution' of the Divisional Court.

C. The Court of Appeal Judgment

The Court of Appeal dismissed Privacy International's appeal, affirming the Divisional Court's decision that the High Court had no jurisdiction to entertain a claim for judicial review of any decision of the IPT, even where such a decision was made on the basis of an erroneous interpretation or application of the law. Like Sir Brian in the Divisional Court, Sales LJ initially focused extensively on the structure and functions of the IPT. His observations are in stark contrast to Leggatt J's opinion on the 'same rank issue', ie whether it is a relevant consideration that an IPT member is, for example, a High Court judge when they are not acting in that capacity.[23] Sales LJ reasoned that the IPT's composition and function was a

[20] *R (Privacy International) v Investigatory Powers Tribunal* (n 16) [44] (emphasis added).

[21] *ibid* [59].

[22] *ibid* [48]–[49].

[23] *ibid* [47]. On this point, see also Hickman, who argues that despite its composition the IPT diverges from a court of law in various important respect: T Hickman, 'The Investigatory Powers Tribunal: A Law Unto Itself?' [2018] *PL* 584, 586.

significant feature that had to be taken into account when construing section 67(8) of RIPA. While acknowledging that the UK courts' 'highly restrictive approach' to the interpretation of ouster clauses 'reflects the fundamental importance of the rule of law in our legal and political system',[24] Sales LJ's subsequent stipulation as to what the rule of law requires is much narrower than the Supreme Court's. An individual's ability to have a complaint against a public authority determined by *some* independent body sufficiently safeguards the rule of law.

Sales LJ agreed with Dinah Rose, who acted as counsel for Privacy International both before the Court of Appeal and the Supreme Court, that the restrictive approach towards ouster clauses is an example of the principle of legality in action. He also endorsed the view that the principle of legality creates a strong presumption in statutory interpretation that 'Parliament intends to legislate for a liberal democracy subject to the rule of law, respecting human rights and other fundamental principles of the constitution'.[25] He further noted that 'the rule of law and the ability to have access to a court or tribunal to rule upon legal claims constitute principles of fundamental character'.[26] However, he ultimately still reduced the case to turning on 'a short point of statutory construction'.[27]

He concluded that while any isolation of a tribunal from the prospect of appeal on a point of law 'involves a substantial inroad upon usual rule of law standards in this jurisdiction',[28] the language of section 67(8) clearly meant that jurisdiction for judicial review had been ousted. *Anisminic* did not, he reasoned, necessitate a different conclusion given the difference in the wording of the two ouster clauses in question (principally the addition of the phrase: 'including decisions as to whether they have jurisdiction') and the context, which was said to be materially different. Thus, the Court of Appeal's legal analysis largely starts and finishes with what the relevant part of the statute, on the face of it, appears to suggest. There are no allowances for the nuance created by constitutional principles, which are recognised and endorsed formalistically without having any material impact on the court's determination.

D. *Privacy International* in the Supreme Court: Is Parliament Truly Sovereign?

Privacy International appealed to the Supreme Court, which determined two questions, the second of which was hypothetical: (i) whether section 67(8) ousts

[24] *R (Privacy International) v Investigatory Powers Tribunal* [2017] EWCA Civ 1868, [2018] 1 WLR 2572, [19].

[25] *ibid* [21].

[26] *ibid.*

[27] *ibid.* The correctness of this one-dimensional approach had been questioned before the Supreme Court judgment was handed down, see, eg, P Daly, 'Three Aspects of Anisminic' (*Admin Law Blog*, 27 November 2018).

[28] *R (Privacy International) v Investigatory Powers Tribunal* (n 24) [25].

the supervisory jurisdiction of the High Court to quash a judgment of the IPT because of an error of law, and (ii) whether – and, if so, on what basis – Parliament may generally by statute oust said jurisdiction to quash the decision of an inferior court or tribunal of limited statutory jurisdiction. Allowing the appeal, the Supreme Court confirmed what some academics had begun to argue, namely that, contrary to Sales LJ's Court of Appeal judgment, 'the legal effect of an ouster clause is never a "short point of statutory construction", and the meaning of ouster clauses cannot be found merely from their language and legislative context'.[29]

As for the first issue, Lord Carnwath takes *Anisminic*[30] as the starting point. He reasons that when the predecessor to the RIPA was drafted in 1985, which was after Lord Diplock's aforementioned explanation as to the legal significance of *Anisminic* in *O'Reilly v Mackman*,[31] it would have been clear to Parliament that a determination which is wrong in law, going to the court's jurisdiction or otherwise, was to be treated as no determination at all. The reference to a 'determination' in section 67(8) of the Act should be read as a reference only to a legally valid determination, not to 'purported' ones.[32]

Apart from *Anisminic*, Lord Carnwath's judgment relies heavily on the Supreme Court judgment in *R (Cart) v Upper Tribunal*,[33] which is said to provide 'the essential background to the resolution of the issues in the present appeal'.[34] In *Cart*, it had been held that unappealable decisions of the Upper Tribunal were in fact reviewable where an important point of principle or practice was at issue, or where there was some other compelling reason for the relevant appellate court to hear the appeal.[35] The way the case law has developed post-*Anisminic*, Lord Carnwath says in obiter dicta, is connected to the development of judicial review itself, which 'has grown from being little more than a method of correcting the errors of law of inferior courts to its present eminence as the remedy for protecting individuals against unlawful action by the Government and other public bodies'.[36] Given the well-established common law presumption against ousting the jurisdiction of the High Court, this is no case of ordinary statutory interpretation. In line with the principle of legality, judicial review can only be excluded by the clearest and most explicit words, which have not been adopted here. Lord Carnwath then proceeds to suggest that a different, more explicit formula

[29] Tucker (n 8).

[30] *Anisminic Ltd v Foreign Compensation Commission* (n 6).

[31] *O'Reilly v Mackman* (n 11).

[32] The Court recognised the leap that was taken in *Anisminic*, whose relatively narrow ratio was transformed by later judgments, most notably *O'Reilly v Mackman, ibid.*

[33] *R (Cart) v Upper Tribunal* (n 18).

[34] *R (Privacy International) v Investigatory Powers Tribunal* (n 1) [85].

[35] *Cart* reviews have been at the centre of recent legislative judicial review reform. Section 2 of the Judicial Review and Courts Act 2022 removes the *Cart*-jurisdiction for judicial reviews through an ouster clause.

[36] Lord Woolf and others (eds), *De Smith's Judicial Review*, 8th edn (Sweet & Maxwell, 2018) para 4-006-7, cited in *R (Privacy International) v Investigatory Powers Tribunal* (n 1) [60].

might have been successful in excluding challenges to both 'determinations' and 'purported determinations'.

Dissenting, Lord Sumption (with whom Lord Reed agreed), reasons that Parliament has expressed itself clearly and that – in light of the judicial character of the IPT – the rule of law is sufficiently vindicated. He notes further, in obiter dicta, that finding, as he does, that section 67(8) ousts the jurisdiction of the High Court, should not be seen as an 'all or nothing' approach; decisions that demonstrate 'the grossest bias', for example, may still be reviewable.[37] Lord Sumption's dissent can be contrasted with Lord Wilson's dissent, which focused more on the precise wording of section 67(8). The latter, according to Lord Wilson, rebuts 'the initial presumption that Parliament did not intend such an exclusion' and, accordingly, there is a need to construct this section strictly.

As for the second, hypothetical question, whether Parliament could ever oust the supervisory jurisdiction of the High Court, Lord Carnwath's judgment clearly suggests that the parameters for this question are set by the courts. In what in parts reads very much like an open endorsement of common law constitutionalism, Lord Carnwath (with whom Lady Hale and Lord Kerr agreed) reasons that it is ultimately for the courts, not the legislature, to determine the limits set by the rule of law, including whether the latter allowed the exclusion of judicial review. He notes that the courts have

> not adopted a uniform approach, but have felt free to adapt or limit the scope and form of judicial review, so as to ensure respect on the one hand for the particular statutory context and the inferred intention of the legislature, and on the other for the fundamental principles of the rule of law, and to find an appropriate balance between the two. Even if this was not always the way in which the decisions were justified at the time, it may be seen as providing a sounder conceptual basis.[38]

This proposition, he reasons, is a natural application of the constitutional principle of the rule of law 'and an essential counterpart to the power of Parliament to make law'.[39] Concluding on the second issue, he considers there to be

> a strong case for holding that, consistently with the rule of law, binding effect cannot be given to a clause which purports wholly to exclude the supervisory jurisdiction of the High Court to review a decision of an inferior court or tribunal, whether for excess or abuse of jurisdiction, or error of law. In all cases, regardless of the words used, it should remain ultimately a matter for the court to determine the extent to which such a clause should be upheld, having regard to its purpose and statutory context, and the nature and importance of the legal issue in question; and to determine the level of scrutiny required by the rule of law.[40]

Lord Lloyd-Jones does not express a view on the second issue. Lord Sumption (with whom Lord Reed agrees) does not consider it helpful to address the latter in

[37] *ibid* [205].
[38] *ibid* [130].
[39] *ibid* [132].
[40] *ibid* [144].

the abstract. The observations he does make confirm the view he takes in his ratio, ie that Parliament *is* able to exclude the High Court's jurisdiction to review the merits of a tribunal's decisions. Finally, Lord Wilson also narrows down the second issue, rephrasing it to establish a link to the current proceedings, and reiterating that the High Court's jurisdiction can be ousted.

II. *R (Miller) v Prime Minister*

The Supreme Court decision in *Miller v Prime Minister* has been described as the 'most significant judicial statement on the constitution in over 200 years',[41] the UK's equivalent of *Marbury vs Madison*,[42] and as making *R (Miller) v Secretary of State for Exiting the European Union*[43] look 'relatively conventional in legal terms'.[44] One of the last judgments by the Supreme Court under the presidency of Lady Hale, and one of the most succinct Supreme Court judgments of all time, the case breaks new ground as far as the recognition, development and enforcement of constitutional principles is concerned. The judgment also has a distinct legal constitutionalist flair to it, both as far as the preliminary question and as far as the substantive matter is concerned.

The case turns on the royal prerogative. By way of introduction, prerogative powers are residual common law powers, rights and immunities the monarch used to have which are now vested in the Crown, and which 'remain in existence to the extent that Parliament has not expressly or by implication extinguished them'.[45] One key example of the royal prerogative today continues to be the Government's power to sign international treaties. Prerogative powers are residual in the sense that no new prerogative powers can be created, and in that existing prerogative powers cannot be broadened. Since the seminal House of Lords decision in *Council of Civil Service Unions v Minister for the Civil Service*,[46] it is clear that the courts can review not only the existence but also the exercise of prerogative powers, and that certain prerogative powers are not justiciable. *Miller v Prime Minister* is a formidable example of a judicial decision which looks at prerogative powers not in the face of conflicting statutory provisions, but in the context of constitutional principles.

[41] T Poole, 'Understanding What Makes "Miller & Cherry" the Most Significant Judicial Statement on the Constitution in Over 200 Years' (Prospect Magazine, 25 September 2019).

[42] M Radley, 'Wightman: A Marbury v Madison Moment?' (2021) 42(7) *European Competition Law Review* 407, 407.

[43] *R (Miller) v Secretary of State for Exiting the European Union* [2017] UKSC 5, [2018] AC 61.

[44] A McHarg, 'The Supreme Court's Prorogation Judgment: Guardian of the Constitution or Architect of the Constitution?' (2020) 24(1) *Edinburgh Law Review* 88, 88.

[45] *R v Secretary of State for the Home Department, ex p Fire Brigades Union* [1995] 2 AC 513 at 552 (per Lord Browne-Wilkinson).

[46] *Council of Civil Service Unions v Minister for the Civil Service* [1985] AC 374, [1984] 3 WLR 1174.

A. The Facts

Following the notification of its intent to leave the European Union on 29 March 2019, Parliament rejected the withdrawal agreement subsequently negotiated between the Government and the European Council on no less than three occasions. The withdrawal date was therefore extended to 31 October 2019. Three months prior to that deadline, Boris Johnson became Prime Minister. He wanted to negotiate a fresh withdrawal agreement but maintained that the UK would leave the EU on 31 October even if no agreement could be reached. In late August 2019 Mr Johnson advised the Queen that Parliament should be prorogued from a date between 9 and 12 September until 14 October. As the Supreme Court judgment explains,

> Prorogation of Parliament brings the current session to an end. The next session begins, usually a short time later, with the Queen's Speech. While Parliament is prorogued, neither House can meet, debate and pass legislation. Neither House can debate Government policy. Nor may members of either House ask written or oral questions of Ministers. They may not meet and take evidence in committees. In general, Bills which have not yet completed all their stages are lost and will have to start again from scratch in the next session of Parliament ...[47]

The power to give this advice constitutes an exercise of prerogative power. The Privy Council made the order in those terms, as approved by the Queen, on 28 August 2019. This meant that, on returning from summer recess on 3 September 2019, Parliament was to be prorogued for five weeks, to return only two weeks before the UK was set to leave the EU. Mrs Miller brought judicial review proceedings challenging the lawfulness of that advice on the same day the prorogation was announced. In parallel to the proceedings of the High Court in England and Wales, separate proceedings had already been underway in Scotland, where, in anticipation of a prorogation, a cross party group of Members of Parliament led by Ms Cherry, a member of the Scottish National Party, had petitioned the Court of Session for a declaration that any future prorogation would be unlawful.

B. *Miller v Prime Minister* in the Court of Sessions and the Divisional Court

As for the Scottish proceedings, initially, on 4 September 2019, the Outer House of the Court of Sessions refused Ms Cherry's petition, saying the issue was not justiciable.[48] On appeal to the Inner House, that decision was reversed.[49] In a short

[47] *R (Miller) v Prime Minister* (n 2) [2].
[48] *Joanna Cherry MP and others v the Advocate General* [2019] CSOH 70.
[49] *Joanna Cherry MP and others v the Advocate General* [2019] CSIH 49.

judgment, Lord Carloway held that the matter was justiciable and the prorogation unlawful. Applying the common law, specifically 'the principles of democracy and the rule of law', a phrase taken from *Moohan v Lord Advocate*,[50] a case concerned with the right to vote, Lord Carloway reasoned that an illegitimately motivated decision to prorogue could be subject to judicial review, as opposed to prerogative decisions 'which are made on the basis of legitimate political considerations alone'.[51] An improper motive had been demonstrated, thereby rendering the prorogation at once both justiciable and null and of no effect.

The Scottish decision stands in sharp contrast to the High Court's judgment,[52] which dismissed the claim for judicial review on the basis that the matter was non-justiciable. That conclusion was reached by a highly distinguished bench, being constituted of Lord Burnett of Maldon, the Lord Chief Justice of England and Wales, Sir Etherton, the Master of the Rolls, and Dame Victoria Sharp, the President of the then Queen's Bench Division of the High Court. The High Court held: (1) that not all exercises of common law prerogative powers were justiciable; (2) that the first question to be answered was whether the subject matter of a prerogative power was justiciable; (3) that the criteria for identifying whether the exercise of a prerogative power was justiciable was whether it was 'political' or entailed matters of 'high policy'; (4) that political decisions would not be reviewable due to the separation of powers and because there were no legal standard by which they could be judged; and (5) that the claimant had failed to show that this consistent approach ought to be modified by what the Court considered to be a 'novel and sophisticated argument resting on Parliamentary Sovereignty'.[53] Following the claimant's approach, which was in part based on *UNISON v Lord Chancellor*,[54] would 'invite the judicial arm of the state to exercise hitherto unidentified power over the Executive branch of the state in its dealings with Parliament'.[55]

C. The Supreme Court's Unanimous, Ground-Breaking Decision

The High Court allowed a leap-frog appeal from its judgment directly to the Supreme Court pursuant to section 12(3A)(c) of the Administration of Justice Act 1969 subject to leave being granted by the Supreme Court, which it was. The Supreme Court said the appeal from both courts raised four issues, recognising that there was a degree of overlap between them:

(1) Is the question of whether the Prime Minister's advice to the Queen was lawful justiciable in a court of law?

[50] *Moohan v Lord Advocate* [2015] UKSC 1 [35] (per Lord Hodge).
[51] *Joanna Cherry MP and others v the Advocate General* (n 49) [50].
[52] *R (Miller) v The Prime Minister* [2019] EWHC 2381 (QB), [2019] ACD 136.
[53] *ibid* [58].
[54] *R (UNISON) v Lord Chancellor* [2017] UKSC 51, [2020] AC 869.
[55] *R (Miller) v The Prime Minister* (n 52) [63].

> (2) If it is, by what standard is its lawfulness to be judged?
> (3) By that standard, was it lawful?
> (4) If it was not [lawful], what remedy should the court grant?[56]

The judgment was given by Lady Hale with whom all ten[57] other Justices agreed. The Court first made a number of preliminary observations. In making the decision to prorogue Parliament, the Prime Minister had a constitutional responsibility 'to have regard to all relevant interests, including the interests of Parliament'.[58] While the courts cannot decide political questions, decisions made by the executive concerned with politics or which have 'a political hue to them' do not prevent the courts from considering the matter.[59] The fact that the Prime Minister is accountable to Parliament does not in itself justify 'the conclusion that the courts have no legitimate role to play' because accountability is impossible when Parliament is prorogued, and because there exists, independently, a judicial duty to give effect to the law.[60] Finally, deciding the matter (if the prorogation was justiciable) reinforces the separation of powers rather than frustrate it.[61]

As for the question of justiciability, the Court draws a distinction between the question, on the one hand, whether a prerogative exists (and, if it does, its extent) and, second, whether a prerogative power that has been exercised within its limits is open to challenge on established judicial review grounds.[62] The parties agreed that the former was justiciable. As for the latter, the Supreme Court relies on the House of Lords decision in *Council of Civil Service Unions v Minister for the Civil Service*, which I referred to above. The Court reiterates that justiciability depends on 'the nature and subject matter of the particular prerogative power being exercised', and which gives the dissolution of Parliament as an example of a power the exercise of which was not justiciable.[63] The Court notes:

> Before reaching a conclusion as to justiciability, the court therefore has to determine whether the present case requires it to determine where a legal limit lies in relation to the power to prorogue Parliament, and whether the Prime Minister's advice trespassed beyond that limit, or whether the present case concerns the lawfulness of a particular exercise of the power within its legal limits. That question is closely related to the identification of the standard by reference to which the lawfulness of the Prime Minister's advice is to be judged.[64]

[56] *R (Miller) v Prime Minister* (n 2) [27].

[57] Given the constitutional significance of the case, similarly to *R (Miller) v Secretary of State for Exiting the European Union* (n 43) (n 43), the Court sat in a special formation.

[58] *R (Miller) v Prime Minister* (n 2) [30].

[59] *ibid* [31]. The *Case of Proclamations* (1611) 12 Co Rep 74 and *Entick v Carrington* (1765) 19 State Tr 1029 were mentioned to illustrate this point.

[60] *ibid* [33]. The latter reason was based on *R v Secretary of State for the Home Department, ex p Fire Brigades Union* (n 45) 572–73.

[61] *R (Miller) v Prime Minister* (n 2) [34].

[62] *ibid* [35].

[63] *ibid*, citing *Council of Civil Service Unions v Minister for the Civil Service* (n 46) 418.

[64] *ibid* [37].

Attempting to answer that question, the Court says that since a prerogative power is recognised by the common law, it is for the court to determine its limits in accordance with the common law and 'the fundamental principles of our constitutional law'.[65] In giving effect to those principles, the courts uphold

> the values and principles of our constitution and making them effective. It is their particular responsibility to determine the legal limits of the powers conferred in each branch of government, and to decide whether any exercise of power has transgressed those limits', including where the 'question raised is political in tone or context.[66]

Having set the scene, the Court then moves on to consider the two fundamental constitutional principles relevant to the question before them: parliamentary sovereignty and parliamentary accountability. After recognising legislation as the 'highest' and 'supreme form of law in our legal system', the Court states that the parliamentary sovereignty goes beyond the recognition of that status, saying it also includes the need to protect Parliament from 'threats posed to it by the use of prerogative powers'.[67] Bringing the constitutional principle back to the question of justiciability, the Court provides:

> The sovereignty of Parliament would, however, be undermined as the foundational principle of our constitution if the executive could, through the use of the prerogative, prevent Parliament from exercising its legislative authority for as long as it pleased. That, however, would be the position if there was no legal limit upon the power to prorogue Parliament (subject to a few exceptional circumstances in which, under statute, Parliament can meet while it stands prorogued). An unlimited power of prorogation would therefore be incompatible with the legal principle of Parliamentary sovereignty.[68]

Having concluded that '… as a concomitant of Parliamentary sovereignty, … the power to prorogue cannot be unlimited …',[69] Lady Hale then proceeds to the second constitutional principle: parliamentary accountability. Three authorities are offered in support of its existence and status: *R (Miller) v Secretary of State for Exiting the European Union*, in which Lord Carnwath equated its fundamental status to that of parliamentary sovereignty,[70] *R v Secretary of State for the Environment, ex p Nottinghamshire*,[71] and *Mohammed (Serdar) v Ministry of Defence*.[72] The link between parliamentary accountability and prorogation, the Court explains, is that 'the longer … Parliament stands prorogued, the greater the risk that responsible government may be replaced by unaccountable government: the antithesis of the democratic model'.[73]

[65] *ibid* [38].
[66] *ibid* [39].
[67] *ibid* [41].
[68] *ibid* [42].
[69] *ibid* [44].
[70] *R (Miller) v Secretary of State* (n 43) [249].
[71] *R v Secretary of State for the Environment, ex p Nottinghamshire, County Council* [1986] AC 240, 250.
[72] *Mohammed (Serdar) v Ministry of Defence* [2017] UKSC 1, [2017] AC 649 [57].
[73] *R (Miller) v Prime Minister* (n 2) [48].

Returning to the question of the legal limits of the power to prorogue, the Court turns to *UNISON v Lord Chancellor*,[74] which, it says, exemplifies how the courts deal with the exercise of a statutory power (which is seen as analogous to a prerogative power in the analysis) that is liable to impact a constitutional principle. The courts' approach in such a case was that 'Unless the terms of the statute indicate a contrary intention, the courts have set a limit to the lawful exercise of the power by holding that the extent to which the measure impedes or frustrates the operation of the relevant principle must have a reasonable justification'.[75]

Bringing all of the above analysis together, Lady Hale proceeds to set out what the limit on the prerogative power to prorogue is:

> the relevant limit upon the power to prorogue can be expressed in this way: that a decision to prorogue Parliament (or to advise the monarch to prorogue Parliament) will be unlawful if the prorogation has the effect of frustrating or preventing, without reasonable justification, the ability of Parliament to carry out its constitutional functions as a legislature and as the body responsible for the supervision of the executive. In such a situation, the court will intervene if the effect is sufficiently serious to justify such an exceptional course.[76]

Thus, a three-stage test is devised. First, there is the factual question of whether Parliament is prevented from carrying out its legislative function and from supervising the executive, which is followed by what might be dubbed the 'reasonable justification' question. Finally, as a third step, the court ought to consider whether the consequences of prorogation are 'sufficiently serious' to call for the courts' intervention and correction.[77] Concluding on the question of justiciability, Lady Hale says the matter is justiciable seeing as it concerns the extent of the prerogative powers, which the Court will determine by reference to the legal standard (the three-stage test) devised. Thus, this case concerns not the exercise of the prerogative power, but instead the limits of the power, which is marked by the boundary between the prerogative and the two constitutional principles in question. A matter '... which can be resolved by the application of that standard is by definition one which concerns the extent of the power to prorogue, and is therefore justiciable'.[78]

Having established that the matter is justiciable, the Court's determination of whether the prorogation was lawful is dealt with comparatively swiftly. The prorogation had the effect of frustrating parliamentary accountability and there was no (good) reason prorogue Parliament (or, if there was one, it was not in evidence before the Court). As for the remedy, counsel for the Prime Minister (and the Advocate General) had argued that, even if the advice was unlawful, no declaration to the effect of rendering the prorogation null and void could be made seeing

[74] *R (UNISON) v Lord Chancellor* (n 54).
[75] *R (Miller) v Prime Minister* (n 2) [49].
[76] *ibid* [50].
[77] *R (Miller) v Prime Minister* (n 2) [51].
[78] *ibid* [52].

as the prorogation constituted 'proceeding in Parliament', thereby commanding parliamentary privilege and protection under article 9 of the Bill of Rights 1688. The Supreme Court did not agree that the prorogation amounted to 'proceeding in Parliament'. Rather, prorogation had been imposed on Parliament through an external decision. Seeing as the advice to prorogue was unlawful, it was 'null and of no effect',[79] 'as if the Commissioners had walked into Parliament with a blank piece of paper'.[80]

III. The Common Law Constitutionalist Side of the Spectrum: Themes, Characteristics and Vulnerabilities

With the exception of *O (A Child)*, the cases discussed in this chapter share one important characteristic. They are marked by significant disagreement between the country's most senior courts and judges as to the meaning and application of constitutional fundamentals. The divergence of opinion is particularly stark in *Privacy International*; the evolution from the Divisional Court judgment in 2017 to the majority's Supreme Court judgment in 2019 signifies a remarkable shift from what started as a parliamentary sovereignty and legislative intention-centric approach to a substantive rule of law one. As the different judgments and individual opinions in these proceedings show, we find serious disagreement on almost every level, which is emblematic of the spectrum of constitutional theory inherent in the nuanced constitution. Indeed, the level of disagreement at the Supreme Court alone has prompted some commentators to say that

> The judgments run all the way along the spectrum, from Lord Carnwath's expression of doubt about the ability of Parliament to legislate to exclude judicial review to Lord Wilson's apparent bafflement at the proposition that s. 67(8) was anything but pellucidly clear.[81]

As I noted in this book's introduction, the UK constitution's 'nuance' is caused by the fact that there is no uniformly recognised justification for the exercise of public power, there being no paramount constitutional theory or principle. Both parliamentary sovereignty and a commitment to limited government and certain values, manifested in the substantive notion of the rule of law, feature in judicial reasoning, but neither command absolute respect. The *Privacy International* proceedings are an exemplification of the nuanced constitution in that beneath the surface we can observe both schools of thought, ie political and legal constitutionalism, across all judgments and within individual opinions

[79] The Supreme Court again relied on *R (UNISON) v Lord Chancellor* (n 54) as authority for the link between unlawfulness and the exercise of the prerogative being void, see [69].

[80] *R (Miller) v Prime Minister* (n 2) [69].

[81] P Daly, 'Of Clarity and Context: *R (Privacy International) v Investigatory Powers Tribunal* [2019] UKSC 22' (Administrative Law Matters, 15 May 2019).

as well as significant disagreement as to which of the two schools of thought deserves primary consideration. Sir Brian's judgment in the High Court, the Court of Appeal's unanimous decision and the dissenting judgments in the Supreme Court are manifestations of political constitutionalist thought being the dominant philosophy followed. All these judgments found – as the IPT had submitted to the Supreme Court – that there was nothing constitutionally offensive about legislative arrangements whereby Parliament reallocates the High Court's judicial review jurisdiction to a judicial body that is both independent of the executive and capable of providing an authoritative interpretation of the law. This is based on the simple understanding that

> The rule of law applies as much to the courts as it does to anyone else, and under our constitution, that requires that effect must be given to Parliamentary legislation. In the absence of a written constitution capable of serving as a higher source of law, the status of Parliamentary legislation as the ultimate source of law is the foundation of democracy in the United Kingdom. The alternative would be to treat the courts as being entitled on their own initiative to create a higher source of law than statute, namely their own decisions.[82]

Meanwhile, closer towards the legal constitutionalism end of the spectrum, we find not just the Supreme Court's majority opinion but also Leggatt J's Divisional Court judgment. As Scott has argued, it is remarkable that judges openly question – as Leggatt J did in his opinion at the Divisional Court – whether it is possible to draft an ouster clause that actually successfully ousts the jurisdiction of the High Court. Leggatt J's reflection that 'it is difficult to conceive how Parliament could have been more explicit than it was' in the Foreign Compensation Act 1950, the statute in question in *Anisminic*, implies that Parliament's absolute legislative competency is openly doubted.[83] This is evident in Lord Carnwath's judgment as well, which goes as far as suggesting the courts may in certain circumstances not recognise primary legislation as having a binding effect where the interest at stake (eg judicial review) is important enough. It is difficult to argue, despite his attempts to convince his readership otherwise by stressing his approach's respect for – and compatibility with – legislative intent, that Lord Carnwath's approach is not a manifestation of common law constitutionalist thought. In seeking 'to resolve disputes in a manner that achieves integrity with past decisions' while simultaneously seeking 'a morally just outcome in the light of the context of the particular dispute',[84] his reasoning resembles the basic premise of common law constitutionalism.

The second feature of the nuanced constitution which is evident from *Privacy International* is linked to the first characteristic identified above: the nuanced constitution is often marked by judicial reasoning – exemplified by Lord Carnwath's reasoning concerning the second, hypothetical issue – which

[82] *R (Privacy International) v Investigatory Powers Tribunal* (n 1) [209] (per Lord Sumption).

[83] PF Scott, 'Ouster Clauses and National Security: Judicial Review of the Investigatory Powers Tribunal' [2017] *PL* 355, 358.

[84] J Jowell, 'Beyond the Rule of Law: Towards Constitutional Judicial Review' [2000] *PL* 671, 673.

attempts the impossible by trying to reconcile what is in essence common law constitutionalist reasoning with the orthodox Diceyan position of unlimited legislative law-making powers.[85] Lord Carnwath's judgment is logically and conceptually vulnerable because it attempts to rationalise the essence of his judgment, which is legal constitutionalism, within a parliamentary sovereignty framework, thereby exposing the inherent tension underlying the nuanced constitution.

If we look at Lord Carnwath's opinion on both issues and Lloyd-Jones' opinion on the second issue, we can see that their combined effect is that the rule of law is thought to be '*as foundational as* Parliamentary Sovereignty'.[86] There is no perceived difficulty with putting the two principles on the same level. Lord Carnwath conceptualises the courts' power to determine the limits on Parliament's ability to exclude judicial review not as a limitation on parliamentary sovereignty but as 'a natural application of the constitutional principle of the rule of law … and as an essential counterpart to the power of Parliament to make law'.[87] This distorts, and ultimately defeats the doctrine of parliamentary sovereignty as it reduces the latter to Parliament's 'power to make law' as opposed to 'power to make *any law it pleases*'. Indeed, that is the key distinction between the two different approaches evident in the *Privacy International* proceedings. Those judges on the parliamentary sovereignty side of the spectrum subscribe to Parliament's unlimited law-making power. The latter demands judicial interpretation that is fully respectful of any legislative choices made, including 'undesirable' ones.

The disagreement in the *Privacy International* litigation stems from there being two clearly defined, clashing visions of the constitutional order. The difference in approach between the High Court and the Supreme Court in *Miller v Prime Minister* on the one hand was perhaps less inevitable, and certainly less foreseeable, in the sense that the reasoning ultimately carrying the case was not firmly based in precedent. In fact, much of the Supreme Court's judgment is either a significant further development of existing public law principals, or a novel approach altogether. As McHarg puts it, the Court 'engaged in considerable *creativity* in casting itself as the guardian at common law of constitutional values hitherto regarded as grounded in the political rather than the legal constitution'.[88]

This is not to say that one of the constitutional principles the Supreme Court relied on, parliamentary sovereignty, was not well-established; of course it was. Rather, it is the Court's acceptance of David Pannick KC's novel development of this principle which makes the judgment break new ground. Thus, the legal maxim not to frustrate the '*expressed will* of Parliament' is expanded into covering also the chronologically prior '*ability to express* that will'.[89] Safeguarding this indirect

[85] *R (Evans) v Attorney-General* [2015] UKSC 21, [2015] AC 1787.
[86] *R (Privacy International) v Investigatory Powers Tribunal* (n 1) [114] (emphasis added).
[87] *ibid* [132].
[88] McHarg (n 44) 89.
[89] *ibid* 95.

aspect of parliamentary sovereignty is, strictly speaking, entirely unprecedented. As Endicott puts it, 'The decision borrowed the legal force of legislation to turn Parliament's need to meet as appropriate into a legal limit on the Prime Minister's power to prorogue'.[90] True, in doing so, the Court does not dictate the elected branches of state 'what to produce',[91] however it nonetheless sets independent new standards about *how* the performance of its functions ought to be achieved, based on abstract novel legal claims such as the contention that the Prime Minister had a 'constitutional responsibility … to have regard to all relevant interests, including the interests of Parliament'.[92] This statement, albeit expressed in passing, and not featuring in the substantive decision of the Court, is an example of the Court imposing legal standards where there was previously a void, including by applying established principles in a novel context and way.

Similarly to *Privacy International*, an attempt is made to ground the Court's actual approach and reasoning in constitutional orthodoxy terms. However, what is in fact happening is the painting of legal rules onto a largely blank canvas. The main way in which this can be observed is the conceptualisation and positioning of the principle of parliamentary accountability. A simple Westlaw search helps us understand just how novel the Supreme Court's reliance on this purported principle is. All in all, there appear to have been ten cases that mention parliamentary accountability, one of which is the Supreme Court's judgment's in *Miller v Prime Minister* itself. This leaves us with nine other judgments. Out of these, three post-date *Miller v Prime Minister*, one is from the German Bundesverfassungsgericht, and one from the European Court of Human Rights in a challenge not involving the UK.[93] Out of the remaining four judgments, one involved the lawfulness of the recommendations of a Local Government Ombudsman[94] while another one was concerned with a lack of parliamentary oversight over executive power in the context of false imprisonment.[95] The third case is the well-known decision in *Padfield v Minister of Agriculture, Fisheries and Food*,[96] which again concerned very different circumstances, and in which the term was used in a different context.

What we are therefore left with is Lord Carnwath's obiter comment in *Miller v Secretary of State*,[97] which was made in the context of discussing the Government's ability to withdraw from treaties, outside the context of Parliament

[90] T Endicott, 'Making Constitutional Principles into Laws' (2020) 136 *LQR* 175, 178.

[91] C Gearty, 'The Supreme Court Judges are Oiling the Democratic Machine, not Telling it What to Produce' (*LSE Brexit Blog*, 25 September 2019).

[92] *R (Miller) v Prime Minister* (n 2) [30].

[93] *Szabo v Hungary* App no 37138/14 (2016) 63 EHRR 3.

[94] *Paula Gallagher & Mary McCarthy) v Basildon District Council v Commission for Local Administration in England* [2010] EWHC 2824 (Admin), [2011] PTSR 731.

[95] *Muuse v Secretary of State for the Home Department* [2010] EWCA Civ 453, [2010] CLY 77.

[96] *Padfield v Minister of Agriculture, Fisheries and Food* [1968] AC 997, [1968] 2 WLR 924.

[97] *R (Miller) v Secretary of State* (n 43).

being prorogued, as Lord Carnwath's next two sentences in the same paragraph indicate: 'The Executive is accountable to Parliament for its exercise of the prerogative, including its actions in international law. That account is made through ordinary Parliamentary procedures'.[98]

Looking at the paragraph citied by the Supreme Court in its entirety, it is of as little help to the Supreme Court as the other two cases mentioned in support of the principle of parliamentary accountability, in so far as the attempt to ground the reasoning in precedent is concerned. All of this is not to say that the Supreme Court did not reach the morally correct decision in *Miller v Prime Minister*. However, from a legal point of view, the judgment is revolutionary in its level of abstract reasoning and transformation of constitutional values into legally enforceable rules. In the absence of direct authority, the Court relies on previous decisions which are either not on point, or which share a loose connection with the principle or reasoning in question, much like the *Moohan* reference in the Inner House's judgment.[99]

As Elliott shows, *Miller v Prime Minister* and *Privacy International* in fact share this characteristic of flexibly transferring certain aspects of legal principles to novel factual situations. Elliott says that this simply reflects that parliamentary sovereignty is

> a fundamental principle that determines and reflects the nature of constitutional democracy in the UK. Looked at in this way the Court's view becomes an entirely unremarkable one: namely, that untrammelled executive power to prorogue Parliament would render the sovereignty of Parliament a dead letter.[100]

That may well be right, however it reveals several things about the nature of the constitution. First, we can observe the sheer power of fundamental constitutional principles in the adjudicative process. Second, those principles are, in most cases, common law based, putting the judiciary in the driving seat. Third, in shaping and applying common law constitutional principles to political decisions, the Supreme Court is spinning a gradual web of substantive values around facts. These values give an increasingly legalistic flair to constitutional adjudication. In this context, it is worth highlighting that the Supreme Court in *Miller v Prime Minister* made it clear that, rather than being something akin to a 'historical fact', the concept of parliamentary sovereignty itself is a common law construct,[101] which is in fact equated, on a legal sources level, with common law constitutional rights.[102] This, perhaps, is the most revolutionary message stemming from this remarkable judgment.

[98] *ibid* [249].
[99] *Moohan v Lord Advocate* (n 50) [51].
[100] M Elliott, 'A New Approach to Constitutional Adjudication? Miller II in the Supreme Court' (*Public Law for Everyone Blog*, 24 September 2019).
[101] *R (Miller) v Prime Minister* (n 2) [40].
[102] *ibid*. The common law right of open justice is given as an example.

IV. *R (Begum) v Special Immigration Appeals Commission*

We now move to the opposite side of the constitutional spectrum, beginning with a decision that generated significant public attention: *R (Begum) v Special Immigration Appeals Commission (SIAC)*,[103] a highly complex and technical judgment. Much of its complexity stems from the fact that the Supreme Court had to determine no less than three appeals concerning Ms Begum. Behind the technical points made by the Court lies a broader theme of judicial deference to executive decisions in the field of national security, and what one might think is an uncharacteristic downplaying of the importance and status of procedural rights, which are normally among the most cherished rights of the English common law.

A. The Facts

Ms Begum, a British national from London, left the UK in 2015 as a teenager to join the so-called Islamic State of Iraq and the Levant. The Supreme Court judgment in her case originated in the Secretary of State for the Home Department's decision to deprive Ms Begum of her British citizenship under the British Nationality Act 1981. The decision was made on the basis that she was purportedly a British-Bangladeshi dual national who had travelled to Syria to align herself with ISIL, which meant that her return to the UK would present a risk to the country's national security. Decisions of this nature are effective immediately, even where appeals or other legal challenges are brought against them.

At the time Ms Begum was notified of the Secretary of State's decision, she was being held at a camp in Syria.[104] Ms Begum appealed to the Special Immigration Appeals Commission (SIAC) against the deprivation decision. SIAC decided three preliminary points.[105] First, the deprivation decision did not make Ms Begum stateless. This point was not challenged. Second, the Secretary of State had not departed from the Home Office's extra-territorial human rights policy when he made the decision. The policy in question is a statement that was made in the context of the adoption of the Immigration Act 2014 by then Home Secretary Theresa May that

> [T]he Secretary of State has a practice of not depriving individuals of British citizenship when they are not within the UK's jurisdiction for ECHR purposes if she is satisfied that doing so would expose those individuals to a real risk of treatment which would constitute a breach of article 2 or 3 if they were within the UK's jurisdiction and those articles were engaged.[106]

[103] *R (Begum) v Special Immigration Appeals Commission* (n 3).
[104] At the time of writing, she continues to be in Syria, albeit at a different camp.
[105] *Begum v Secretary of State for the Home Department* [2020] SC/163/2019.
[106] *R (Begum) v Special Immigration Appeals Commission* (n 3) [21].

Third, SIAC determined that while Ms Begum could not have an effective appeal against the deprivation decision given where she was, this did not mean that her case should succeed.

Ms Begum challenged SIAC's determination of the second and third issue by judicial review in the High Court, which found in her favour on the policy issue, but not on the fair and effective appeal issue. The Secretary of State appealed to the Supreme Court saying the High Court wrongly concluded that SIAC had erred in determining the policy issue. Ms Begum cross-appealed, saying the High Court wrongly dismissed her argument that her appeal against the deprivation decision should automatically be allowed because she could not fairly and effectively pursue it due to the negative leave to enter decision.

Separately, Ms Begum made an application outside the Immigration Rules[107] for leave to enter the UK to be able to pursue her appeal against the deprivation decision (and also to avoid the risk of mistreatment abroad). That application was refused by the Secretary of State because Ms Begum had failed to provide a record of her fingerprints and a photograph of her face and, as far as her reliance on human rights was concerned, the European Convention on Human Rights (ECHR) had no application to her. The Secretary of State also considered, in the alternative, that even if it did apply, none of her rights had been breached. Like the initial deprivation decision, the leave to enter decision was taken partly in reliance on information which is not open to the public.

Ms Begum challenged the leave to enter decision. For those kinds of decisions, individuals only have a statutory right to appeal on the basis of a conflict with the Human Rights Act 1998 (HRA). She made an appeal under the HRA, which was refused by SIAC but then subsequently succeeded before the Court of Appeal. The Secretary of State appealed to the Supreme Court against the Court of Appeal's decision, arguing that the latter had been wrong to find that leave to enter must be granted to Ms Begum because, otherwise, she could not have a fair and effective hearing of her appeal against the deprivation decision.

Finally, there is the third litigation, which concerned the leave to enter decision outside the HRA. Seeing as there is no statutory right of appeal to SIAC against leave to enter decisions other than on grounds of the HRA, Ms Begum tried to challenge the leave to enter decision through a separate High Court claim as well. She initially lost,[108] but was then successful in the Court of Appeal, whose judgment the Secretary of State appealed against. The legal question arising before the Supreme Court in that appeal was the same as the one arising under the second issue, namely whether the Court of Appeal was wrong to conclude that leave to enter must be granted if a fair and effective hearing of her appeal against the deprivation decision could not be facilitated from outside the jurisdiction.

[107] The Immigration Act 1971, s 3.

[108] Laing J granted permission for judicial review of the leave to enter decision, but dismissed her application on substance.

B. The Court of Appeal Decision

This is a highly complex case, and I will, for the purposes of this chapter's discussion, only highlight the Court of Appeal's and the Supreme Court's decision.[109] The Court of Appeal bench was made up of Flaux LJ, King LJ and Singh LJ.[110] The Court unanimously allowed Ms Begum's appeal against SIAC's decision in the leave to enter appeal, and her appeal against Elisabeth Laing J's decision to dismiss the application for judicial review of the leave to enter decision. The Secretary of State was ordered to grant Ms Begum leave to enter the country and to provide her with the necessary travel documents,[111] and the matter was remitted to SIAC to (re-) determine the question of risk of transfer, and the associated human rights implications.

In the Court's judgment, given by Flaux LJ, chancellor of the High Court, the Court first highlighted SIAC's 'clear and categorical' finding that Ms Begum 'cannot play any meaningful part in her appeal, and that, to that extent, the appeal will not be fair and effective'.[112] After finding that the circumstances in which Ms Begum left the UK and the fact that she did so of her own volition were irrelevant for the question of the legal and procedural consequences of SIAC's conclusion that she cannot have a fair and effective appeal, Flaux LJ considered what legal and procedural consequences should follow from the conclusion of SIAC that Ms Begum could not have a fair and effective appeal. He did not accept her legal team's submissions that SIAC's finding would automatically result in her appeal being allowed. This would, especially in light of the expert evidence around the national security risk, 'potentially set a dangerous precedent'.[113] Rather, he said, the critical question was what steps could be taken 'to alleviate the unfairness and lack of effectiveness'.[114] He did not consider that a stay, one of the three options proposed by SIAC, was satisfactory. A stay would be 'wrong in principle' because it 'would in effect render her appeal against an executive decision to deprive her of her British nationality meaningless for an unlimited period of time'[115] and it would not address the foreseeable risk of her being transferred to another country where she might face mistreatment or worse.[116]

Approaching the matter pragmatically, the Court determined,

> since neither allowing the appeal as Mr Hickman QC [counsel for Ms Begum] submitted nor staying the appeal as Sir James [counsel for the Government] submitted, is a

[109] A helpful summary of SIAC's decision can be found in the Court of Appeal judgment.

[110] *Begum v Special Immigration Appeals Commission and Others* [2020] EWCA Civ 918, [2020] 1 WLR 426.

[111] However, this was stayed pending the determination of the appeal to the Supreme Court.

[112] *Begum v Special Immigration Appeals Commission and Others* (n 110) [92], citing [143] of the SIAC judgment. The difficulties highlighted included the giving of effective instructions, see [93].

[113] *ibid* [95].

[114] *ibid* [111].

[115] *ibid* [117].

[116] *ibid* [116].

> legally satisfactory outcome, the only way in which there can be a fair and effective appeal is to allow the appeals in respect of the refusal of [leave to enter].[117]

Put differently, Ms Begum should be allowed, subject to safeguards, to enter the country to fight the deprivation of her citizenship. Flaux LJ proceeded to compare the national security threat Ms Begum appeared, on the evidence available, to present to those prevalent in SIAC's judgment in *U2 v Secretary of State for the Home Department*,[118] concluding that her return to the UK could be addressed and managed. For instance, she could be arrested and charged with terrorist offences upon arrival, and be remanded in custody pending trial, or be made the subject of terrorist prevention and investigation measures. Flaux LJ concluded that

> In all the circumstances, although I would refuse Ms Begum's challenge to SIAC's decision that, it did not follow that because she could not have a fair and effective appeal, her appeal should be allowed, I consider that fairness requires that we allow her [leave to enter] appeals against the decisions of SIAC and the Administrative Court.[119]

Turning to the second issue, the correct approach to the Secretary of State's extra-territorial policy, the Court of Appeal disagreed with SIAC that this issue should be reviewed on judicial review grounds only. Rather than limiting itself to a judicial review rationality review, SIAC ought to have conducted a full merits appeal. Executive policy or practice ought to have been considered on the same basis as the issue of statelessness, which SIAC *had* decided for itself. Because SIAC had not made an independent assessment of the issue of risk of Ms Begum being transferred to another country in breach of her Article 2 and Article 3 rights, her judicial review succeeded on that point. The Court remitted the matter to SIAC to 'consider the question of risk on the basis that it has to decide that issue de novo for itself on the totality of the evidence before it'.[120]

C. The Supreme Court Decision

The Supreme Court considered both the scope of an appeal against the refusal of entry clearance, and the scope of an appeal against a deprivation decision. The practical result of the Supreme Court's judgment is that Ms Begum is not allowed to re-enter the UK to pursue the appeal against the Secretary of State's decision to deprive her of her British nationality. To put it shortly, the Supreme Court recognised that Ms Begum could not have an effective right of appeal in light of her whereabouts and circumstances. This being the case, however, the solution was not to therefore allow her to re-enter the jurisdiction, but, rather, the appeal would have to be stayed until it could be fairly heard, which might never be the case.

[117] *ibid* [118].
[118] *U2 v Secretary of State for the Home Department* [2019] SC/130/2016.
[119] *Begum v Special Immigration Appeals Commission and Others* (n 110) [122].
[120] *ibid* [129].

Central to the judgment are the different natures of appeal under the respective statutory framework. Lord Reed, who gives the judgment with which all other Justices[121] agreed, first highlights the assessments the Secretary of State had received in the run-up to the deprivation decision, including a Mistreatment Risk Statement which had been prepared in light of SIAC's case law on how to comply with the extra-territorial policy, and the Security Service's conclusion

> that a repatriation to Bangladesh is [not] a foreseeable outcome of deprivation and as such the Home Secretary may consider that there is no real risk of return – let alone of mistreatment on return – for the purpose of complying with his practice.[122]

Considering SIAC's jurisdiction with regard to the deprivation decision, Lord Read highlights that section 2B of the Special Immigration Appeals Commission Act 1997 does not contain – and there is no other statutory provision which sets out – the grounds on which an appeal can be brought. Marshalling the case law cited by the parties, Lord Reed highlights the House of Lords decision in *Secretary of State for the Home Department v Rehman*,[123] which was concerned with an appeal to SIAC under section 2 of the Special Immigration Appeals Commission Act 1997 against a deportation decision. He emphasises the House of Lords' focus on the separation of powers and the Secretary of State's expertise in questions of national security, noting Lord Hoffmann's reasoning that there were 'inherent limitations, first, in the powers of the judicial branch of government and secondly, within the judicial function, in the appellate process',[124] saying that the same limitations 'being inherent in the judicial function and in the appellate process, must also apply to SIAC (and to the Divisional Court and the Court of Appeal) under the current legislation'.[125] He goes on to cite with approval Lord Hoffmann's statement, in the same judgment, that the question of whether something is *in the interest of* national security is not a question of law, but, rather,

> It is a matter of judgment and policy. Under the constitution of the United Kingdom and most other countries, decisions as to whether something is or is not in the interests of national security are not a matter for judicial decision. They are entrusted to the executive.[126]

Naming other decisions which underline the correctness of the approach taken in *Rehman*, Lord Reed concludes that while SIAC's jurisdiction is appellate rather than supervisory,[127] that 'does not determine the principles of law which the appellate body is to apply. As has been explained, they depend upon the nature of the

[121] Lords Hodge, Lloyd-Jones and Sales, and Lady Black.

[122] *R (Begum) v Special Immigration Appeals Commission* (n 3) [24].

[123] *Secretary of State for the Home Department v Rehman* [2001] UKHL 47, [2003] 1 AC 153.

[124] *ibid* at 49 (per Lord Hoffmann).

[125] *R (Begum) v Special Immigration Appeals Commission* (n 3) [55].

[126] *ibid* [56] citing *Secretary of State for the Home Department v Rehman* (n 123) at 50 (per Lord Hoffmann).

[127] *ibid* [69].

decision under appeal and the relevant statutory provisions'.[128] The deprivation decision could be challenged on a number of bases including Wednesbury unreasonableness, a failure to take into account relevant considerations, procedural impropriety. To put it shortly, deprivation decisions are reviewable on judicial review grounds only. SIAC could not put itself '"in the shoes" of the decision-maker and treat it as competent to re-consider the matter de novo or to re-take the decision itself'.[129]

This is in contrast to the jurisdiction and powers of SIAC with regard to the leave to enter decision, the discussion of which is highly technical in nature. In short, the Court held, noting the parties' agreement on this point, that the provisions of the Nationality, Immigration and Asylum Act 2002 which are listed in section 2(2) of the Immigration Act 1971 Act apply to Ms Begum's appeal against the refusal of her human rights claim as part of the leave to enter decision. Human rights based appeals are limited to the ground that the impugned decision unlawfully infringes on Article 6 ECHR, which SIAC has jurisdiction to decide for itself (rather than merely review the Secretary of State's decision).[130]

Having explained the different natures of review,[131] Lord Reed first dismisses – with regard to the issue of whether the High Court was wrong to reject Ms Begum's argument that the deprivation appeal should automatically be allowed if it could not be fairly and effectively pursued due to being refused leave to enter the UK – Ms Begum's natural justice argument. Where, in a situation such as the present, Parliament has not stipulated what an appeal tribunal ought to do if a person's right to appeal could not be effectively exercised,

> it is necessary to consider how such a body should reasonably respond to a problem of that kind, having regard to its responsibility for the administration of justice, the nature and consequences of the decision in question, and any relevant provisions of the legislation.[132]

Citing Eleanor Roosevelt ('justice cannot be for one side alone'),[133] which he says would be the case if Ms Begum was allowed to re-enter on the basis that she could not conduct the appeal effectively from abroad, Lord Reed draws a distinction between an obstacle liable to be temporary and a disadvantage which cannot be overcome. In respect of the former, a stay or adjournment may be appropriate whereas in respect of the latter the court would normally proceed with the case, which may well lead to the disadvantaged party losing the case. On the other hand, where the difficulty is of such an extreme nature that one party placed is at a forensic disadvantage and it is impossible for the case to be fairly tried, the interests of justice may require a stay of proceedings. This approach, Lord Reed says,

[128] *ibid.*
[129] *ibid* [81].
[130] *ibid* [37].
[131] *ibid* [82]–[83].
[132] *ibid* [89].
[133] *ibid* [90].

is illustrated by a number of cases. The first case mentioned, *Carnduff v Rock*,[134] involved action by a police officer to recover reasonable remuneration for information that had been supplied, which involved issues of confidentiality and the public interest. The second case referred to is *Tariq v Home Office*,[135] in which the Supreme Court referred to *Carnduff*, apparently to defeat the argument that a closed material procedure should not be employed to protect national security material essential to the defence of the claim but deemed contrary to the public interest.

Recognising the serious consequences of a deprivation decision on individuals as well as the public interest in preventing them from returning to the UK, Lord Reed dismisses Ms Begum's cross-appeal against the High Court's decision in relation to the deprivation appeal, concluding that,

> it would be irresponsible for the court to allow the appeal without any regard to the interests of national security which prompted the decision in question, and it is difficult to conceive that the law would require it to do so.[136]

Lord Reed proceeds to criticise the Court of Appeal's decision in strong terms. First, he says there was no basis for allowing the leave to enter appeal because no Article 6 ground was argued before the Court of Appeal, only common law principles were invoked. Second, he states that the exercise in comparative risk analysis by reference to *U2* was flawed; a lower risk was not necessarily one which could be managed. Third, Lord Reed remarks that there was no basis for the finding that the national security concerns about Ms Begum could be addressed and managed without any evidence or submissions to that effect. The Court of Appeal had 'overlooked the limitations to its competence, both institutional and constitutional, to decide questions of national security'.[137] Fourth, Lord Reed criticises the Court of Appeal for treating the right to an effective appeal as a 'trump card'.[138]

In offering his conclusions on the case, Lord Reed explained that, in his view, the Court of Appeal committed four significant errors. It misunderstood the role of SIAC and the courts on an appeal against the Home Secretary's decision refusing leave to enter the UK. It erroneously decided that when a person's right to have a fair hearing of an appeal conflicts with the requirements of national security, the former must prevail over the latter. It mistakenly treated the Home Secretary's policy, which was 'intended for his own guidance in the exercise of the discretion conferred on him by Parliament, as if it were a rule of law which he must obey',[139] and,

> the Court of Appeal erred in its approach to the appeal against the dismissal of Ms Begum's application for judicial review of the Home Secretary's refusal of leave

[134] *Carnduff v Rock* [2001] EWCA Civ 680, [2001] 1 WLR 1786.
[135] *Tariq v Home Office* [2011] UKSC 35, [2012] 1 AC 452.
[136] *R (Begum) v Special Immigration Appeals Commission* (n 3) [94].
[137] *ibid* [119].
[138] *ibid* [110].
[139] *ibid* [136].

> to enter the United Kingdom. It made its own assessment of the requirements of national security, and preferred it to that of the Home Secretary, despite the absence of any relevant evidence before it, or any relevant findings of fact by the court below. Its approach did not give the Home Secretary's assessment the respect which it should have received, given that it is the Home Secretary who has been charged by Parliament with responsibility for making such assessments, and who is democratically accountable to Parliament for the discharge of that responsibility.[140]

In sum, the Supreme Court overturned the Court of Appeal's judgment on the grounds that, first, it had misunderstood the scope of an appeal against the Secretary of State's decision to refuse Ms Begum leave to enter, second, the Court had wrongly made its own assessment of national security requirements despite there being no evidence before it, third, the Court had unduly placed Ms Begum's right to a fair hearing above conflicting national security requirements, and, finally, it had mistakenly treated the extraterritorial human rights policy in question as a rule of law instead of guidance.

V. *R (O (A Child)) v Secretary of State for the Home Department*

In stark contrast to *Begum*, *O (A Child)* is a case which quietly, out of the spotlight, produced a number of constitutionally relevant and indeed constitutionally significant judicial statements. It has all of the necessary ingredients for an important decision, discussing the principle of legality (or rather, the inapplicability thereof), the status of statutory rights, common law constitutional rights (or, rather, the lack thereof), statutory interpretation and the use of external materials, and, as many public law cases appear to include these days, a discussion on the implications of *UNISON v Lord Chancellor*.[141] In much the same way as *Miller v Prime Minister* takes some of its force from its brevity, which gives the impression that its legal reasoning is clear and uncontroversial, *O (A Child)* makes a number of fundamental statements in a succinct way. Its impact has been significant, too. In the short space of time since its publication, *O (A Child)* has been referred to by no less than nine cases. Judgments citing it range from a decision concerning PAYE regulations, in which *O (A Child)* was relied on as authority for the 'well-established approach to statutory construction',[142] to another Supreme Court decision concerning pilot schemes introducing voter identification requirements at local elections, in which *O (A Child)* was referred to as reiterating 'that the primary source by which meaning is ascertained is by

[140] *ibid* [134].
[141] *R (UNISON) v Lord Chancellor* (n 54).
[142] *Stephen Hoey and Others v Commissioners for Her Majesty's Revenue and Customs* [2022] EWCA Civ 656, [2022] STC 902 [66].

way of conducting an analysis of the language used by Parliament'.[143] Similar statements and references to the decision have been made in the planning context[144] and the European Union law/constitutional law context (in Northern Ireland).[145]

A. The Facts

Section 1(4) of the British Nationality Act 1981 entails a statutory right to acquire British citizenship:

> A person born in the United Kingdom after commencement who is not a British citizen by virtue of subsection … shall be entitled, on an application for his registration as a British citizen made at any time after he has attained the age of ten years, to be registered as such a citizen if, as regards each of the first ten years of that person's life, the number of days on which he was absent from the United Kingdom in that year does not exceed 90.

The Immigration Act 2014 Act enables the Home Secretary to set fees for an application by children meeting those requirements. The maximum that can be charged is specified in the Immigration and Nationality (Fees) Order 2016, which was made under the 2014 Act. The maximum amount at the time of the judgment was £1,500. The actual fees are set out in secondary legislation, the Immigration and Nationality (Fees) Regulations 2018. They can be, and indeed are, vastly in excess of the costs associated with the processing of the application. Indeed, costs are only one of the matters the Secretary of State must have regard to in devising the fee under section 68(9) of the Immigration Act 2014. Other factors include the benefits the Secretary of State thinks are likely to accrue to any person in connection with the exercise of the function, the costs of exercising any other function in connection with immigration or nationality, the promotion of economic growth, fees charged by or on behalf of governments of other countries in respect of comparable functions and any relevant international agreement.

The facts of this case are very straightforward. O,[146] the first claimant in this matter, said the fees imposed by the Secretary of State in the Regulations were ultra vires the Immigration Act 2014 because the Secretary of State did not have the power to set the fee at the level which renders nugatory the underlying primary statutory right to become a British citizen. O, who was joined by the second claimant, the Project for the Registration of Children as British Citizens, was born in the UK in 2007, where she had been attending school since. She held a Nigerian

[143] *R (Coughlan) v Minister for the Cabinet Office* [2022] UKSC 11, [2022] 1 WLR 2389 [13].

[144] *London Historic Parks and Gardens Trust v Minister of State for Housing* [2022] EWHC 829 (Admin), [2022] JPL 1196 [55].

[145] *Allister v Secretary of State for Northern Ireland* [2022] NICA 15, [2022] 3 CMLR 8.

[146] Judgments involving children and other vulnerable or uncapacious individuals are often anonymise to protect their identity.

passport and never left the UK. She applied for British citizenship in 2017 but was only able to pay a fraction of the fee associated with the application, namely £386 instead of the then required £973 (the fee was subsequently increased). Due to the shortfall, the Secretary of State refused to process O's application.

B. The High Court's and Court of Appeal's Decisions

The High Court claim included more grounds than the ones pursued before the Supreme Court. O had additionally argued, for example, that in setting the fee for the registration of children as British citizens under the British Nationality Act 1981 at the relevant level, the Secretary of State had failed to discharge her duty towards the welfare of children under section 55 of the Borders, Citizenship and Immigration Act 2009, and that the fees breached the Secretary of State's public sector equality duty. Jay J recognised 'that O and her mother cannot as a matter of practical reality pay the full fee'[147] and said the evidence suggested the registration fee was unaffordable in the *UNISON* sense, meaning the majority of children growing up in households on low or middle incomes, could only pay the fee if unreasonable sacrifices were made.

Jay J held that the present case did not involve fundamental rights, but merely an 'important' statutory right.[148] He dismissed the claim on the ultra vires ground, saying he was bound by the decision of the Court of Appeal in *R (Williams) v Secretary of State for the Home Department*.[149] In *Williams*, the legal challenge had also involved section 1(4) of the 1981 Act, however on a slightly different basis in that the claimant had said the fees were ultra vires because there was no fee exemption for applications by children in receipt of local authority assistance due to destitution. The Court of Appeal held that the fact that the fee was unaffordable to some did not undermine the statutory purpose and intent of the 1981 Act and that the entitlement to apply for registration as a citizen was not a constitutional right. Jay J considered that *Williams* had not been sufficiently altered by the Supreme Court's subsequent judgment in *UNISON*, but said that the full effect of *UNISON* on *Williams* ought to be considered by a higher court. The High Court did, however, allow the claim under section 55 of the 2009 Act. Jay J granted a declaration to that effect but refused to quash the Regulations, and did not grant any substantive relief.

Jay J granted the appellants a certificate for a leapfrog appeal on the ultra vires ground, however the Supreme Court refused permission, indicating the Court of Appeal should be given the opportunity to consider the *Williams* decision in the

[147] *R (Project for the Registration of Children as British Citizens and others) v Secretary of State for the Home Department* [2019] EWHC 3536 (Admin), [2020] 1 WLR 1486 [9].

[148] *ibid*, see [72].

[149] *R (Williams) v Secretary of State for the Home Department* [2017] EWCA Civ 98, [2017] 1 WLR 3283.

light of *UNISON*. The Court of Appeal dismissed the Home Secretary's appeal against Jay J's decision on section 55 as well as the claimant's cross-appeal as to relief.[150] As for the ultra vires challenge part of the appeal, the Court of Appeal unanimously held that *UNISON* had not overturned *Williams*.

C. The Supreme Court's Decision: Limiting the Effect of *UNISON* by Creating a New Constitutional Principle

The Supreme Court judgment, given by Lord Hodge with whom Lord Briggs, Lord Stephens and Lady Rose agreed, starts the legal analysis by recognising that 'There is no dispute as to the importance to an individual of the possession of British citizenship'[151] before stating that the appeal before it was, principally, concerned with statutory interpretation. The question, Lord Hodge says, was 'whether Parliament has authorised in *primary* legislation the imposition by *subordinate* legislation of the fees which the appellants challenge'.[152]

The appellant relied on the 'constitutional principle'[153] stemming from *UNISON* that 'specific statutory rights are not to be cut down by subordinate legislation passed under the vires of a different Act'. In *UNISON*, Lord Reed had derived this principle from *R v Secretary of State for Social Security, ex p Joint Council for the Welfare of Immigrants* (hereinafter referred to as *JCWI*).[154] In *JCWI* the claimants had challenged subordinate legislation made under the Social Security Contributions and Benefits Act 1992, which removed the right to apply for urgent case payments pending one's claim for asylum being finally determined. Specifically, the regulations excluded those who sought asylum not on first arrival to the UK as well as asylum seekers whose claims for asylum had been adversely determined by the Secretary of State and who had appealed said determination from the payments, which meant they would face destitution. The Court of Appeal by a majority held that the regulations were ultra vires as they rendered nugatory the rights conferred on those groups of asylum seekers to seek refugee status under the Asylum and Immigration Appeals Act 1993. In his concurring judgment, Waite LJ stated 'Subsidiary legislation must not only be within the vires of the enabling statute but must also be so drawn as not to conflict with statutory rights already enacted by other primary legislation'.[155]

[150] *R (Project for the Registration of Children as British Citizens and others) v Secretary of State for the Home Department; R (O (A Child) v Secretary of State for the Home Department* [2021] EWCA Civ 193, [2021] 1 WLR 3049.

[151] *R (O (A Child)) v Secretary of State for the Home Department* (n 4) [26].

[152] *ibid* [27] (emphasis added).

[153] *ibid* [39].

[154] *R v Secretary of State for Social Security, Ex p Joint Council for the Welfare of Immigrants* [1997] 1 WLR 275, CA.

[155] *ibid* at 293E.

In its judgment, the Supreme Court from the beginning emphasises the need to ascertain the meaning of the words used by Parliament, which 'involves an objective assessment of the meaning which a reasonable legislature as a body would be seeking to convey in using the statutory words which are being considered'.[156] The Court also highlights that it was accepted by all parties that the appeal was not concerned with constitutional or fundamental common law rights, and that none of the ECHR rights were engaged. Lord Hodge also appears to suggest that the statutory right in question is not fundamental in nature.

As for *JCWI*, Lord Hodge says he has 'difficulty' with the statement made by Waite LJ cited above.[157] He disagrees that, as a matter of constitutional law, one must look beyond the vires of the enabling statute. Given parliamentary sovereignty, Parliament is free to legislate and, in legislating, expressly or by implication amend or repeal an earlier statute. In analysing subordinate legislation, one must simply look to the enabling power contained in the primary legislation that authorises the subordinate legislation, regardless of what was enacted before it. In engaging in that interpretative exercise, courts must take account of presumptions based on 'long-standing principles of constitutional and administrative law', such as the principle of legality, when they ascertain whether a later Act of Parliament has empowered the executive to make subordinate legislation which restricts or removes rights conferred by an earlier Act of Parliament. However, 'the central task of the court is to ascertain the extent of the enabling power in statute 2'.[158] The Supreme Court therefore instructs us to view as a '*presumption* rather than a *rule of law* which predetermines the vires of'[159] the later statutes the following statement made in *JCWI*:

> the Regulations now in force [are] so uncompromisingly draconian in effect that they must indeed be held ultra vires. I would found my decision … on the wider ground that rights necessarily implicit in the Act of 1993 are now inevitably being overborne. Parliament cannot have intended a significant number of genuine asylum seekers to be impaled on the horns of so intolerable a dilemma: the need either to abandon their claims to refugee status or alternatively to maintain them as best they can but in a state of utter destitution. Primary legislation alone could in my judgment achieve that sorry state of affairs.[160]

In reading this as a presumption rather than a strict legal rule, if the conclusion is still that the later Act of Parliament expressly or impliedly empowers the executive to make subordinate legislation which has the effect of removing the rights conferred by an earlier statute, those rights have been removed intra vires.

[156] *R (O (A Child)) v Secretary of State for the Home Department* (n 4) [31].
[157] *ibid* [40].
[158] *ibid* [41]–[42].
[159] *ibid* [42] (emphasis added).
[160] *R v Secretary of State for Social Security, Ex p Joint Council for the Welfare of Immigrants* (n 154) at 293C-D (per Brown LJ).

Lord Hodge then proceeds to say that, in this case, the normal canons of statutory interpretation apply, seeing as no constitutional or fundamental right was at stake. Consequently, Lord Hodge reasons, 'the special rule of construction, which is embodied in the principle of legality, has no application' and that, similarly, the principle stemming from *UNISON* 'that where a statutory power authorises an intrusion upon [a right], it is interpreted as authorising only such degree of intrusion as is reasonably necessary to fulfil the objective of the provision in question' does not apply either.[161]

Turning to the statutory provision at stake, Lord Hodge highlights that the Immigration Act 2014, the later of the two Acts of Parliament: (a) authorises the Secretary of State to make a fees order that must specify the maximum chargeable amount if the fee is a fixed fee, subject to the affirmative resolution in the House of Lords and the House of Commons; (b) authorises the Secretary of State to make regulations setting out the fee, subject to the negative resolution procedure in Parliament; (c) sets out the only matters to which the Secretary of State can have regard in setting the fee amount in the regulations; and (d) empowers, but does not require, the Secretary of State to introduce exceptions, fee waivers, refunds, etc. Lord Hodge then proceeds to note that there is no criterion of affordability in the 2014 Act. In fact, the Act

> expressly empowered the Secretary of State to set fees at levels which (i) took account of benefits likely to accrue from citizenship and (ii) could subsidise the cost of the exercise of other functions in connection with immigration or nationality, thereby moving part at least of the financial burden of such functions from the UK taxpayer to the applicants. The mechanism of control of the level of fees of fixed amount which Parliament enacted was by empowering the Secretary of State to specify maximum fees in a fees order, over which Parliament could exercise a degree of control through the affirmative resolution procedure. Similarly, in the 2014 Act Parliament did not specify that there must be adjustments made to the level of the fees charged or the waiver of such fees for children who could not afford to pay the specified fee. On the contrary, Parliament delegated to the Secretary of State the task of making such provision in the fees regulations, which were subject only to the negative resolution procedure.[162]

Consequently, it follows that the later Act of Parliament authorises the subordinate legislation by which the Secretary of State has fixed the fee that must be paid for applications to be registered as a British citizens under section 1(4) of the earlier of the two Acts of Parliament. As for the fee itself, its 'appropriateness' is not a question of law but a

> question of policy which is for political determination. It is not a matter for judges for whom the question is the much narrower one of whether Parliament has authorised the Secretary of State to set the impugned fee at the level which it has been set.[163]

[161] *R (O (A Child)) v Secretary of State for the Home Department* (n 4) [33].
[162] *ibid* [49].
[163] *ibid* [51].

VI. Rights, Reasoning and Precedent on the Political Constitutionalist Side of the Spectrum

As was highlighted in subsequent case law, 'the question in Begum concerned the proper approach to review by a specialist tribunal of a decision which Parliament had decided should be entrusted to the Secretary of State ….'[164] The Supreme Court's decision is the most recent in a line of cases at the highest level establishing that special respect must be paid to the judgments of the executive on national security matters.[165] It proposes that SIAC should take a public law approach to challenges to the Secretary of State's assessment of national security, rather than conduct its own assessment. Where the public interests prayed in aid by the executive relate to national security, the courts are expected to show great respect to the judgment of the executive about whether the relevant risk is made out and about the weight to be attached to it. Subsequent case law has established that, whether a case involves the protections offered by the HRA or not, the executive's assessment will be tested in limited ways. This is because SIAC

> does not have the institutional competence to assess the risk for itself as a primary decision-maker. Nor is it democratically accountable. If SIAC were to call the risk incorrectly, the executive, not SIAC, would suffer the political fallout. The executive can be removed at a general election; SIAC cannot.[166]

The focus in *Begum* on deference needing to be shown to the decisions of democratically accountable institutions is emblematic of the political constitutionalist component of the nuanced constitution. Taking a step back, the decision is a reminder of two things in particular. First, *Begum* shows that, in certain contexts, what is considered 'institutional legitimacy' will easily trump legal rights. Second, the Supreme Court's judgment highlights that there is a category of executive action which is accorded higher levels of deference than others while, at the same time, certain rights ordinarily cast as beacons of our constitutional rights protection in certain situations are not really instrumental to a decision's reasoning, let alone its outcome.

As for the first point, as Martin notes,

> While the reasoning of the Supreme Court regarding the nature of appeals under [the legislative framework] and the approach to be taken to the extraterritorial human rights policy is relatively uncontroversial, the court's repeated reference to constitutional catchphrases such as 'institutional competence', 'democratic accountability' and 'respect' is notable.[167]

[164] *Attorney General v BBC* [2022] EWHC 826 (QB), [2022] 4 WLR 74 [29].

[165] For previous authorities on this point, see *R (Carlile) v Secretary of State for the Home Department* [2014] UKSC 60, [2015] AC 945 and *Secretary of State for the Home Department v Rehman* (n 123), both of which were referred to in *R (Begum) v Special Immigration Appeals Commission* (n 3).

[166] *Secretary of State for the Home Department v P3* [2021] EWCA Civ 1642, [2022] 1 WLR 2869 [102] (per Laing LJ).

[167] S Martin, 'Deference, "Fairness" and Accountability in the National Security Context' (2021) 80(2) *CLJ* 209, 212.

Rather than engaging with a substantive rights discussion at common law, the institutional credentials of one of the parties submitting legal arguments tilts, it seems, the scales in that party's favour, and it is difficult to see on what basis any such initial imbalance could be overcome. The implications of the UK's rights framework, which allows certain substantive rights to be outshone simply because the limitation imposed on them was made by the political branches of state is discussed in more detail in chapter five. As for the instant discussion, at the heart of this case lies the assumption, as discussed in later chapters, that 'decisions about national security should be made by people who can be elected and removed'.[168]

As for the second point, Hooper has highlighted that Lord Reed himself, in the much celebrated decision of *R (Osborn) v Parole Board*, which is discussed in greater detail in chapter four, stated that 'justice is intuitively understood to require a procedure which pays due respect to persons whose rights are significantly affected by decisions taken in the exercise of administrative or judicial functions'.[169] Yet, in this process, the person affected by the decision has not been heard, and has in fact been unable to give meaningful instructions to her lawyer. The judgment leaves the individual the judgment is about in legal limbo, in such a dramatic way that one cannot help but think that the phrase invoked by Lord Reed in *Begum*, that 'justice cannot be for one side alone', had in fact no impact on the reasoning or outcome of this case. As properly recognised by the Court of Appeal, no discernible justice appears to have been achieved for Ms Begum, who will continue to live in circumstances which SIAC had accepted breached her human rights under the ECHR, and which is likely to have led to the death of one of her children. On the other hand, the Secretary of State's discretion in the context of highly controversial powers has been considerably strengthened, which has set a helpful precedent for future decisions, as subsequent judgments show. Thus, as Sir Stephen Irwin noted in his concurring judgment in *Secretary of State for the Home Department v P3*, which followed *Begum* and in which, contrary to *Begum*, Convention rights had been pleaded, 'SIAC is bound to show deference at all stages and at all levels, to the assessments of those responsible for making those assessments professionally. In matters of high policy, that deference will be effectively simply acceptance'.[170] In a further subsequent decision by the Administrative Court, this has been interpreted to suggest that 'in practical terms, the threshold for judicial interference will be high even in the court's consideration of individual pieces of intelligence'.[171]

Much like in *Miller v Prime Minister*, the Court in *Begum* painted on an essentially blank canvas as far as directly applicable precedent is concerned. In *Miller*,

[168] *Secretary of State for the Home Department v P3* (n 166) [79].

[169] *R (Osborn) v Parole Board* [2013] UKSC 61, [2014] AC 1115 [68], cited in H Hooper, 'Justice for One Side Alone? R. (on the application of Begum) v Special Immigration Appeals Commission' [2022] *PL* 1, 8.

[170] *Secretary of State for the Home Department v P3* (n 166) [126].

[171] *QX v Secretary of State for the Home Department* [2022] EWHC 836 (Admin) (appeal outstanding) (7 April 2022, unreported at time of writing) [38].

the Supreme Court's reasoning inflated the legal aspects of the constitution. In *Begum*, political institutions were strengthened at the expense of judicial oversight and fundamental due process rights. In effect, looking beyond the technicalities of the decision around the question of standards of review, what we are left with, despite the UK's much-hailed human rights framework, is a system in which the executive, because of their 'democratic credentials', can unilaterally strip its citizens of their nationality without guaranteeing a truly available appeal system. Morally, this is problematic in particular seeing as the changes brought in by the Immigration Act 2014, which, for instance, allows for the deprivation of citizenship of those born in the UK but who have some purported theoretical claim to another country's passport, predominantly affects minorities. Minorities have less political agency, and are therefore much less able to simply 'vote out office holders' whose performance they disagree with. The reference to *Carnduff v Rock*[172] as authority for the suggestion that the interest of justice requires a stay of proceedings adds insult to injury. There the interest at stake was remuneration under a purported contract, which is far removed from the situation in *Begum*.

Begum was widely regarded as a 'win' in the political constitutionalist camp. For example, Ekins, who said the decision was 'a powerful and welcome, if somewhat overdue, affirmation of constitutional principle and the limits of judicial power', noted while there may be

> good reasons to think that the power to deprive a person of their British citizenship is overly broad and should be more strictly limited, if not abolished … this is an argument that should be advanced in Parliament not in a courtroom.[173]

In short, the legal value and enforceability of a right is dependent on majority approval. As the legal analysis in both *Begum* and *O (A Child)* shows, that institutional legitimacy-centric approach, which is another aspect of the nuanced constitution, can extend to the most basic of rights. Citizenship, whether denied at the stage of application due to insufficient funds or deprived at a later stage in life, acts as a 'conduit pipe' for the realisation of other rights. Furthermore, as a government report highlights, deprivation of citizenship 'paves the way for possible immigration detention, deportation or exclusion from the UK and otherwise removes an individual's right of abode in the UK'.[174]

Yet, *Begum* and *O (A Child)* leave one with the distinct impression that, rather than being a constitutionally priced, and accordingly legally protected value, the significance of citizenship is but a small factor, perhaps even an afterthought, in both decisions despite judicial assurances to the contrary. Importantly, the bridge between *Begum* and *O (A Child)* is not just the fact that both concerned citizenship of individuals with a migration background. Another commonality is the common law's persistent refusal to accord certain rights a 'fundamental' or 'constitutional'

[172] *Carnduff v Rock* (n 134).

[173] R Ekins, 'The Significance of the Supreme Court's Begum judgment' (*Policy Exchange Blog*, 3 March 2021).

[174] HM Government Transparency Report: Disruptive Powers 2018/19 (March 2020) 21, para 5.9.

status, despite them being core rights for democratic participation, the very essence and justification for political constitutionalism. As highlighted by Sandro, citizenship is the basis for democratic participation. Therefore, *O (A Child)*

> ends up betraying the limits of the orthodox constitutional doctrine upon which it is based. Destitute children born in the UK who are entitled to British citizenship might never have the financial means to pay the fees to register as such, and thus might never enjoy the right to co-determine that very policy that prices them out of political representation. Our constitution is said to be political, but for whom?[175]

As we will see in later chapters, the nuanced constitution places similarly contradictory restrictions on the 'right to vote', which is equally important in a system that considers itself based on, and assigns moral value to, being a democracy.

Another characteristic of the nuanced constitution brought out by *O (A Child)* is the lack of consistency in approach across different judgments. How is it, for example, that in *Miller v Prime Minister* Lord Carnwath's one sentence in *Miller v Secretary of State*[176] can be taken to effectively set parliamentary accountability on par with parliamentary sovereignty as far as constitutional status and weight is concerned, whereas *O (A Child)* proceeded on the basis that the right to citizenship was not fundamental or constitutional despite Jay J expressly recognising that *in R (Bancoult) v Foreign Secretary (No 2)*, a Supreme Court case, Lord Mance characterised the right of abode as 'fundamental and, in the informal sense in which that term is necessarily used in a United Kingdom context, constitutional'?[177] Also, much like in *Miller v Prime Minister*, the Supreme Court in *O (A Child)* constructed a new analytical approach, here by devising the 'presumption vs legal rule' dichotomy, which, in the event, did not add anything to the ordinary approach to statutory interpretation. Yet, in devising this test, the Supreme Court departs from its own endorsement, in *UNISON*, of the constitutional principle stemming from *JCWI*.

Finally, *O (A Child)* signifies the immaturity and uncertainty embedded into our system of human and constitutional rights protection, which is also emblematic of the nuanced constitution. All three courts in *O (A Child)* characterised the fee, unaffordable for many, not as an unlawful barrier to a legal right, but, instead, as 'simply a *pre-condition* for the existence of the statutory right to apply for citizenship'.[178] Contrast this with the decision in *UNISON*, where the fees individuals were charged by the Secretary of State to bring a claim in the employment law sphere were classified as an unlawful infringement of the common law

[175] P Sandro, 'A Political Constitution, but for whom? Citizenship Fees, Legality, and the Limits of Doctrine' (*UK Constitutional Law Association Blog*, 23 February 2022).

[176] see text associated with n 98.

[177] *R (Project for the Registration of Children as British Citizens and others) v Secretary of State for the Home Department* (n 147) [14], citing *R (Bancoult) v Foreign Secretary (No 2)* [2008] UKHL 61, [2009] 1 AC 453 [151].

[178] A Richardson, 'The Legality of Home Office Fees' (*UK Constitutional Law Association Blog*, 26 May 2021) (emphasis added).

constitutional right of access to justice. Does this suggest that common law constitutional rights rank higher than legislated rights, including by affording the former judicial protection through the principle of legality, despite them being developed by the unelected branch of state?

Having compared and contrasted these four authorities through the lens of the spectrum of the nuanced constitution, in the next two chapters of this book the focus shifts to one concept or phenomenon of the latter: common law constitutional rights.

PART II

Common Law Constitutional Rights

3

A Short History of Common Law Constitutional Rights

Two of the four decisions discussed in chapter two were linked by a common law constitutional rights case: *R (UNISON) v Lord Chancellor*,[1] in which the Supreme Court held that tribunal fees of up to £1,200 had been unlawful from the outset because they unduly restricted the constitutional right of access to justice. Giving the Court's lead judgment,[2] Lord Reed said that the fees in question had 'the practical effect of making it unaffordable for persons to exercise rights conferred on them by Parliament, or of rendering the bringing of claims to enforce such rights a futile or irrational exercise', thereby 'rendering those rights nugatory'.[3] The Court quashed the Employment Tribunals and the Employment Appeal Tribunal Fees Order[4] as well as rules 11 and 40 of the Employment Tribunals Rules of Procedure 2013.

As is discussed in greater detail in the second half of this chapter as well as in chapter four, *UNISON* broke new ground for common law constitutional rights jurisprudence. Moreover, the Supreme Court's decision has had a significant impact on the conceptualisation of the rule of law and other constitutional principles, including the principle of legality. *UNISON* is also an important, and, certainly at the Supreme Court level, a rare example of a decision in which the bench was willing to critically engage with statistics and socio-economic evidence to determine the real life as opposed to the theoretical impact of a measure put in place by the executive. As for the judgment's practical effects, following *UNISON* the Ministry of Justice and HM Courts and Tribunals Service rolled out a refund scheme, with initial estimates suggesting the total refund costs would amount to thirty-three million pounds.[5] There has also been a considerable increase in cases at the Employment Tribunals and the Employment Appeal Tribunal since the fees were scrapped.[6]

[1] *R (UNISON) v Lord Chancellor* [2017] UKSC 51, [2020] AC 869.

[2] The Court's decision was unanimous; however, Lady Hale produced a second shorter judgment, with which all other Justices including Lord Reed agreed, focusing on the link between the fees and the Equality Act 2010.

[3] *R (UNISON) v Lord Chancellor* (n 1) [104].

[4] 2013 (SI 2013/1893).

[5] UK Parliament, House of Lords written answer, HL1770, 19 October 2017.

[6] House of Commons Library Research Briefing, 'Employment Tribunals after R (Unison) v Lord Chancellor' (5 November 2018).

Common law constitutional rights decisions like *UNISON* are important to study, not only in their own right but also with a view to developing a better understanding of the UK constitution more generally. Indeed, the jurisprudence surrounding these rights lends itself particularly well to an in-depth exploration of public law adjudication under the nuanced constitution. First, common law constitutional rights are a product of the English common law. Accordingly, they reveal how the latter, as an important component of the constitution, protects rights, and particularly what aspects of the English common law are conducive towards basic rights adjudication, and which ones are not. Second, common law constitutional rights operate in a public law context. This means they inhabit a sphere defined by other constitutional principles. Accordingly, they offer a unique opportunity for scholars to explore the broader nature of the constitution. Third, common law constitutional rights, by virtue of what they seek to protect and by virtue of the mechanisms they employ, are among the most legislation-resilient concepts the English common law possesses. Accordingly, the study of these rights allows us to explore the boundaries of the principle of parliamentary sovereignty, the reach of the substantive notion rule of law, and their interplay.

This chapter takes a chronological approach, setting out a summary of how common law constitutional rights have developed, focusing in particular on the last few decades. Judicial emphasis on the legal protections offered by the common law has seen a strong resurgence in recent years, especially in the Supreme Court.[7] As will become clear, however, there is nothing particularly new about judges developing the law and 'construing statutes in a way that protects higher notions of justice and rights'.[8] The English common law, the source of common law constitutional rights, has always, albeit inconsistently, been influenced and shaped by the idea that the supreme authority of the land is subject to limits and that individuals bear negative and positive rights. Historically, these were often conceptualised and enforced through various areas of private law. Thus, many of the common law's rights protections were, and some continue to be found in tort law,[9] property law[10] and criminal law.[11] Private law provided a fertile ground for the development of rights as it remained relatively undisturbed by the political branches of the state until well into the nineteenth century.[12] However, as the

[7] Lord Woolf and others, *De Smith's Judicial Review*, 8th edn (Sweet & Maxwell, 2021) Ch 11 – 'Substantive Review and Justification, Violation of Common Law Rights and Constitutional Principles', 11-053.

[8] D Meagher, 'The Common Law Principle of Legality in an Age of Rights' (2011) 35(2) *Melbourne University Law Review* 449, 452.

[9] See, eg, *Sir W De Crespigny v Wellesley* (1829) 5 Bingham 392, 130 ER 1112 and *Hollins v Fowler* (1874–75) LR 7 HL 757.

[10] See, eg, *Tapling v Jones* (1865) 11 HLC 290, (1865) 20 Common Bench Reports (New Series) 166 and *Western Counties Railway Co v Windsor and Annapolis Railway Co* (1882) 7 App Cas 178.

[11] The law of battery, for example, indirectly protects personal rights such as the right to be free from physical harmful contact.

[12] J Hasnas, 'Toward a Theory of Empirical Natural Rights' (2005) 22(1) *Social Philosophy and Policy* 111, 132, fn 51.

following section shows, there are also famous historical case law examples within the public law sphere that were conceptualised as free-standing rights.

In looking at this country's constitutional rights history, a note of caution is necessary. Especially when it comes to homegrown rights protection, historical reality is regularly mixed with a fair bit of mythmaking, hyperbole and selection bias. The English common law 'is a story, prompted by lawyers, and told by judges',[13] and it is, increasingly perhaps, leveraged by politicians. One example of the latter is the aftermath of the Government commissioned Independent Human Rights Act Review to examine how (well) the Human Rights Act 1998 (HRA) operates in practice. In its December 2021 report,[14] the panel tasked with the review concluded that, overall, the HRA was working well, but made recommendations for certain changes.[15] Concomitantly with the publication of the report, the Boris Johnson Government announced its plans to replace the HRA with a different bill of rights.[16] The subsequently published Bill of Rights bill appears to have been abandoned following the selection of Liz Truss as Prime Minister. Relevantly for this chapter's theme, the proposal's underlying narrative was that the UK has a history of strong human rights protection, and that there should be a stronger emphasis on the English common law, which was shaped by that history, and vice-versa. For example, the Government's consultation document postulated,

> The United Kingdom has a long, proud, and diverse history of freedom. This stretches from Magna Carta in 1215, the 1689 Claim and Bill of Rights, and the Slave Trade Act of 1807, through to the 1918 Representation of the People Act.[17]

The principles lying behind some of these laws are said to have 'inspired the writers of the Declaration of Independence, the US Constitution and subsequent Bill of Rights' as well as 'international treaties and obligations'.[18] Albeit true in part, these sweeping statements need to be taken with a pinch of salt. Contrary to the impression created by the Government's rhetoric, our history of human rights protection is far more ambivalent than often suggested. Specifically, it is important to recognise that the narrative around the UK's history of the pursuit of the rule of law and human rights is often detached from the common law's persistent moral failings both at home and, particularly, abroad. As Friedman puts it, we can find 'extraordinary (and shameful) variation[s] in its own standards'.[19] How the common law has developed, and spread through parts of the Empire, and how, in fact, the level of protection it offers compares to other jurisdictions requires thorough analysis and critical thinking. In what follows, I only scratch the surface

[13] D Friedman, 'A Common Law of Human Rights: History, Humanity and Dignity' (2016) *European Human Rights Law Review* 378, 383.

[14] The Independent Human Rights Act Review (December 2021).

[15] *ibid*, vi onwards.

[16] Ministry of Justice, 'Plan to Reform Human Rights Act' (Press Release, 14 December 2021).

[17] Ministry of Justice, 'Human Rights Act Reform: A Modern Bill of Rights' – Consultation, Foreword.

[18] *ibid* [19].

[19] Friedman (n 13) 384.

of a topic that warrants much closer scholarly attention. My aim is a modest one. I attempt to set out, on a high level basis, some of the factors, themes and precedents that have shaped common law constitutional rights protection.

I. Three Famous Antecedents: A Tale of Precedents, Mythmaking and Common Law Legacy

One cannot with certainty point to the first case reflecting a rights-based focus. Notably, however, there are several famous cases originating in earlier centuries whose judicial reasoning rely heavily on the idea that the common law is able to protect individuals from interference with their rights by the state or other individuals. These decisions have echoed down the centuries as a source of pride and inspiration. One of the most treasured of them, and certainly one of the most contemporaneously relevant, is *Entick v Carrington*,[20] which has been described as 'one of the canons of English public law'.[21] Among many other things, it stands for the recognition of property rights at common law,[22] the case having been brought as one of trespass for unlawful seizure of personal property. However, *Entick v Carrington* also has another significant, broader dimension. It has been interpreted as one of the first judicial recognitions of the rule that express legal authority is necessary for the interference with individual rights. As Lord Neuberger has extra-judicially summarised,

> Nathan Carrington and three other King's messengers, acting under the orders of Lord Halifax, Secretary of State, had broken into John Entick's home and removed various supposedly pernicious pamphlets, causing significant damage in the process. Lord Camden the Chief Justice of Common Pleas said that Mr Carrington had been guilty of trespass to Mr Entick's land as the 'silence of the books' meant that the King and therefore the executive had no statutory or common law power to enter forcibly onto a citizen's land.[23]

Thus, public action will not be permitted unless legal authority is established. Put differently, *Entick v Carrington* provides that the state has no 'residual freedom' to act within the bounds set by legal prohibitions. In so deciding, *Entick v Carrington* marked an important turning point in the history of public law. In fact, it is one of the few famous cases which is still regularly cited in court today, including in our jurisdiction's most senior courts. One example that links this important eighteenth century case to contemporaneous rights litigation are the *Privacy International*

[20] *Entick v Carrington* (1765) 2 Wilson, KB 275, 95 ER 807, 19 Howell's St Tr 1029.

[21] A Tomkins and P Scott, 'Introduction' in A Tomkins and P Scott (eds), *Entick v Carrington 250 Years of the Rule of Law* (Hart Publishing, 2015).

[22] For a detailed analysis of the case see D Baranger, 'Law, Liberty and *Entick v Carrington*' in A Tomkins and P Scott *ibid.*

[23] D Neuberger, 'Reflections on Significant Moments in the Role of the Judiciary' (Personal Support Unit Fundraising Breakfast, 16 March 2017).

proceedings, which were discussed in detail in chapter two. Since the Supreme Court held[24] that decisions by the Investigatory Powers Tribunal (IPT) were subject to judicial review, Privacy International has succeeded on the substance of its complaint. In January 2021 the High Court quashed the ITP's decision and made a declaration as to the scope of section 5 of the Intelligence Services Act 1994.[25] The High Court's judgment contains an important discussion on fundamental rights, and repeats the well-established mechanism of the principle of legality in a particularly succinct way:

> Parliamentary sovereignty means that Parliament may legislate to override fundamental rights. However, Parliament is and must be subject to political constraints: if Parliament decides to enact legislation that is contrary to fundamental rights, it must squarely confront what it is doing and accept the political cost. That Parliament has confronted a breach of rights may be demonstrated not only in the express language of a statute but also by necessary implication. In the absence of either of those mechanisms, the courts will presume that fundamental rights are untouched …[26]

How does *Entick v Carrington* relate to this? The High Court proceeded to highlight, in discussing fundamental rights and the impugned computer hacking warrants, the long history of case law and influential writings demonstrating the common law's aversion to general warrants:

> We take from Blackstone, Hale and the general warrant cases that it is a fundamental right of an individual under the common law that he or she should not be apprehended, or have property seized and searched, save by decision of the person legally charged with issuing the warrant. Expressed in modern legal language, a general warrant is one which requires the exercise of judgment or discretion by the official executing the warrant as to which individuals or which property should be targeted. It follows that a general warrant gives rise to an unlawful delegation of authority by the legally entrusted decision-maker to the executing official. This unlawful delegation breaches a fundamental right.[27]

Linking these general historical references to *Entick v Carrington*, the Court proceeded, saying counsel for Privacy International,

> was correct to say that the right not to have property searched other than by the authority of the law has always been treated as a fundamental right. The great case of *Entick v Carrington* … held that the Secretary of State could not order searches of private property without authority conferred by an Act of Parliament or the common law. In doing so, the court emphasised the connection between property and privacy: a person's papers (containing private information) are their owner's 'dearest property' whose secret nature cannot be the subject of intrusion without legal authority.[28]

[24] *R (Privacy International) v Investigatory Powers Tribunal* [2019] UKSC 22, [2019] 2 WLR 1219.
[25] *R (Privacy International) v Investigatory Powers Tribunal* [2021] EWHC 27 (Admin), [2021] QB 936.
[26] *ibid* [37].
[27] *ibid* [45].
[28] *ibid* [46].

Finally, the High Court confirmed the continued legal force of *Entick v Carrington* 'and the other general warrant cases of the 1760s', which were not 'a mere historical footnote, nor … of only "marginal relevance"' but, rather, the case's 'fundamental message remains good law. Indeed, the common law's insistence that the Government cannot search private premises without lawful authority has been recently confirmed by a unanimous Supreme Court as having the status of a constitutional principle'.[29] The latter reference is to *R (Miller) v Prime Minister*, in which Lady Hale said *Entick v Carrington* established that the Secretary of State 'could not order searches of private property without authority conferred by an Act of Parliament or the common law'.[30] The computer network exploitation warrants issued under section 5 of the Intelligence Services Act 1994 were unlawful in that they were insufficiently specific for the property concerned to be objectively ascertainable on the face of the warrants. Clear statutory words would have been necessary to override the well-established historical aversion of the common law to general search warrants.

Entick v Carrington's continued legal relevance can be contrasted with the second famous antecedent, arguably the best-known in popular discourse, *Somerset v Stewart*.[31] The Government's consultation document, referred to above, suggested, 'Famously, in Somerset v Stewart in 1772, Lord Mansfield found that the law did not permit someone to be forcibly removed from England and sold into slavery'.[32] That is not a true statement of what the case was about, nor of what the Court decided. As for the facts, a black man who had been given the name 'Somerset' and held captive by a slave-owner in Virginia had been brought over to England, where he refused to continue in bondage. As he tried to escape, he was captured and held on a vessel that was about to leave for Jamaica. The case was decided by Lord Mansfield during what is sometimes referred to as the 'golden age' of *habeas corpus*, following the enactment of the Habeas Corpus Act 1679. The Act itself is a source of mythmaking, as is the history around *habeas corpus* preceding it. As Brown explains, looking at the history of the writ of *habeas corpus* shows that it is wrong to suggest

> that from time immemorial (or at any rate, as many suppose, since Magna Carta) habeas corpus has been the central foundation of all our liberties. It is not so. … The writ had its origins not in securing freedom from detention at all, but rather in ensuring a person's attendance before a court of law so that justice (whether civil or criminal) might be administered in his presence. Later on, hardly its finest flowering, the writ became a weapon in the armoury of the common-law courts in their jurisdictional war with the courts of equity.[33]

[29] *ibid* [47].
[30] *R (Miller) v Prime Minister; Cherry and others (Respondents) v Advocate General for Scotland* [2019] UKSC 41, [2020] AC 373 [32].
[31] *Somerset v Stewart* (1772) Lofft 1, 98 ER 499.
[32] Ministry of Justice, 'Human Rights Act Reform' (n 17) [17].
[33] S Brown, ' Habeas Corpus – A New Chapter' [2000] *PL* 31, 34.

Notably, it was not 'Somerset' himself that could rely on this piece of legislation. His English godparents had made an application to the Court of King's Bench for a writ of *habeas corpus*.[34]

Somerset v Stewart is an example of a judgment whose subsequent misunderstanding and romanticising has created an enduring illusion as to the long-standing virtue and strength of the English common law, which is often used to imply present-day virtue. Counsel for Somerset sought to persuade Lord Mansfield by passionate appeals, including 'Ought we not, on our part, to guard and preserve that liberty by which we are distinguished by all the earth!'.[35] There are different accounts as to the words used by Lord Mansfield. One source suggests that he said,

> The state of slavery is of such a nature, that it is incapable of being introduced on any reasons, moral or political; but only positive law, which preserves its force long after the reasons, occasion, and time itself from whence it was created, is erased from memory: it's so odious, that nothing can be suffered to support it, but positive law. Whatever inconveniences, therefore, may follow from a decision, I cannot say this case is allowed or approved by the law of England; and therefore the black must be discharged.[36]

This statement has been much celebrated. Undoubtedly, the allusion to the Anglo-American model of slavery being immoral is welcome. However, four observations can be made which contextualise and put this famous decision into perspective. First, the actual impact of the case is heavily disputed. In particular, it is highly doubtful to what extent this case had any implications beyond its individual application. Instead of outlawing slavery, it merely settled a narrow point of law, namely that a slave master could not seize a slave and remove him from the jurisdiction against his will.[37] The case does not pronounce a legal ruling on the legality of holding fellow human beings in bondage in the country itself. Accordingly, one cannot sensibly conclude that Lord Mansfield's judgment signified – in any meaningful way – that the English common law 'provided certain minimum levels of substantive protection to anyone who came to England'.[38] In fact, in the opening paragraphs of Lord Mansfield's judgment, he says 'The question is, if the owner had a right to detain the slave, for the sending of him over to be sold in Jamaica'.[39] Second, it is equally wrong to suggest that the judgment implies that 'the master-slave relationship rested on a dubious legal foundation because

[34] A Jackman, 'Judging a Judge: A Reappraisal of Lord Mansfield and *Somerset*'s Case' (2018) 39(2) *The Journal of Legal History* 140.

[35] *Somerset v Stewart* (n 31) 503.

[36] *ibid* 510.

[37] WM Wiecek, 'Somerset: Lord Mansfield and the Legitimacy of Slavery in the Anglo-American World' (1974) 42 *University of Chicago Law Review* 86, 87. Note that Wiecek says the second legal point that was determined by this case was that slaves could bring *habeas corpus* applications, however this may have to be qualified, see Jackman (n 34).

[38] G Van Cleve, '"Somerset's Case" and Its Antecedents in Imperial Perspective' (2006) 24(3) *Law and History Review* 601, 636.

[39] *Somerset v Stewart* (n 31) 509.

of slavery's contrariness both to natural law and to the substantive principles of the English Constitution'.[40] If this statement was true, slavery could certainly not have continued in the UK for more than six decades after *Somerset v Stewart* was decided, and beyond that in parts of the British Empire. Indeed, the judgment itself states 'Contract for sale of a slave is good here; the sale is a matter to which the law properly and readily attaches, and will maintain the price according to the agreement'.[41] Third, the fact that Lord Mansfield in the later *Gregson v Gilbert* decision equated slaves who had been killed while being shipped across the Atlantic with livestock further undermines the suggestion that English judges have historically been morally opposed to slavery or to the inequitable treatment of human beings.[42] Fourth, an important aspect of *Somerset v Stewart* is that Lord Mansfield very clearly stated that positive law could legalise slavery despite it being 'odious'. This highlights the common law's inherent and historically recognised vulnerability as far as constitutional rights protection is concerned while at the same time reminding us that orthodox constitutional theory suggests that nothing is beyond legislative reach, no matter how morally appalling.

The third famous antecedent is *Dr Bonham's Case*,[43] which is not in fact an example of constitutional rights protection, but rather an authority that speaks to the common law's interpretative power.[44] Having studied medicine at Cambridge, Dr Bonham had been fined and imprisoned by the College of Physicians for practising in London without becoming a member of the College first. The College had continuously refused to issue him a licence.[45] The College had been authorised by statute to fine and imprison individuals. Dr Bonham brought a claim based on false imprisonment against the college, which was heard in the Court of Common Pleas. The key question concerned the legality of the College's decision in light of its statutory powers. Sir Edward Coke CJ, who was versed in the medieval rights debate,[46] and who is often cited as an authoritative source of support for common law constitutional rights today, found in favour of Dr Bonham. Appalled at the multifaceted power the College had been vested with, he famously said, when interpreting the statutory power in question,

> It appears in our Books, that in many Cases, the Common Law does control Acts of Parliament, and sometimes shall adjudge them to be void: for when an Act of Parliament

[40] JB Dyer, 'After the Revolution: *Somerset* and the Antislavery Tradition in Anglo-American Constitutional Development' (2009) 71(4) *The Journal of Politics* 1422, 1422.

[41] *Somerset v Stewart* (n 31) 509.

[42] *Gregson v Gilbert* 99 ER 629, better known as the 'Zong' case, see also J Krikler, 'The Zong and the Lord Chief Justice' (2007) 64(1) *History Workshop Journal* 29.

[43] *Dr Bonham's Case* 77 ER 638, (1608) 8 Co Rep 107.

[44] See also JW Tubbs, *The Common Law Mind: Medieval and Early Modern Conceptions* (Johns Hopkins University Press, 2000) 158–59; R Berger, 'Doctor Bonham's Case: Statutory Construction or Constitutional Theory?' (1969) 117(4) *University of Pennsylvania Law Review* 521.

[45] For a detailed summary of the facts, see HJ Cook, 'Against Common Right and Reason: The College of Physicians versus Dr. Thomas Bonham' (1985) 29(4) *The American Journal of Legal History* 301.

[46] C Palley, 'The United Kingdom and Human Rights' (42nd series, The Hamlyn Lectures, Sweet & Maxwell, 1991) 20.

> is against Common right and reason, or repugnant, or impossible to be performed, the Common Law will control it, and adjudge such Act to be void.[47]

To this day, the meaning and implication of this statement,

> is a matter of contention among scholars. Did Coke mean that if a judge finds a particular statute unreasonable, he or she may render the statute ineffective? Or did Coke mean that there can and should be a judicial review of legislation when it isn't in keeping with the common law or with a country's constitution, to the point that the statute is voidable?[48]

Some suggest that this statement must be read in its historical context. At the relevant time, the branches of state were not clearly established, and, both Parliament and the courts were attempting to seize control from the monarch, which is why the above quote has been suggested to be best interpreted as representing attempts to secure a pluralistic government.[49] Further, subsequent qualifications by Coke, focusing on statutory construction in cases entailing uncertain or general words, are said to give a more nuanced view of what he was trying to say.[50] Finally, it has been highlighted that there was, at the time the judgment was handed down, a lack of a consistent or technical meaning of the word 'void' and that, therefore, the supposed force of the statement needs to be qualified to the extent that 'controlling' a statute may have simply meant to 'prevent the application of the full rigour of a statute in a single case, and certainly does not support claims for judicial review of statutes'.[51] Scholars have, sometimes in light of these qualifications and sometimes regardless of them, debated whether the case merely stands for common law rules on statutory interpretation[52] or whether it attempts to insinuate the superiority and supremacy of the common law,[53] thereby providing a historical upset to more contemporary orthodox constitutional theory.

Like *Somerset v Stewart*, *Dr Bonham's Case* is not successfully invoked in our courts today. However, it is worth noting that litigants in person have in recent memory attempted to rely on this authority and other historical legal sources which have been characterised as important constitutional rules in public discourse.[54]

[47] *Dr Bonham's Case* (n 43) 652.

[48] N McWha, 'Coke in Dr Bonham's Case: His Meaning Revisited' (*University of Southern Queensland School of Law and Justice Blog*, 5 August 2021).

[49] DE Edlin: *Judges and Unjust Laws: Common Law Constitutionalism and the Foundations of Judicial Review* (University of Michigan Press, 2008) 55.

[50] JWF Allison, *The English Historical Constitution: Continuity, Change and European Effects* (Cambridge University Press, 2007) 5.

[51] I Williams, 'Dr Bonham's Case and "Void" Statutes' (2006) 27(2) *The Journal of Legal History* 111, 126.

[52] SE Thorne, 'Dr Bonham's Case' (1938) 54 *LQR* 543.

[53] For an overview see RH Helmholz, 'Bonham's Case, Judicial Review, and the Law of Nature' (2009) 1(1) *Journal of Legal Analysis* 325 and RA Edwards, 'Bonham's Case: The Ghost in the Constitutional Machine' (1996) 11(1) *The Denning Law Journal* 74. P Craig, for example, regards Coke's remarks about the controlling power of the common law as the underpinning of the judiciary to interpret statutes in 'Ultra Vires and the Foundations of Judicial Review' (1998) *CLJ* 63, 88.

[54] See *R (Wilson George) v Mayor of London* [2003] EWHC 1257 Admin (8 April 2003, unreported).

For the purposes of our discussion, *Dr Bonham's Case* exemplifies that there is an early legacy to the contemporary debate around the close connection between rights, institutional legitimacy and statutory construction.

More broadly, all three judgments share a special affinity with powerful language and imagery, and their combined legacy is the perception that the English common law is a source of justice and reason. Indeed, 'justice' has, as it still does today, historically influenced judicial decision-making, complementing and influencing the interpretation of established sources of law, including legislation. Appearing somewhat haphazard in their historical expression, today some of the reasoning highlighted in this section would be perceived as aspects of the substantive rule of law. In what follows, I outline the contemporary judicial recognition of common law constitutional rights, which continues the theme of judges finding in the common law what is deemed ought to be there.

II. The First Modern Phase of Common Law Constitutional Rights Jurisprudence

Notably, the first modern phase of common law constitutional rights was developed in the context of the UK's obligations under the European Convention on Human Rights (ECHR). The UK was one of the first countries to ratify the ECHR in 1951, having previously played a role in drafting it.[55] However, it was only from 1966 onwards that individuals had the right to petition the European Court of Human Rights (ECtHR).[56] The first case was brought before what was then the Commission rather than the ECtHR in 1967.[57] By the time the HRA was passed, the UK had been the respondent state before the ECtHR more than 100 times.[58] However, this did not make up for the fact that individuals could not seek redress before domestic courts, a situation which stood in sharp contrast to what individuals in the civil law based signatory states could do.[59] When the HRA was passed, the UK was the only Member State apart from Ireland that had not incorporated provisions of the Convention into domestic law. Initially, the UK appeared to delay implementation out of concern that such a step would

> compromise the doctrine of the sovereignty of parliament and [it] flattered itself that there was no need, assuming that the rights and freedoms guaranteed by the Convention

[55] For details see G Marston, 'The United Kingdom's Part in the Preparation of the European Convention on Human Rights, 1950' (1993) 42(4) *ICLQ* 796.

[56] See Lord Lester, 'U.K. Acceptance of the Strasbourg Jurisdiction: What Really Went on in Whitehall in 1965' [1998] *PL* 237.

[57] *Alam and Khan v United Kingdom* App no 2991/66 (1967) 24 CD 116.

[58] Council of Europe, *European Court of Human Rights, Forty Years of Activity* (1998) 26.

[59] L Clements and J Young, `Human Rights: Changing the Culture' (1999) 26 *Journal of Law and Society* 1.

could be delivered under the common law. Aggrieved parties would have to exhaust domestic remedies before they could resort to Strasbourg.[60]

This situation was far from ideal, and there were judicial[61] statements in favour of, and political[62] voices campaigning for, the ECHR's transposition into domestic law.

Politically, one could detect a serious will to incorporate the ECHR into domestic law from the late 1990s.[63] It was through the Labour Party's initiative that the rights guaranteed under the ECHR were eventually transposed into national law, via the HRA. In early 1993, incorporation of the Convention was officially endorsed by John Smith, the Labour leader at the time. That position was maintained by his successor Tony Blair in 1995 and strengthened by a 1996 consultation paper.[64] Finally, the planned transposition was announced in the Queen's speech following the Labour's Party's victory in the 1997 General Election. The HRA, which was passed in 1998, entered into force on 2 October 2000. Its passing into law formed part of the most comprehensive constitutional overhaul to date.[65]

A. Examples of Common Law Constitutional Rights and their Claim to Sufficiency During the First Phase

It is in this political and legal context that the initial rise of common law constitutional rights has to be analysed. By 'initial rise' I do not mean to suggest that common law constitutional rights did not exist prior to this point in time. As some of the famous antecedents show, common law constitutional rights have, arguably, always been around to varying degrees. Rather, the phase discussed here represents a relatively defined space of time within which common law constitutional rights were not only enforced relatively frequently, but where judgments grounded in them also spoke, to some degree, to their conceptualisation. With this clarification in mind, perhaps the most unequivocal commitment to common law constitutional rights in this first phase, which loosely coincides with the run-up to the incorporation of the HRA, was shown in *R v Lord Chancellor, ex p Witham*.[66]

[60] H Potter, *Law, Liberty and the Constitution: A Brief History of the Common Law* (Boydell Press, 2015) 286.

[61] See particularly Lord Scarman, '*English Law – The New Dimension*' (26th series, The Hamlyn Lectures, Stevens & Sons Ltd, 1974).

[62] See, eg, the Lords Select Committee, *Report of the Select Committee on a Bill of Rights* (HL 176, 1978) and the two bills introduced into Parliament by Lord Lester of Herne Hill in the 1990s.

[63] For an overview of this development, see R Singh, *The Future of Human Rights in the United Kingdom: Essays on Law and Practice* (Hart Publishing, 1997) Ch 2.

[64] 'Rights Brought Home: The Human Rights Bill' (Cm 3782, 1997).

[65] See Lord Irvine, 'Constitutional Reform and a Bill of Rights' (1997) 5 *European Human Rights Law Review* 483 for a comprehensive overview of other key developments.

[66] *R v Lord Chancellor, ex p Witham* [1998] QB 575 (QB).

The applicant had applied for judicial review of a decision by the Lord Chancellor to introduce an order which had the effect of reversing the prior rule according to which litigants in persons receiving income support did not have to pay a fee to initiate proceedings in the High Court. He argued that this would deny him his constitutional right of access to the courts.[67] In his judgment, Laws J went into some detail in answering the preliminary question of whether such a right existed in the first place. His conclusion can be seen as the prelude to the principle of legality-based approach in *R v Secretary of State for the Home Department, ex p Simms*,[68] which was decided two years after *Witham*. To Laws J, what makes a common law right *constitutional* is the intrinsic mechanism that it cannot be abrogated unless abrogation is specifically permitted by Parliament.[69] Substantively, determining the content of the right he identified at common law, he could draw on the authoritative pair of cases that is *Leech*[70] and *Raymond v Honey*,[71] both prisoners' rights cases. These cases and others, he stated, provided the basis for arriving at his legal conclusion. There was therefore no need to refer to Strasbourg jurisprudence.

Prior to *Witham*, *Derbyshire CC v Times Newspaper Ltd*,[72] which determined that a local authority could not bring an action for damages for libel against a newspaper that had questioned the propriety of investments made for the authority's superannuation fund, had established that non-incorporation was not an obstacle to relying on the Convention. Borrowing from US case law, the House of Lords reasoned that the threat of a civil action for defamation would inevitably have an inhibiting effect on the common law right to freedom of speech. For the purposes of this chapter, the following are the most important parts of Lord Keith of Kinkel's speech, which drew on the 'no inconsistency between foreign and domestic sources' approach adopted in *Attorney-General v Observer Ltd (No 2)*,[73] better known as the 'Spycatcher case', and which warrant being spelled out at length. He said,

> The conclusion must be, in my opinion, that under the common law of England a local authority does not have the right to maintain an action of damages for defamation.

[67] The right of access to justice is centuries old, see, eg, *R and W Paul Ltd v Wheat Commission* [1937] AC 139, [1936] 2 All ER 1243. It is widely regarded as the most developed common law right: J Beatson and others, *Human Rights: Judicial Protection in the United Kingdom* (Sweet & Maxwell, 2008) 1-11–1-14; M Elliott and K Hughes, *Common Law Constitutional Rights* (Hart Publishing, 2020) 13 ('The Nature and Role of Common Law Constitutional Rights').

[68] *R v Secretary of State for the Home Department, ex p Simms* [2000] 2 AC 115 (HL).

[69] *R v Lord Chancellor, ex p Witham* (n 66) 585G.
The proposition that general words should not be construed to allow interference with individual rights and freedoms was adopted in many other judgments around the same time, see *Morris v Beardmore* [1981] AC 446; *Wheeler v Leicester City Council* [1985] AC 1054 and *Marcel v Commissioner of Police of Metropolis* [1992] Ch 225, [1991] 2 WLR 1118.

[70] *R v Secretary of State for the Home Department, ex p Leech (No 2)* [1994] QB 198, [1993] 3 WLR 1125.

[71] *Raymond v Honey* [1983] 1 AC 1 (HL).

[72] *Derbyshire CC v Times Newspaper Ltd* [1993] AC 534 (HL).

[73] *Attorney-General v Observer Ltd (No 2)* [1990] 1 AC 109 (HL).

> That was the conclusion reached by the Court of Appeal, which did so principally by reference to article 10 of the European Convention for the Protection of Human Rights and Fundamental Freedoms …, to which the United Kingdom has adhered but which has not been enacted into domestic law … I have reached my conclusion upon the common law of England without finding any need to rely upon the European Convention. My noble and learned friend, Lord Goff of Chieveley, in *Attorney-General v. Guardian Newspapers Ltd. (No. 2)* … expressed the opinion that in the field of freedom of speech there was no difference in principle between English law on the subject and article 10 of the Convention. I agree, and can only add that I find it satisfactory to be able to conclude that the common law of England is consistent with the obligations assumed by the Crown under the Treaty in this particular field.[74]

Many other cases stressed the comparative strength as well as the *sufficiency* of the common law. They include *Morris v Beardmore*, in which the House of Lords relied on the common law right to keep one's home free from unauthorised intruders[75] and *R v Secretary of State for the Home Department, ex p Pierson*, in which the House of Lords said that prisoners in this jurisdiction retained all such (common law) rights that are not expressly taken away from them by Parliament.[76]

B. Enabling and Contributing Factors: Constitutional Trajectory and the European Mirror

One crucial step towards the facilitation of common law constitutional rights in the late 1980s and 1990s was the watershed moment marked by several judgments in the 1960s. During the wars and shortly thereafter the acquisition of new powers by the Government had been largely uncontrolled. Famous cases from the first half of the last century that gave successive governments somewhat of a blank cheque with regard to governmental power and ministerial discretion included *R v Local Government Board, ex p Arlidge*,[77] *Liversidge v Anderson*,[78] *Associated Provincial Picture Houses Ltd v Wednesbury Corporation*[79] and *R v Metropolitan Police Commissioner, ex p Parker*.[80] Then, as is well known, from the 1960s onwards, UK administrative law entered a transformative period.[81] During this time, 'judicial review expanded exponentially …, as the judiciary regained confidence lost during two wartime regimes'.[82] It is generally accepted that the rise of the administrative state and the connected growth of public power was at the heart

[74] *Derbyshire CC v Times Newspaper Ltd* (n 72) 550E, 551F-G.
[75] *Morris v Beardmore* (n 69).
[76] *R v Secretary of State for the Home Department, ex p Pierson* [1998] AC 539 (HL).
[77] *R v Local Government Board, ex p Arlidge* [1915] AC 120 (HL).
[78] *Liversidge v Anderson* [1942] AC 206 (HL).
[79] *Associated Provincial Picture Houses Ltd v Wednesbury Corporation* [1948] 1 KB 223 (CA).
[80] *R v Metropolitan Police Commissioner, ex p Parker* [1953] 1 WLR 1150.
[81] TT Arvind and L Stirton, 'The Curious Origins of Judicial Review' (2017) 133 *LQR* 91.
[82] C Harlow and R Rawlings, *Law and Administration*, 3rd edn (Cambridge University Press, 2009) 98.

of the reasons why the courts' attitudes shifted. Writing extra-judicially in 1992, Lord Browne-Wilkinson said politicians were intervening in many aspects of citizens' daily lives, such as education and health, and that large areas of intervention were covered by subordinate legislation which lacked effective parliamentary scrutiny.[83] The reaction by the courts was to develop the law of judicial review.[84] The courts 'dusted off old doctrine and writs' and developed a more modern system of public law that would be capable of controlling this growing 'post-war state apparatus'.[85]

During this time, statutory interpretation became more nuanced through recourse to constitutional principles such as fairness and natural justice, both of which are viewed as common law constructs. Furthermore, the courts began to introduce and reinforce constitutional principles which impose restrictions on the elected branches of state. For instance, *Padfield and Others v Minister of Agriculture, Fisheries and Food*[86] established that even if legislation confers upon a decision-maker an 'unfettered' discretion,

> The use of that adjective, even in an Act of Parliament, can do nothing to unfetter the control which the judiciary have over the executive, namely, that in exercising their powers the latter must act lawfully and that is a matter to be determined by looking at the Act and its scope and object in conferring a discretion upon the minister rather than by the use of adjectives.[87]

The background to this case was a statutory requirement in place at the time that milk producers should sell their milk only to the Milk Marketing Board. Producers in the South East of England complained to the responsible minister about the price paid to them by that board. The relevant legislation provided that 'if the Minister … so directs', a committee had to consider complaints. The Minister declined to refer the matter to a committee, stating amongst other things that he had an unfettered discretion in this respect. The House of Lords upheld the claim of the producers. Where discretion was exercised, it would need to be done in a way that accommodates for the underlying purpose of the Act in question. Parliament,

> must have conferred the discretion with the intention that it should be used to promote the policy and objects of the Act [and] the policy and objects of the Act must be determined by construing the Act as a whole and construction is always a matter for the Court.[88]

Other cases decided around the same time defined some of the standards imposed by the common law. In *Ridge v Baldwin*[89] it was held that a chief constable who

[83] Lord Browne-Wilkinson, 'The Infiltration of a Bill of Rights' [1992] *PL* 397, 397.
[84] *ibid* 398.
[85] T Hickman, *Public Law after the Human Rights Act* (Hart Publishing, 2010) 13.
[86] *Padfield and Others v Minister of Agriculture, Fisheries and Food* [1968] AC 997 (HL).
[87] *ibid* 1060 (per Lord Upjohn). See also CJS Knight, 'A Framework for Fettering' (2009) 14(1) *Judicial Review* 73.
[88] *Padfield and Others v Minister of Agriculture, Fisheries and Food* (n 86) 1030.
[89] *Ridge v Baldwin* [1964] AC 40 (HL).

had been dismissed was entitled to prior notice of the charge against him and an opportunity to be heard. A breach of the common law requirement to have a fair hearing would render a decision void.[90] This initiated the development towards the modern understanding of procedural justice.[91] *Ridge v Baldwin* initiated a new era 'in which the courts have subjected the working of government to a degree of judicial scrutiny, on substantive as well as procedural grounds, which shows little sign yet of diminishing'.[92]

Then came *Anisminic Ltd v Foreign Compensation Commission*,[93] which, as was discussed in chapter two, provided the foundation for the Supreme Court decision in *Privacy International*.[94] To repeat briefly, the appellants in *Anisminic* had applied to the Foreign Compensation Commission claiming they were entitled to parts of the Egyptian Compensation Fund in respect of property requisitioned by Egypt in 1956. The Commission provisionally found that they had not established a valid claim, so the company brought an action for a declaration that the Commission's determination was a nullity. The legislation vesting power in the Commission, the Foreign Compensation Act 1950, stated in section 4(4) that 'the determination by the commission of any application made to them under this Act shall not be called in question in any court of law'. However, the House of Lords held that this ouster clause did not prevent it from considering whether a *purported* decision was actually a nullity due to procedural irregularity. As the Commission had based its decision on an inquiry it did not have the power to make – considering the nature of the company – it had gone outside its jurisdiction, and the determination was accordingly a nullity. This being the case, the House of Lords found that there was no problem with a court calling it into question. In short, 'the ouster was ousted'.[95]

Had the courts not moved from construing powers granted to public bodies *literally* to interpreting them *purposively* in *Anisminic*, *Padfield* and *Ridge v Baldwin*, thereby creating a system of robust judicial oversight, there would have been less room for rights under the common law in statutory construction in the 1980s and 1990s, and today. As Lord Diplock put it in *In Re Racal Communications Ltd*, commenting on *Anisminic*, the basic presumption in judicial review was now that

> where Parliament confers on an administrative tribunal or authority, as distinct from a court of law, power to decide particular questions defined by the Act conferring the power, Parliament intends to confine that power to answering the question as it has been so defined: and if there has been any doubt as to what that question is, this is a

[90] D Feldman, 'Error of Law and Flawed Administrative Acts' (2014) 73(2) *CLJ* 275, 276.

[91] C Forsyth, '"Blasphemy against Basics": Doctrine, Conceptual Reasoning and Certain Decisions of the UK Supreme Court' in J Bell and others, *Public Law Adjudication in Common Law Systems: Process and Substance* (Hart Publishing, 2016) 151. *Ridge v Baldwin* also signified a shift in emphasis from whether the process was judicial to whether it affected a person's rights.

[92] Lord Woolf and others (n 7) Ch 6 – 'Historical Development Since the 1960s' 6-044.

[93] *Anisminic Ltd v Foreign Compensation Commission* [1969] 2 AC 147 (HL).

[94] *R (Privacy International) v Investigatory Powers Tribunal* (n 24).

[95] J Metzer, 'Anisminic 2.0' (*UK Human Rights Blog*, 15 May 2019).

> matter for courts of law to resolve in fulfilment of their constitutional role as interpreters of the written law and expounders of the common law and rules of equity.[96]

In other words, these authorities contributed significantly to the UK constitution's contemporary nuanced approach. Moving from the facilitative wider public law background to the actual first phase of common law constitutional rights, one cannot explain their development without acknowledging the considerable impact the UK's membership of the Council of Europe and its obligations under the ECHR had on domestic judicial developments. The apparent gap at the time between human rights protection on the domestic front and the rights guaranteed under the ECHR facilitated and incentivised their development under the common law. Indeed, the Command Paper accompanying the Human Rights Bill had criticised that the UK was falling behind other European countries whose acceptance of the Convention had gone hand in hand with the Convention's incorporation into their domestic law.[97] It became increasingly clear that the UK's record before the ECtHR was meagre. Only Italy had found itself in violation of Convention rights more often than the UK.[98] Further, in comparison to other jurisdictions that had seen many cases brought against them before the ECtHR, what distinguished the UK's record was the serious nature of the cases brought in combination with a notable absence of speedy and effective domestic remedies to address these.[99]

Lord Neuberger recently said that it was a frustrating time for UK judges, 'as they realised that they were deciding cases which they knew would be held to be wrong by the Strasbourg court, while being unable to do anything about it'.[100] However, as Harlow and Rawlings point out, the UK's record may need to be qualified. There was in the UK at the time a longstanding tradition of political litigation and a generous system of legal aid, and, in contrast to the UK, other jurisdictions only allowed for individual petitions at a later point in time.[101] Nonetheless, there was an important human factor at play. To avoid repeatedly being told the UK legal system offered insufficient human rights protection, courts had to very actively engage with the particulars of their international obligations under the Convention to limit the risk of having their judgments 'overturned'. I therefore suggest that the development of common law constitutional rights and their first significant peak in the late 1980s and 1990s cannot be separated from the UK's

[96] *Re Racal Communications Ltd* [1981] AC 374 (HL).

[97] This applies to dualist states. In monist states such as France the Convention was directly enforceable.

[98] It is estimated that two-thirds of these violations involved primary or secondary legislation: JUSTICE, 'The Human Rights Bill: Briefing for the Second Reading in the House of Commons' (16 February 1998) 1.

[99] J Straw and P Boateng, 'Bringing Rights Home: Labour's Plans to Incorporate the European Convention on Human Rights into UK Law' (1997) 1 *European Human Rights Law Review* 71.

[100] Lord Neuberger, 'The Role of Judges in Human Rights Jurisprudence: A Comparison of the Australian and UK Experience' (Supreme Court of Victoria, August 2014).

[101] C Harlow and R Rawlings, *Pressure through Law* (Routledge, 1992) 254–55.

membership of the Council of Europe. The common law became a vehicle for the *indirect* and *undisclosed* fulfilment of ECHR obligations during that period, and individual common law rights were introduced or strengthened to secure compliant standards.

Apart from domestic developments and the influence of the UK's obligations under the ECHR, one should also not underestimate the role EU law played at this time. By the 1990s, the Court of Justice of the European Union (CJEU) had on numerous occasions declared domestic legislation to be incompatible with (then) Community legislation, having first read fundamental human rights into the latter.[102] Further, it was already the practice of the CJEU to refer to the ECHR in its judgments.[103] For example, in *Johnston v Chief Constable of the Royal Ulster Constabulary*[104] part of the statutory instrument implementing the Equal Treatment Directive[105] was held to be invalid as it did not comply with Directive itself, nor with the requirements under articles 6 and 13 ECHR. In that sense, the Convention had been, at least partially, indirectly incorporated into domestic law through the mandatory application (and supremacy) of EU law.

Finally, there was a large amount of influential extra-judicial writings which promoted both the value of the ECHR and the capacity and tradition of the common law to protect fundamental rights. Sir John Laws, one of the early judicial figures developing and promoting common law constitutional rights, argued that the courts could domestically secure basic rights by building on existing public law principles, and that these would essentially cover the substantive rights protected by the ECHR.[106] The latter was described as a 'legitimate aid' to determine what the 'policy of the common law' should be.[107] Other important extra-judicial statements from the time of the first phase were made by Lord Bingham,[108] Sir Stephen Sedley,[109] Lord Scarman[110] and Lord Irvine.[111] Furthermore, as Hickman points out,[112] this first phase also benefitted from the

[102] Case 29/69 *Stauder v City of Ulm* [1969] ECR 419; Case 11/70 *Internationale Handelsgesellschaft mbH v Einfuhr- und Vorratsstelle fur Getreide und Futtermittel* [1970] ECR 1125.

[103] For an insightful analysis of this phenomenon, see N Grief, 'The Domestic Impact of the European Convention on Human Rights as Mediated through Community Law' [1991] *PL* 555. See also M Demetriou, 'Using Human Rights through EC Law' [1999] *European Human Rights Law Review* 484.

[104] Case 222/84 *Johnston v Chief Constable of the Royal Ulster Constabulary* [1986] ECR 1651.

[105] Council Directive 76/207/EEC of 9 February 1976 on the implementation of the principle of equal treatment for men and women as regards access to employment, vocational training and promotion, and working conditions [1976] OJ L39/40.

[106] SJ Laws, 'Is the High Court the Guardian of Fundamental Constitutional Rights?' [1993] *PL* 59.

[107] *ibid* 64.

[108] Lord Bingham, 'The European Convention on Human Rights: Time to Incorporate' (1993) 109 *LQR* 390.

[109] S Sedley, 'Human Rights: A Twenty First Century Agenda' [1995] *PL* 386 and 'A Bill of Rights for Britain' [1997] *European Human Rights Law Review* 458.

[110] Lord Scarman, 'English Law – The New Dimension' (26th series, The Hamlyn Lectures, Stevens & Sons Ltd, 1974).

[111] Lord Irvine, 'Judges and Decision-Makers: The Theory and Practice of Wednesbury Review' [1996] *PL* 59.

[112] Hickman (n 85) 17.

theoretical account of rights provided by Ronald Dworkin,[113] which had been further developed and 'domesticised' by a handful of prominent English law academics,[114] most notably Sir Jeffrey Jowell KC[115] and Trevor Allan.[116]

III. Phase Two: In the Shadow of the Human Rights Act?

Co-existence between domestic and international law is expressly mentioned both in the HRA, and in the ECHR. As for the former, section 11 provides,

> A person's reliance on a Convention right does not restrict (a) any other right or freedom conferred on him by or under any law having effect in any part of the United Kingdom; or (b) his right to make any claim or bring any proceedings which he could make or bring apart from sections 7 to 9.

Along the same lines, article 53 of the ECHR states,

> Nothing in this Charter shall be interpreted as restricting or adversely affecting human rights and fundamental freedoms as recognized, in their respective fields of application, by Union law and international law and by international agreements to which the Union, the Community or all the Member States are party, including the European Convention for the Protection of Human Rights and Fundamental Freedoms, and by the Member States' constitutions.

However, during the second phase, the courts' focus increasingly began to shift towards the HRA. That said, it would be wrong to suggest that 'the coffin lid of constitutional rights' was 'well and truly screwed down'[117] by the passing of the Act. In fact, also during this phase there were cases which were decided in a rather similar fashion to how common law constitutional rights cases are sometimes decided today, namely by reference to the common law and the HRA in the alternative. For instance, in *R v Shayler*[118] a former employee of the security service had without lawful authority disclosed confidential documents to the media. He argued that he had a defence to the charges under the Official Secrets Act 1989 because disclosure had been necessary in the public interest. The House of Lords affirmed previous decisions that no such defence was available under the

[113] R Dworkin, *Taking Rights Seriously* (Duckworth, 1977); *Law's Empire* (Fontana Press, 1986).

[114] See, eg, D Oliver, 'Is the Ultra Vires Rules the Basis of Judicial Review?' [1987] *PL* 543; P Craig, 'What should Public Lawyers do? A Reply' (1992) 12(4) *OJLS* 564.

[115] Sir J Jowell, 'Restraining the State: Politics, Principle and Judicial Review' (1997) 50(1) *Current Legal Problems* 189.

[116] Selected works include TRS Allan, 'Legislative Supremacy and the Rule of Law: Democracy and Constitutionalism' (1985) 44(1) *CLJ* 111; TRS Allan, 'Dworkin and Dicey: The Rule of Law as Integrity' (1988) 8(2) *OJLS* 266.

[117] B Dickson, *Human Rights and the United Kingdom Supreme Court* (Oxford University Press, 2013) 28.

[118] *R v Shayler* [2002] UKHL 11, [2003] 1 AC 247.

legislation in question. In his judgment, Lord Bingham turned to the common law first, before discussing the position under the Convention, saying,

> The fundamental right of free expression has been recognised at common law for very many years ... The reasons why the right to free expression is regarded as fundamental are familiar, but merit brief restatement in the present context ... Despite the high value placed by the common law on freedom of expression, it was not until incorporation of the European Convention into our domestic law by the Human Rights Act 1998 that this fundamental right was underpinned by statute.[119]

Also, in *R (Daly) v Secretary of State for the Home Department* the House of Lords decided that the common law constitutional right to privileged legal advice would be infringed where prison policy mandated inspection of certain correspondence, suggesting that it was essential that the common law remained a sufficient source for the protection of this right.[120]

There are many other cases that challenge the notion of an incapacitation of human rights protection under the common law, sometimes through constitutional principles rather than specific constitutional rights. For example, in the 2003 House of Lords decision in *R (Anufrijeva) v Secretary of State for the Home Department*,[121] the Court found that the termination of an asylum seeker's income support benefit took effect not from the time the rejection of the claim had been recorded. It was effective from the moment the decision had been communicated to her. The Court's majority placed a strong emphasis on the guiding public law principle of fairness.

Meanwhile, in *Iraqi Civilians v Ministry of Defence and another*,[122] the Supreme Court recognised that 'the continuing importance of the common law, which continues to develop in parallel to the system of ECHR rights introduced by the Human Rights Act 1998, has been recognised since soon after that statute came into force', citing *McCartan Turkington Breen v Times Newspapers Ltd*[123] and the above mentioned *R v Shayler*[124] as examples.

In light of these authorities and others, it is not the case that human rights protection under the common law was altogether abandoned. Instead, it co-existed, often in the 'shadow of the Convention'.[125] Gradually, the HRA became increasingly dominant, being viewed as 'synonymous with human rights protection'[126] to the point that, in the third, current phase of common law constitutional rights protection, the Supreme Court felt the need to reiterate the common

[119] *ibid* [21]–[22].
[120] *R (Daly) v Secretary of State for the Home Department* [2001] UKHL 26, [2001] 2 AC 532.
[121] *R (Anufrijeva) v Secretary of State for the Home Department* [2003] UKHL 36, [2004] 1 AC 604.
[122] *Iraqi Civilians v Ministry of Defence and another* [2017] UKSC 1, [2017] AC 649.
[123] *McCartan Turkington Breen v Times Newspapers Ltd* [2001] 2 AC 277, 297.
[124] *R v Shayler* (n 118) [21].
[125] M Arden, *Human Rights and European Law: Building New Legal Orders* (Oxford University Press, 2015) 27.
[126] M Elliott, 'Beyond the European Convention: Human Rights and the Common Law' (2015) 68 (1) *Current Legal Problems* 85.

law's continued relevance. For instance, in *Watkins v Secretary of State for the Home Department*,[127] a post-HRA case, Lord Rodger said that since the HRA had entered into force, references to common law constitutional rights had become superfluous. He suggested they had only ever been 'preparatory' in character, and intrinsically linked to the Convention. Thus,

> In using the language of 'constitutional rights', the judges were, more or less explicitly, looking for a means of incorporation *avant la lettre*, of having the common law supply the benefits of incorporation without incorporation. Now that the Human Rights Act is in place, such heroic efforts are unnecessary.[128]

The HRA's initial dominance can be explained by a number of factors. The most decisive one is undoubtedly that the HRA is statute law, which is typically regarded as 'the apex of the hierarchy of legal norms'.[129] The HRA makes it explicitly unlawful for public authorities, including courts, to act in a manner inconsistent with the rights guaranteed under it, and requires the judiciary to read national legislation 'so far as it is possible' in a way that is compatible with Convention rights. This is a key mechanism under the HRA, 'not an optional canon of construction'.[130] Indeed, there is no need to detect any ambiguity in the legislation.[131] Thus, UK courts are, by virtue of what has been recognised as a 'constitutional statute',[132] under an obligation to assess human rights compliance. The same cannot be said to be a feature of the English common law. The legal authority of common law constitutional rights cases is therefore comparatively weaker than the protection offered by the HRA. Finally, constitutional orthodoxy also dictates that domestic administrative law allows limited room for substantive review,[133] whereas under the Convention substance forms part of the legal test when considering whether there has been a violation.

Another main reason for the dominance of the HRA is that 'whilst the protection of rights and interests through the common law had the benefits of vintage and domesticity on its side, it also lacked force and precision'.[134] Focusing on precision, there is in general no real difficulty in identifying which right of the HRA to rely on. This can be contrasted with the fact that, as I argue in chapter five, there is today still no equivalent comprehensive list of common law constitutional rights and, indeed, while it is possible to draw one up, there remains uncertainty as to the scope of common law constitutional rights due to the nuanced constitution's

[127] *Watkins v Secretary of State for the Home Department* [2006] UKHL 17, [2006] 2 AC 395.

[128] *ibid* [64].

[129] Harlow and Rawlings (n 82) 40.

[130] *Ghaidan v Godin-Mendoza* [2004] UKHL 3, [2004] 2 AC 557 [29].

[131] A small selection of what is by now an extensive body of case law includes *Re S (Minors) (Care Order: Implementation of Care Plan)* [2002] UKHL 10, [2002] 2 AC 291 and *R v A (No 2)* [2001] UKHL 25, [2002] 1 AC 45.

[132] *R (Buckinghamshire CC) v Secretary of State for Transport* [2014] UKSC 3, [2014] 1 WLR 324 [207].

[133] T Poole, 'The Reformation of English Administrative Law' (2009) 68(1) *CLJ* 142.

[134] R Masterman and S Wheatle, 'A Common Law Resurgence in Rights Protection?' [2015] *European Human Rights Law Review* 57, 58.

uncertain philosophical footing. In the context of the HRA, neither counsel nor the courts need to engage in any guess-working or tracing exercise. One can point with ease to one or several of the rights listed in the HRA and then refer to what is by now an extensive body of case law, not only from domestic courts but also from the ECtHR itself. As Mavronicola puts it, 'Convention rights are, although not perfect or perfectly ascertained, both more substantial and better substantiated than the common law constitution's equivalent guarantees'.[135]

Additionally, there is a systematised reasoning pattern associated with the HRA, which facilitates the orderly preparation and resolution of disputes. To illustrate, but many other examples could be chosen, in *R (L) v Commissioner of Police of the Metropolis*[136] the appellant claimed that her human rights had been violated when the police issued an enhanced criminal records certificate which stated that she had been accused of neglecting her child and that she had allegedly not cooperated with social services. The question was whether section 115(7) of the Police Act 1997, as interpreted in *R (X) v Chief Constable of the West Midlands Police*,[137] was incompatible with her right to respect for private life under article 8 ECHR, or would otherwise need to be read down to avoid incompatibility. The Supreme Court held that article 8 was engaged and, it not being an absolute right, moved on to consider whether interference could be justified as being proportionate. The vast majority of cases will typically follow the same reasoning pattern, asking whether behaviour falls within the ambit of a Convention right, whether there has been an infringement of such right and whether such an infringement is, if the right is not an absolute one,[138] proportionate and pursuant of one of the legitimate aims listed in the respective Convention article. One of the main attractions under this approach is the reasoning template based on the principle of proportionality,[139] which the UK courts were at the time the HRA was passed already familiar with due to its pertinence in EU law.[140] In contrast, and I will discuss this in detail in chapter four, while there are certain key characteristics

[135] A Mavronicola, 'The Mythology and the Reality of Common Law Constitutional Rights to Bodily Integrity' in Elliott and Hughes (n 67) 42.

[136] *R (L) v Commissioner of Police of the Metropolis* [2009] UKSC 3, [2010] 1 AC 410.

[137] *R (X) v Chief Constable of the West Midlands Police* [2004] EWCA Civ 1068, [2005] 1 WLR 65.

[138] Four Convention rights are absolute, ie their restriction or suspension can never be justified, not even in a state of emergency: the right not to be subjected to torture or unhuman or degrading treatment; the right not to be held in slavery or servitude; the right not to be convicted for conduct which was not an offence at the time it occurred; and the right to be punished for an offence as was applicable at the time the offence was committed.

[139] See J McBride, 'Proportionality and the European Convention on Human Rights' in E Ellis (ed), *The Principle of Proportionality in the Laws of Europe* (Oxford University Press, 1999); E Bjorge, *Domestic Application of the ECHR: Courts as Faithful Trustees* (Oxford University Press, 2015). See also A Legg, *The Margin of Appreciation in International Human Rights Law: Deference and Proportionality* (Oxford University Press, 2012) 178–81.

[140] See R Gordon, *EU Law in Judicial Review* (Oxford University Press, 2014) Ch 11. For the concept of a 'multi-stream jurisdiction' and how different remedies and principles influence each other, see Harlow and Rawlings (n 82) Ch 15; see also N Bamforth and P Leyland (eds), *Public Law in a Multi-Layered Constitution* (Hart Publishing, 2003) 311–35.

that we also find in common law constitutional rights jurisprudence, including references to proportionality,[141] there is no coherent underlying orthodoxy yet. This makes it difficult to predict, amongst other things, which way a case will be decided.

Finally, another factor is the appeal of the new. Having been described as having 'the potential for being one of the most fundamental constitutional enactments since the Bill of Rights over 300 years ago' prior to its entering into force,[142] the HRA was expected to initiate 'a shift in the legal tectonic plates'.[143] It indeed led to an unprecedented awareness and emphasis on human rights protection in this jurisdiction. The second phase was marked not only by litigation under the HRA but also by the amassment of literature engaging with human rights, and an increasing offering of dedicated human rights courses and degrees at UK universities. The new found appetite for and fascination with human rights apparent under the new regime could be witnessed at the judicial level, too. The 'attitude of many lawyers and judges in the UK to the Convention was not unlike that of a child to a new toy … fascinated with the new toy, the old toy, the common law, was left in the cupboard'.[144]

IV. Contemporary Common Law Constitutional Rights Jurisprudence in the Supreme Court: Putting the Common Law Back on the Map

The substantive expansion of the rights protected under the Convention, the exponential increase in case law from Strasbourg and other factors meant that common law constitutional rights were enforced more subtly, or not enforced at all, for approximately the first ten years of the HRA's lifetime. In a 2015 speech, the late Lord Toulson, who at the time was a Justice of the Supreme Court, reflected on the significance of the changes to domestic law brought about by the HRA, and that those changes were not intended to stifle domestic rights protection:

> When we come to the Human Rights Act the most striking features are not so much the language of the rights in themselves which the Act was intended to protect, but rather its provisions for their application and interpretation. In that respect Parliament took a number of novel steps. It made it a tort for a public body to breach Convention rights. It required the Minister promoting a bill to make a statement to Parliament as to its compliance with the Convention in its considered opinion. It placed an express duty on courts to interpret legislation as far as possible so as to be compatible to the convention.

[141] *Kennedy v Charity Commission* [2014] UKSC 20, [2015] AC 455 [54].

[142] L Clements and J Young, 'Human Rights: Changing the Culture' (1999) 26(1) *Journal of Law and Society* 1, 1.

[143] F Klug, *Values for a Godless Age: The Story of the United Kingdom's New Bill of Rights* (Penguin, 2000) 11.

[144] Lord Neuberger (n 100) [29].

> If that was not possible, it provided for the court to make a declaration to that affect, in which case the matter would return to Parliament for its consideration. It required courts to have regard to any decision of the European Court of Human Rights. The words were carefully chosen and mean what they say, no less and no more. Parliament deliberately did not subordinate the courts of the UK to the Strasbourg Court. If after careful consideration the UK court reaches a different view from that reached by the Strasbourg Court, the domestic court must rule as it believes to be right. None of this was intended to put a stranglehold on the common law.[145]

Lord Toulson's understanding of and approach to the interaction between international and domestic law protection, which is evident from other speeches too, found judicial expression in the 2012 Court of Appeal judgment in *R (Guardian News and Media Ltd) v City of Westminster Magistrates' Court*,[146] which was the first in a line of cases that openly questioned the way in which the relationship between the Convention and the common law had developed. The newspaper publisher had made an application to the respondent magistrates' court to inspect or have disclosure of certain documents in proceedings concerning the extradition of two British citizens alleged to have been involved in corruption. The respondent had refused the application, saying that the principle of open justice in criminal proceedings did not encompass a right for the press (or indeed the public) to inspect documents placed before the court. The court also said that there were no provisions in the Criminal Procedure Rules 2010 that gave the appellant a right to inspect the documents requested.

Toulson LJ (as he then was) said that the open justice principle 'is a constitutional principle to be found not in a written text but in the common law',[147] and, allowing the appeal, held that the right to open justice was to be determined by the courts, that the power to allow access to documents before the court derived from the common law rather than the Criminal Procedure Rules, which merely set out a process for the exercise of that common law power, and that where documents had been placed before a judge and referred to in the course of proceedings, the default position was that the open justice principle allowed access to them, but that such access was subject to a fact-specific proportionality exercise.

The judgment in *Guardian News* has served as a template for other common law constitutional rights cases. Since its inauguration in 2009, the Supreme Court has given more than two dozen judgments in which common law constitutional rights have featured. The judgments in *R (Osborn) v Parole Board* (right to a fair hearing),[148] *A v BBC*,[149] *Kennedy v Charity Commission* (the right to accountability and

[145] Lord Toulson, 'Fundamental Rights and the Common Law' (Keynote address given at the Fundamental Rights Conference: A Public Law Perspective, LSE, 10 October 2015).

[146] *R (Guardian News and Media Ltd) v City of Westminster Magistrates' Court* [2012] EWCA Civ 420, [2013] QB 618.

[147] *ibid* [69].

[148] *R (Osborn) v Parole Board* [2013] UKSC 61, [2014] AC 1115.

[149] *A v BBC* [2014] UKSC 25, [2015] AC 588.

transparency),[150] *R (UNISON) v Lord Chancellor* (right of access to justice),[151] and *R (Elgizouli) v Secretary of State for the Home Department*,[152] all of which are discussed in detail in chapter four, are the key judgments of this third, contemporary phase of common law constitutional rights jurisprudence. They are united by powerful ratios and obiter dicta. For example, in *R (UNISON) v Lord Chancellor*, Lord Reed held that the constitutional right of access to the courts, which is synonymously referred to as the right of access to justice, was inherent in the rule of law, and was 'not an idea recently imported from the continent of Europe, but has long been deeply embedded in our constitutional law'.[153] Meanwhile, in *Kennedy v Charity Commission*, which precedes *UNISON*, the Supreme Court explained the general approach to the interaction between domestic and international rights protection, citing Toulson LJ's Court of Appeal judgment in *Guardian News*,[154] as follows,

> Since the passing of the Human Rights Act 1998, there has too often been a tendency to see the law in areas touched on by the Convention solely in terms of the Convention rights. But the Convention rights represent a threshold protection; and, especially in view of the contribution which common lawyers made to the Convention's inception, they may be expected, at least generally even if not always, to reflect and to find their homologue in the common or domestic statute law. Not surprisingly, therefore, Lord Goff of Chieveley in *Attorney General v Guardian Newspapers Ltd (No 2)* [1990] 1 AC 109, 282-284 and the House in *Derbyshire County Council v The Times Newspapers Ltd* [1993] AC 534, 551E both expressed the view that in the field of freedom of speech there was no difference in principle between English law and article 10. In some areas, the common law may go further than the Convention, and in some contexts it may also be inspired by the Convention rights and jurisprudence (the protection of privacy being a notable example). And in time, of course, a synthesis may emerge. But the natural starting point in any dispute is to start with domestic law, and it is certainly not to focus exclusively on the Convention rights, without surveying the wider common law scene. …[155]

Apart from these cases, those with the strongest impact on this line of jurisprudence include *R (Prudential Plc) v Special Commissioner of Income Tax* (the right to professional privilege),[156] *Moohan v Lord Advocate* (the right to vote),[157] *R (C) v Secretary of State for Justice* (the right to open justice),[158] and *PJS v News Group Newspapers Ltd* (the right to privacy).[159] In their aggregate, common law constitutional rights present an important jurisprudential phenomenon, which can be expected to shape public law adjudication significantly beyond the individual rights protected.

[150] *Kennedy v Charity Commission* (n 141).
[151] *R (UNISON) v Lord Chancellor* (n 1).
[152] *R (Elgizouli) v Secretary of State for the Home Department* [2020] UKSC 10, [2021] AC 937.
[153] *R (UNISON) v Lord Chancellor* (n 1) [64].
[154] *R (Guardian News and Media Ltd) v City of Westminster Magistrates' Court* (n 146) [46] (per Lord Mance with whom Lord Neuberger and Lord Clarke agreed).
[155] *Kennedy v Charity Commission* (n 141).
[156] *R (Prudential Plc) v Special Commissioner of Income Tax* [2013] UKSC 1, [2013] 2 AC 185.
[157] *Moohan v Lord Advocate* [2014] UKSC 67, [2015] AC 901.
[158] *R (C) v Secretary of State for Justice* [2016] UKSC 2, [2016] 1 WLR 444.
[159] *PJS v News Group Newspapers Ltd* [2016] UKSC 26, [2016] AC 1081.

This latest phase of common law constitutional rights is more powerful than the first. In large part, this is due to the institution in charge of the recognition and development of these rights. During the first phase, the phenomenon of common law constitutional rights was not as well supported by precedent at the highest level.[160] Now it is the highest court of the land that openly and powerfully endorses this line of reasoning, often in single majority judgments.[161] Also, the contemporaneous phase is characterised by the endorsement of other unwritten constitutional concepts that had not been as strongly pronounced during the first phase, including the principle of proportionality and an 'advanced' notion of the principle of legality that appears to further restrict Parliament's ability to abrogate fundamental constitutional principles, even where this is done expressly.[162] Finally, as the previous chapter showed, there have been a number of significant constitutional judgments which have further strengthened the substantive notion of the rule of law in certain respects. Judgments such as *R (Privacy International) v Investigatory Powers Tribunal*[163] and *R (Evans) v Attorney-General*[164] contribute to a wider constitutional landscape in which common law constitutional rights have a greater opportunity to prosper.[165] There is thus an overall *constitutionalisation effect*.

Given the HRA's initial dominance and its apparent advantages in comparison to the common law, the question arises why the common law re-emerged when it did, especially given the factors I suggested offer some explanation for why the HRA's initial dominance have remained roughly the same, with the exception of the novelty aspect of the legislation. I suggest that there are three main reasons for the common law's revival, which I set out in a non-hierarchical order. First, there is the continuing political ambition to scrap the HRA. This 'threat' has become more tangible over the past couple of years, culminating in the Bill of Rights being introduced in Parliament in June 2022.[166] However, talk of the HRA being abrogated has been there from the start.[167] Likewise, the idea of a replacement bill of rights is not a new one, and indeed not solely attributable to the Conservative party.[168] However, it is under the governance of the Conservative

[160] See also Dickson (n 117) 26.

[161] See, eg, Lord Reed in *A v BBC* (n 149), *R (Osborn) v Parole Board* (n 148) and *R (UNISON) v Lord Chancellor* (n 1).

[162] *R (UNISON) v Lord Chancellor, ibid* [88].

[163] *R (Privacy International) v Investigatory Powers Tribunal* (n 24).

[164] *R (Evans) v Attorney-General* [2015] UKSC 21.

[165] Note though the observations made about judgments such as *R (Begum) v Special Immigration Appeals Commission* [2021] UKSC 7, [2021] 2 WLR 556 in chapter two. This judgment and others have prompted some to suggest that the Supreme Court's public law jurisprudence has entered a 'shallow end': C Gearty, 'In the Shallow End – Conor Gearty on the UK Supreme Court' (London Review of Books, 27 January 2022).

[166] Bill 117 2022–23 (as introduced).

[167] For an overview of this development, see C Gearty, 'Beyond the Human Rights Act' in T Campbell, KD Ewing and A Tomkins (eds), *The Legal Protection of Human Rights: Sceptical Essays* (Oxford University Press, 2011).

[168] See, eg, the Labour Party's Green Paper, 'The Governance of Britain' (Cm 7170, 2007).

party that political views of the HRA have become increasingly hostile. Political support for the HRA seemed to be at a particular low after a judgment was handed down by the ECtHR which found that the UK's blanket ban on prisoner voting was incompatible with article 3 of the First Protocol of the Convention.[169] Eventually, the Conservatives in their 2015 manifesto pledged to scrap the HRA and replace it with a 'British Bill of Rights'. Further details on this endeavour did not crystallise beyond what was originally formulated in the Conservatives' 2014 proposal,[170] which was unfavourably received (even by some Conservative party members).[171] Subsequently it was announced that any legislative changes to the UK's human rights regime would be put on hold until after Brexit, a statement supported by the Conservatives' Manifesto for the 2017 General Election. It is in this political context that common law constitutional rights began to be 're-discovered' and re-asserted. Given the continuing political threat to human rights protection in this jurisdiction, it is not unreasonable to suggest that the current renewed emphasis on domestic human rights protection is in some ways reactive to a rather hostile human rights environment. Indeed, some members of the Supreme Court have expressed negative opinions about the potential scrapping of the HRA.[172] Therefore, it is perhaps no coincidence that judgments such as *R (Osborn) v Parole Board*[173] were handed down just after the 'Prisoners Voting Saga'[174] unfolded. There is an obvious incentive to 'get the common law up to speed' to avoid a human rights vacuum should the HRA be repealed.

However, the continuing uncertainty around the future of the HRA and what might replace it is too one-dimensional to explain the resurgence of common law constitutional rights. One might also argue that the resurgence is a manifestation of the constitutional role and status of the Supreme Court. 1 October 2009 marked a defining moment in the constitutional history of the United Kingdom, as the highest judicial authority in this jurisdiction was transferred from the House of Lords to the Supreme Court for the United Kingdom.[175] It was established to achieve a complete separation between the UK's senior judges and the Upper House of Parliament, thereby emphasising independence and increasing the transparency between Parliament and the courts. There are signs of the Court asserting itself as a confident and assertive stakeholder in the development of the UK constitution.

[169] *Hirst v the United Kingdom* (2006) 42 EHRR 41.

[170] 'Protecting Human Rights in the UK: The Conservatives' Proposals for Changing Britain's Human Rights Laws'.

[171] See, eg, I McDonald, 'Dominic Grieve and the Human Rights Act, St Hugh's College, Oxford – 13 November 2015' (*OxHRH Blog*, 24 November 2015).

[172] J Rozenberg, 'Judges Would Regret Human Rights Act Repeal, warns Lady Hale' *The Guardian*, 14 March 2013.

[173] *R (Osborn) v Parole Board* (n 148).

[174] See also E Bates, 'Analysing the Prisoner Voting Saga and the British Challenge to Strasbourg' (2014) 14(3) *Human Rights Law Review* 503.

[175] Constitutional Reform Act 2005, Part 3. For a detailed account of the creation of the Court, see A Le Sueur, 'From Appellate Committee to Supreme Court: A Narrative' in L Blom-Cooper, B Dickson and G Drewry (eds), *The Judicial House of Lords, 1876–2009* (Oxford University Press, 2009).

Indeed, only recently Lady Hale said in *R (Miller) v Prime Minister* that '... the courts have the responsibility of upholding the values and principles of our constitution and making them effective'.[176] Speaking extra-judicially, Lady Hale has set out '... three ways in which [the Supreme Court has] definitely become the guardians of the United Kingdom Constitution'.[177]

Putting the case law of the contemporary phase of common law constitutional rights in perspective, it becomes clear that the resurgence of the latter, especially up until Lady Hale's retirement as the Court's President, was or has been part of a bigger wave of constitutionalism at the Supreme Court. Other strands include the Supreme Court's recognition of constitutional statutes,[178] which I briefly discussed in chapter one, a renewed emphasis on the rule of law in the face of arguably unequivocal statutory language,[179] and a more flexible approach to the ECtHR's case law.[180] I accept that the suggestion that the establishment of the Supreme Court has led to changes on a substantive level is somewhat intangible. Clearly, the House of Lords was no stranger to assertive judgments with significant constitutional implications itself.[181] Also, there have of course been numerous judgments in which the Supreme Court has shown significant deference to the state.[182] Yet, it seems that this institutional change and the ensuing exposure of the Supreme Court have led to a different appreciation of what it means to be the main judicial body developing the UK constitution.[183]

Third, as I have already touched upon in chapter one, UK courts have become more accustomed to human rights thinking, making it more natural to develop the English common law accordingly. The increasing engagement not only with European sources but also with other international human rights jurisprudence

[176] *R (Miller) v Prime Minister* (n 30) [39].

[177] Lady Hale, 'The Supreme Court: Guardian of the Constitution? (Sultan Azlan Shah Lecture 2016, Kuala Lumpur, 9 November 2016).

[178] *R (Buckinghamshire CC) v Secretary of State for Transport* (n 132) and *R (Miller) v Secretary of State for Exiting the European Union* [2017] UKSC 5, [2018] AC 61. See also P Craig, 'Constitutionalizing Constitutional Law: HS2' [2014] *PL* 373.

[179] See *R (Evans) v Attorney General* (n 164) and *R (Privacy International) v Investigatory Powers Tribunal* (n 24).

[180] The 'mirror principle', developed by Lord Bingham in *Ullah v Special Adjudicator* [2004] UKHL 26, [2004] 2 AC 323 meant that it was regarded as the duty of national courts to 'keep pace with the Strasbourg jurisprudence as it evolves over time: no more, but certainly no less'. A summary of the judicial move away from this principle can be found in Lord Hodge's majority judgment in *Moohan v Lord Advocate* (n 157) [104]. See also *R (Nicklinson) v Ministry of Justice* [2014] UKSC 38, [2015] AC 657. For a short overview of the contemporary position, see A Young, 'Human Rights Act Review: Whose Rights are they Anyway?' (*Constitutional Law Matter Blog*, 9 February 2022).

[181] *R (Jackson) v Attorney General* [2005] UKHL 56, [2006] 1 AC 262 highlights this point.

[182] *R (Lord Carlile of Berriew QC and others) v Secretary of State for the Home Department* [2014] UKSC 60, [2015] AC 945. See also EC Ip, 'The Institutional Foundations of Supreme Court Power in Britain's Representative Democracy' (2013) 49(3) *Representation: Journal of Representative Democracy* 281.

[183] For a more comprehensive account of the development from 'Handmaids to Parliament's will' to vindicator of the rule of law in the early years of the Supreme Court. see R Masterman and JEK Murkens, 'Skirting Supremacy and Subordination: The Constitutional Authority of the United Kingdom Supreme Court' [2013] *PL* 800.

has over the past two decades led to a partial adaptation in legal analysis. It has become more natural for lawyers and judges to look at a legal problem from a rights-based angle. Where the common law is relied on as a legal source it therefore becomes natural to consider its compatibility with human rights.

The UK courts' renewed interest in the constitutional properties of the English common law raises a plethora of questions about legitimacy. Specifically, it brings to the fore debates around the separation of powers, the boundaries of judicial reasoning, the relationship between domestic and international human rights protection, and the conceptualisation of the rule of law. As I will show in the following chapter, and analyse further in chapter five, these fundamental questions are largely bypassed in the jurisprudence. It will also become apparent that the precedents relied on to shape and enforce individual common law constitutional rights often amount to nothing more than normative claims. This has serious consequences for the strength and comprehensiveness of this jurisprudence, and it reveals some truths about the insecure foundations of the nuanced constitution more broadly.

4

The Nature and Characteristics of Common Law Constitutional Rights

When approaching the subject of public law rights inherent in our domestic legal framework, it is worth recalling that, historically, it was often deemed that individuals were subjects of the Crown 'without the benefit of positive and fundamental constitutional rights … against the public authorities of the state'.[1] According to this view, the English common law merely entailed concepts referred to as negative freedoms or 'liberties', meaning behaviour that is not prohibited by the state, and therefore lawful. Such negative freedoms are residual in character, existing in the gaps between laws; they remain after legal restraints have been subtracted.[2] Thus, even where 'rights' were recognised under this traditional view, they were 'rights' in name only but did not actually possess the qualities of contemporary jurisprudence associated with rights. Evidence for this historical residual freedom narrative can be found in the case law, including *Somerset v Stewart*,[3] which was discussed in chapter three. More recently, Lord Browne-Wilkinson LJ said in *R (Wheeler) v Leicester City Council*:

> Basic constitutional rights in the country such as freedom of the person and freedom of speech are based not on any express provision conferring such a right but on *a freedom of an individual to do what he will save to the extent that he is prevented from doing so by law*.[4]

One of the freedoms that was recently characterised as a quintessentially British right by the UK Government, the right to free speech, has traditionally suffered in its development from the residual freedom approach. As Barendt has highlighted,

> Traditionally, freedom of speech, like other fundamental freedoms, has been regarded in English law as merely residual in character. It enjoys no positive status, but is merely that freedom which individuals enjoy when there is no legal rule limiting its exercise.

[1] A Lester, 'Citizenship and the Constitution' (2008) 79(3) *The Political Quarterly* 388, 393.

[2] Thus, they are at risk of being abrogated by statute (or the common law itself): M Allen and B Thompson, *Cases and Materials on Constitutional and Administrative Law*, 10th edn (Oxford University Press, 2011) 407.

[3] *Somerset v Stewart* (1772) Lofft 1, 98 ER 499. For a discussion on how *Entick v Carrington* 95 ER 807 can be read through the residual freedom lense, see A Perry, 'The Crown's Administrative Powers' (2015) 131 *LQR* 652, 653.

[4] *R (Wheeler) v Leicester City Council* [1985] AC 1054 (HL) 1065 (emphasis added).

> The perspective is that of Dicey, who wrote in one of his best-known passages: 'Freedom of discussion is … in England little else than the right to write or say anything which a jury, consisting of twelve shopkeepers, think it expedient should be said or written.' This view receives a bleak echo when judges decide what should be regarded as free speech cases without reference to the freedom or after an explicit denial that it is in any way in issue.[5]

Contemporary common law constitutional rights jurisprudence suggests that rights cannot accurately be described as having an exclusively negative or gap-filling character. Rather, they are an independent source of law with heightened legal status.[6] The approach is no longer one of investigating what has not been taken away. Rather, courts set out to ascertain what is positively in existence in the English common law. Once such a legal value has been established, through the principle of legality, that value has an 'upward effect' on any conflicting legislation, which is, effectively, read compatible with the identified right unless the latter is expressly abrogated by it and, as *R (UNISON) v Lord Chancellor* suggests, the abrogation represents what is minimally necessary.[7]

This evolution from the concept of a freedom closer to the concept of a fully-fledged right signifies an important development in the English legal tradition. The concept of a residual liberty is understood to signify a 'private sphere … with which others cannot interfere'.[8] However, the key characteristic of a residual liberty is that it can be taken away very easily, particularly under the traditional reading of the UK constitution, by laws adopted by Parliament or indeed changes made to the English common law.[9] Thus, the concept of a residual liberty cannot be characterised as an independent, resilient legal value. Its existence is always conditional upon non-interference. There is nothing that cannot be taken away easily. The vulnerability embedded in the traditional characterisation of rights is increased further by the fact that liberties have been treated as an 'undifferentiated mass, rather than an enumerated list',[10] thus leading to legal uncertainty.

As alluded to in the Diceyan reference above, this traditional adherence to the concept of residual freedoms is perfectly aligned with the orthodox understanding of the nature of the constitution and public power as outlined in chapter one, and further discussed in chapter five. The notion of the political constitution is premised on the assumption that Parliament is legally omnipotent.

[5] E Barendt, 'Libel and Freedom of Speech in English Law' [1993] *PL* 449, 459.

[6] Compare TRS Allan's terminology: 'perceived as an important value entitled to independent weight in adjudication' in *Law, Liberty, and Justice: The Legal Foundations of British Constitutionalism* (Oxford University Press, 1993) 139.

[7] *R (UNISON) v Lord Chancellor* [2017] UKSC 51, [2017] 3 WLR 409 [88]. See also S Wheatle, 'Access to Justice: From Judicial Empowerment to Public Empowerment' in M Elliott and K Hughes (eds), *Common Law Constitutional Rights* (Hart Publishing, 2020) 51, 53.

[8] F von Hayek, *The Constitution of Liberty: The Definite Edition* (Routledge, 2013) 60.

[9] On this point more broadly, see KD Ewing and CA Gearty, *The Struggle for Civil Liberties: Political Freedom and the Rule of Law in Britain, 1914–1945* (Oxford University Press, 2000).

[10] D Feldman, *Civil Liberties and Human Rights in England and Wales*, 2nd edn (Oxford University Press, 2002) 70.

Accordingly, values cannot be entrenched in such a way that they could not be (easily) taken away by the political branches of state. The associated philosophical position that residual liberties are afforded no protection from interference, limitation and abolition makes them undeserving to be called 'rights'.[11] This is not to suggest that, historically, concepts akin to what we today call the principle of legality have not existed. In the 1927 Privy Council decision in *Colonial Sugar Refining Company Ltd v Melbourne Harbour Trust Commissioners*, the Court said that,

> In considering the construction and effect of this Act, the Board is guided by the well known principle that a statute should not be held to take away private rights of property without compensation unless the intention to do so is expressed in clear and unambiguous terms.[12]

However, the property right in question was not based on the common law and, as Young points out, the principle of legality has recently undergone a 'constitutionalisation' process.[13] That said, it would be wrong to suggest that there is a complete split between a historically prevalent residual freedoms approach and a more modern 'rights' approach. Historically, we *can* find examples that resemble the current approach.[14] Conversely, some rights recognised today still do not always benefit from some of the interpretative protections other rights are protected through.[15] However, overall, we have moved away from the residual freedoms narrative. The contemporary equivalent, common law constitutional rights, form part of the expansion of judicial review of legality. Constitutional rights 'are now seen as fundamental features of a constitutional democracy'.[16] This is encouraged by the increasingly prevalent judicial view that it is of great importance that the common law is being recognised as a sufficient source of rights which are fundamental.[17]

Thus, common law constitutional rights can be characterised as a legal source in their own right. The notion of a right implies either that government action cannot interfere or that special justification is needed for government or legislative action to override the right in question. Of course, a 'rights' character does not necessarily mean that any right in question is *adequately* protected in English law.

[11] On this see R Stevens, *Torts and Rights* (Oxford University Press, 2007) 4, referring to HLA Hart, *Essays on Bentham: Jurisprudence and Political Philosophy* (Oxford University Press, 1982).

[12] *Colonial Sugar Refining Company Ltd v Melbourne Harbour Trust Commissioners* [1927] AC 343, 359.

[13] AL Young, 'Fundamental Common Law Rights and Legislation' in Elliott and Hughes (n 7) Ch 10.

[14] See, eg, *Metropolitan Asylum District Managers v Hill* (1881) 6 AC 193 in which Lord Blackburn said at 208 the burden 'lies on those who seek to establish that the legislature intended to take away the private rights of individuals, to shew that by express words, or by necessary implication, such an intention appears'.

[15] See, by reference to the right to property, T Allan, 'Constitutional Rights to Property' in Elliott and Hughes (n 7) Ch 4.

[16] Lord Woolf and others, *De Smith's Judicial Review*, 8th edn, (Sweet & Maxwell, 2021) Ch 1 – 'The Nature of Judicial Review' 1-007.

[17] See, eg, *Secretary of State for the Home Department, ex p Daly* [2001] UKHL 26, [2001] 2 WLR 1622 [30] (per Lord Cooke).

Indeed, as I argue in chapter five, the inbuilt fragility of common law constitutional rights means that the nuanced constitution is ultimately difficult to defend normatively. On the basis of that analysis, common law constitutional rights are best conceptualised as a weak variant of rights.[18]

Nonetheless, the protection is stronger compared to the residual freedoms model, principally for one main reason. When a freedom clashes with legislative interference or an opposing common law rule, the freedom is annihilated.[19] It is not a legal source, and therefore simply cannot compete. They are two different species altogether. When the gaps between the laws are filled, no space remains for a residual freedom. The legal analysis starts and finishes with the focus being solely on the interference of the legal source higher up in the hierarchy. However, where a right meets legislative or common law interference, the starting point is to assert the importance of the right, which ordinarily becomes the focal point of the legal analysis. Any conflicting legal source will be interpreted accordingly or, where constitutional law permits, quashed or invalidated[20] to safeguard the content of the right. Thus, there are implications both in terms of emphasis and potentially in terms of outcome, too.

I. The Positive and Negative Dimensions of Common Law Constitutional Rights

As stated above, common law constitutional rights, once recognised, typically require express statutory language to be overridden and, post-*UNISON*, even such express statutory language may be interpreted restrictively by the courts.[21] It is worth highlighting that common law constitutional rights are not necessarily negative rights, ie rights individuals hold not to be subjected to a specific kind of harmful action. Negative rights are said to be easier to respect as they merely require individuals and/or the state to refrain from interfering with them, whereas it may prove more difficult, time-consuming and expensive to fulfil a positive duty.[22] The European Court of Human Rights (ECtHR) increasingly recognises

[18] I will not explore in more detail the definition of human rights; others have elaborated on this in, eg, R Cruft, SM Liao and M Renzo (eds), *Philosophical Foundations of Human Rights* (Oxford University Press, 2015); M Liao and A Etinson, 'Political and Naturalist Conceptions of Human Rights: A False Polemic?' (2012) 9(3) *Journal of Moral Philosophy* 327. For a civil rights-based account, see C Gearty, *Principles of Human Rights Adjudication* (Oxford University Press, 2005) Ch 3.

[19] See, eg, *R (Bancoult) v Secretary of State for Foreign and Commonwealth Affairs* (No 2) [2001] QB 1067, [2001] 2 WLR 1219.

[20] As is the case in jurisdictions such as Germany and the USA, subject to their respective constitutional rules.

[21] *R (UNISON) v Lord Chancellor* (n 7).

[22] L Wenar, 'Negative and Positive Rights' (2015) The Stanford Encyclopaedia of Philosophy https://plato.stanford.edu/entries/rights/; M Klatt, 'Positive Obligations under the European Convention on Human Rights' (2011) 71 *Zeitschrift für ausländisches öffentliches Recht und Völkerrecht* (ZaöRV) 691, 693. It may perhaps be more sensible to view all rights as giving rise to a wide range of both positive and

implied positive obligations on signatory states to the European Convention on Human Rights (ECHR).[23] This has caused some difficulty in this jurisdiction as the English common law is traditionally seen as not imposing liability for pure omissions or the acts of third parties.[24] Exceptions such as the care required in certain professional relationships[25] traditionally depend on some level of foreseeability and proximity.[26]

Furthermore, generally, public authorities do not owe a duty of care in negligence towards individuals who suffer harm as the consequence of a failure to perform duties,[27] as was exemplified in *In Re McKerr*,[28] in which the House of Lords held that there was, under the common law, no procedural obligation to investigate a death after fatal shootings. More recently, in *Commissioner of Police of the Metropolis v DSD and another*,[29] the Supreme Court held that while the police were liable to two of the black cab driver Worboys' rape victims for investigative failures under article 3 of the ECHR, no similar positive duty existed at common law and the latter should not be adapted to allow harmonisation of the two sources of law.

However, it is evident that UK courts today regularly require the state to do more than just not interfere. In the context of several rights, the courts have vested in the state a duty to positively act to secure the content of the right. In other words, some common law constitutional rights are positive in nature, requiring affirmative duties to benefit the individual bearing that right.[30] *R (Osborn) v Parole Board*,[31] which is one of the main cases discussed in the remainder of this chapter, is a case in point. It concerns the right to procedural fairness, specifically the circumstances in which individuals affected by decisions of the Parole Board are entitled to a hearing.

Mr Osborn was one of two individuals whose appeals made it to the Supreme Court. He had been sentenced to six years' imprisonment following a conviction for having intimidated his estranged wife with a fake firearm. As is normally the case, he was released from prison at the half-way point, after three years. As part of his licence conditions, he was meant to arrive at the hostel where he was

negative duties, see S Fredman, *Human Rights Transformed: Positive Rights and Positive Duties* (Oxford University Press, 2008). See further H Shue, who has classified three types of duty: duties to avoid, duties to protect, and duties to aid in *Basic Rights* (Princeton University Press, 1980) 51.

[23] AR Mowbray, *The Development of Positive Obligations under the European Convention on Human Rights by the European Court of Human Rights* (Hart Publishing, 2004) 229.

[24] *Michael and others (FC) v The Chief Constable of South Wales Police and another* [2015] UKSC 2, [2015] AC 1732 [174].

[25] See *Lanphier v Phipos* (1838) 8 C&P 475, 173 ER 581.

[26] *Kent v Griffiths (No 3)* [2001] QB 36, [2000] 2 WLR 1158; *Capital & Counties Plc v Hampshire CC* [1997] QB 1004.

[27] *Stovin v Wise* [1996] AC 923 (HL); *Gorringe v Calderdale Metropolitan Borough Council* [2004] UKHL 15, [2004] 1 WLR 1057.

[28] *In Re McKerr* [2004] UKHL 12, [2004] 1 WLR 807.

[29] *Commissioner of Police of the Metropolis v DSD and another* [2018] UKSC 11, [2019] AC 196.

[30] AX Fellmeth, *Paradigms of International Human Rights Law* (Oxford University Press, 2016) Ch 5.

[31] *R (Osborn) v Parole Board* [2013] UKSC 61, [2014] AC 1115.

supposed to stay at a certain time, but arrived 20 minutes late. Consequently, his licence was revoked by the Secretary of State on the same day he was released from prison. The question arose whether Mr Osborn ought to be re-released. His case was considered by a 'paper panel' comprising an anonymous member of the Parole Board who issued a written decision that Mr Osborn should not be released. Mr Osborn was notified of the decision by a letter from the Ministry of Justice, which informed him that he was entitled to request an oral hearing within 14 days. His solicitors requested a hearing, alleging that certain information had not been taken into account by the paper panel, and suggesting there were several witnesses who could explain why there had been a delay on the day of Mr Osborn's release. Their request was rejected, again by an anonymous single member panel.

The Supreme Court held that the Parole Board was required to hold an oral hearing before determining an application for release, or for a transfer to open conditions, of a prisoner, otherwise it may fall foul of the common law right of procedural fairness. Lord Reed, giving a single majority judgment, said the Parole Board should hold an oral hearing whenever fairness to the prisoner required one looking at the facts of the case and the importance of what was at stake. While not prescribing when a hearing would be required, he gave some guidance, stating, among other things, that a hearing would often be necessary where 'psychological assessment produced by the Ministry of Justice is disputed on tenable grounds, or where the board may be materially assisted by hearing evidence, for example from a psychologist or psychiatrist'.[32]

Thus, *Osborn v Parole Board* is a prime example of a case in which a constitutional right found at common law was held to vest positive obligations (to hold an oral hearing) in a state institution. In addition to express rights, there are other, more indirect ways in which the state can be required to fulfil certain positive rights. For example, in *R (Wagstaff) v Secretary of State for Health*[33] it was said that although there was no free-standing right to an investigation under the common law (outside an inquest), a refusal to hold such an investigation may be successfully challenged through judicial review on the ground of irrationality.[34] Finally, the judgment in *R (Elgizouli) v Secretary of State for the Home Department* highlights, in the context of its discussion as to whether a common law right ought to be recognised, the following:

> If there is a common law principle that the UK should not facilitate the carrying out of the death penalty in any circumstances whatever, there should not be a valid distinction between taking positive steps to prevent an execution and taking an action that facilitates the execution.[35]

[32] *ibid* [2(ii)(b)].
[33] *R (Wagstaff) v Secretary of State for Health* [2001] 1 WLR 292 (QB), [2000] HRLR 646.
[34] See *R (Amin) v Secretary of State for the Home Department* [2003] UKHL 51, [2004] 1 AC 653.
[35] *R (Elgizouli) v Secretary of State for the Home Department* [2020] UKSC 10, [2021] AC 937 [121] (per Lord Kerr).

This plainly indicates that the contemporary judicial view is that, in principle, the common law can entail both positive and negative rights.[36]

II. The Six Characteristics Stemming from Five Leading Cases: Approach, Summary and Facts

Having characterised common law constitutional rights as – the clue is in the name – 'rights', the remainder of this chapter is concerned with the characteristics commonly shared by these rights. My analysis is based predominantly on *R (UNISON) v Lord Chancellor*[37] and four other important cases, three by the Supreme Court and one Court of Appeal authority. These are, in chronological order, *R (Guardian News) v City of Westminster Magistrates' Court*,[38] *R (Osborn) v Parole Board*,[39] *Kennedy v Charity Commission*[40] and *A v BBC*.[41] *Guardian News*, *Kennedy v Charity Commission* and *A v BBC* were concerned with the principle of open justice, whereas *Osborn v Parole Board*, which I discussed above, was about the right to procedural fairness. Meanwhile, *UNISON v Lord Chancellor* was concerned with the right of access to justice. As should be apparent from this headline description, the key common law constitutional rights cases of recent years all concern some aspect of the administration of justice. They signify the jurisprudential strength of the common law with regard to procedural rights as opposed to substantive rights.

As I noted in chapter three, these cases form part of the third – and current – phase of common law constitutional rights jurisprudence. They have triggered some academic attention, having been analysed in academic articles,[42] speeches,[43] book chapters[44] and case comments.[45] However, analyses have predominantly

[36] Lord Kerr's judgment was in the minority, however no issue was taken by any of the other Justices as to the positive-negative dimension discussed by Lord Kerr.

[37] *R (UNISON) v Lord Chancellor* (n 7).

[38] *R (Guardian News and Media Ltd) v City of Westminster Magistrates' Court* [2012] EWCA Civ 420, [2013] QB 618.

[39] *R (Osborn) v Parole Board* (n 31).

[40] *Kennedy v Charity Commission* [2014] UKSC 20, [2015] AC 455.

[41] *A v BBC* [2014] UKSC 25, [2015] AC 588.

[42] A selection includes Sir P Sales, 'Rights and Fundamental Rights in English Law' 75(1) *CLJ* 86; E Bjorge, 'Common Law Rights: Balancing Domestic and International Exigencies' (2016) 75(2) *CLJ* 220; M Elliott, 'Beyond the European Convention: Human Rights and the Common Law' (2015) 68(1) *Current Legal Problems* 85; R Masterman and S Wheatle, 'A Common Law Resurgence in Rights Protection?' [2015] *European Human Rights Law Review* 57.

[43] Lady Hale, 'UK Constitutionalism on the March?' (Constitutional and Administrative Law Bar Association Conference, 12 July 2014).

[44] See S Wheatle, *Principled Reasoning in Human Rights Adjudication* (Hart Publishing, 2017) Ch 8. See also Elliott and Hughes (n 7).

[45] See E Bjorge, 'Fundamental Rights at English (and European?) Common Law' (2015) 131 *LQR* 192; B Pillans, 'Another Serving of Alphabet Soup: A v British Broadcasting Corporation (Scotland)' (2014) 19(4) *Communications Law* 130.

focused on the angle of this being an ostensibly new movement in UK public law that relies on common law rights instead of, or prior to, the ECHR; the focus is on endemism[46] and on the comparison of domestic rights and European human rights. For example, Elliott has compared common law constitutional rights with the protection offered by the ECHR/Human Rights Act 1998 (HRA) by looking at 'three vectors': normative reach, protective rigour and constitutional resilience.[47]

This book suggests that the relationship between the ECHR and domestic common law rights is only one aspect of common law constitutional rights that is worth exploring. By identifying and analysing the other main characteristics of this concept, I aim to provide a more holistic account of contemporary common law constitutional rights jurisprudence. To do so comprehensively, I also refer to common law constitutional rights judgments other than the ones that are typically associated with this development, including *Beghal v DPP*,[48] *Moohan v Lord Advocate*[49] *and R (Elgizouli) v Secretary of State for the Home Department.*[50] It is important to stress that it is not possible to treat the vast variety of common law constitutional rights as one homogenous mass or standardised jurisprudential concept. As the various contributions to the collection of essays edited by Elliott and Hughes[51] convincingly show, common law constitutional rights can differ significantly from each other, including in terms of how firmly recognised they are and how effective they are on a practical level. This chapter adds to that scholarship, arguing that if we look at common law constitutional rights' domestic constitutional dimension we can find some insightful characteristics, many of which support the view that there is a lack of consistency and clarity. Specifically, the six key characteristics emerging from this jurisprudence are:

1) the absence of a consistent conceptual basis for the courts' jurisdiction to develop common law constitutional rights;
2) principal enforcement through the principle of legality, which is, however, not always applied uniformly;
3) an attempted redefinition of the relationship between the common law and the ECHR, in which the former is accorded primacy;
4) a broad conceptualisation of domestic precedent;
5) extensive reliance on judicial reasoning from other common law jurisdictions; and
6) the use, in the vast majority of cases, of proportionality review.

[46] See particularly S Stephenson, 'The Supreme Court's Renewed Interest in Autochthonous Constitutionalism' [2015] *PL* 394. By way of contrast, Wheatle (n 44) Ch 8 briefly explores the constitutional dimension.

[47] Elliott (n 42) 85.

[48] *Beghal v DPP* [2015] UKSC 49, [2016] AC 88.

[49] *Moohan v Lord Advocate* [2014] UKSC 67, [2015] AC 901.

[50] *R (Elgizouli) v Secretary of State for the Home Department* (n 35).

[51] Elliott and Hughes (n 7).

I will discuss each of these in turn. First, however, I summarise the facts in *Kennedy v Charity Commission* and *A v BBC*, having set out the basic facts of *Osborn v Parole Board* earlier in this chapter. I also include a summary of the facts and judicial reasoning in *UNISON v Lord Chancellor* and *Guardian News v City of Westminster Magistrates' Court* which have already been discussed in preceding chapters.

A. *R (Guardian News) v City of Westminster Magistrates' Court*

As summarised briefly in chapter three, *Guardian News v City of Westminster Magistrates' Court*[52] concerned the newspaper publisher's application to the respondent magistrates' court to inspect or have disclosure of certain documents in proceedings concerning the extradition to the United States of two British citizens alleged to have been involved in corruption. The court had refused the application, saying that the principle of open justice in criminal proceedings did not encompass a right for the press (or indeed the public) to inspect documents placed before the court and that there were no provisions in the Criminal Procedure Rules 2010 that gave the appellant a right to inspect the documents requested.

The Court of Appeal held that the purpose of open justice was not simply to deter impropriety by the judge hearing the case. It was wider, enabling the public to understand and scrutinise the justice system of which the courts were the administrators. Credible evidence had been advanced that the publisher was hampered in its ability to report without access to the documents. To make litigation sufficiently intelligible to the public and press, access to documents referred to in open court might be necessary in some cases. The default position was that access should be permitted on the open justice principle and, where access was sought for a proper journalistic purpose, the case for allowing it would be particularly strong. Here, the newspaper had a serious journalistic purpose in seeking access to the documents; it wanted to stimulate an informed debate about how the justice system dealt with suspected international corruption and the system for extradition of British subjects to the United States. Therefore, 'Unless some strong contrary argument can be made out, the courts should assist rather than impede such an exercise'.[53] In delivering his judgment, which served as the template for other early judgments in the current common law constitutional rights phase, Toulson LJ (as he then was) said that the open justice principle 'is a constitutional principle to be found not in a written text but in the common law',[54] which was to be determined by the courts.

[52] *R (Guardian News and Media Ltd) v City of Westminster Magistrates' Court* (n 38).
[53] *ibid* [77].
[54] *ibid* [69].

B. *Kennedy v Charity Commission* and *A v BBC*

Kennedy v Charity Commission[55] is not the most straightforward Supreme Court judgment to follow. It concerned access to information held by public authorities. Mr Kennedy, a journalist, had made requests to the Charity Commission under section 1 of the Freedom of Information Act 2000 (FOIA) to disclose information about the three statutory inquiries it had carried out under the Charities Act 1993 into the affairs of the Mariam Appeal. For context, as summarised by Earle,

> The Appeal had been used to raise money for sick children in Iraq after the first Gulf War, but its status and the source and application of its funds were something of a mystery. The Commission's inquiries had apparently generated 10,000 pages of documentation and a transatlantic trip by Commission employees, but the resulting published Statements of Results of Inquiry totalled ten pages.[56]

Mr Kennedy deemed the Commission's two brief reports insufficient. The Charity Commission refused his request on the basis of the absolute exemption under sections 2(2) and 32(2) FOIA, which the Commission thought continued to apply beyond the conclusion of the relevant inquiry. Upon complaining to the UK's Information Commissioner, the Charity Commission's refusal was upheld.

The Supreme Court held that section 32 FOIA treated an inquiry as being subject to an absolute exemption from disclosure. Applying the common law rules of statutory interpretation, and looking at common law powers and the provisions of the Charities Act 1993, the Court said that exemption did not cease immediately at the end of the inquiry but continued once it was concluded, persisting until the documents became historical records (after a prescribed number of years) or were destroyed. Accordingly, the Court dismissed Mr Kennedy's appeal. Article 10 ECHR was held not to be engaged as there was no freestanding right to disclosure from public authorities discernible from the Strasbourg jurisprudence.

What relevance did common law constitutional rights have for the judges' decision? *Kennedy* stands foremostly for the primacy of domestic interpretative principles, and it also contains very important obiter dicta on the proportionality test in domestic settings. The Court disagreed with Mr Kennedy's argument that unless a prima facie right to disclosure could be found in the FOIA, domestic law had to be defective due to being in breach of Article 10 ECHR. That approach, the Court said, 'misreads the statutory scheme, and omits to take into account the statutory and common law position to which … attention must be addressed'.[57]

[55] *Kennedy v Charity Commission* (n 40).

[56] R Earle, 'A New Right to Information: Kennedy v Charity Commission' (2014) 25(6) *Entertainment Law Review* 214, 214.

[57] *Kennedy v Charity Commission* (n 40) [6].

One of the most often cited paragraphs of the decision is para 46, in which Lord Mance said,

> Since the passing of the Human Rights Act 1998, there has too often been a tendency to see the law in areas touched on by the Convention solely in terms of the Convention rights. But the Convention rights represent a threshold protection; and, especially in view of the contribution which common lawyers made to the Convention's inception, they may be expected, at least generally even if not always, to reflect and to find their homologue in the common or domestic statute law.

In the present case, the common law helped ascertain the meaning and significance of the relevant provisions of the Charities Act 1993, which were, in Lord Mance's view, underpinned and to be interpreted not by reference to the ECHR but by the common law presumption in favour of openness. Evidently, this presumption did not assist Mr Kennedy on this occasion. The statutory scheme was deemed to be sufficiently clearly against him. The approach in *Kennedy* can be compared to *Elgizouli v Secretary of State for the Home Department*, in which Lord Carnwath said that the Supreme Court's recent jurisprudence suggests that 'the development of the common law in line with the European Convention, but not beyond …'.[58]

As for *A v BBC*,[59] the appellant, the BBC, appealed against a decision of the Court of Session[60] which had upheld the dismissal of the broadcasting service's application to revoke or vary directions made under section 11 of the Contempt of Court Act 1981 in the course of judicial review proceedings brought by the respondent, A, in relation to his deportation. The directions prohibited the publication of his name and any other identifying matters. A had been granted indefinite leave to remain but was subsequently notified of his intended deportation following his conviction for child sex offences. In the proceedings that followed the notice, A had argued that his deportation would violate his rights under articles 2 (right to life), 3 (right not to be subjected to torture or degrading treatment) and 8 (right to private and family life) of the ECHR, claiming that, as a sex offender, he would be at risk of violence or death.

The First-tier Tribunal found that any such risk depended on his deportation being publicised. Given his anonymity in the court proceedings since 2001, there was no such publicity. The Upper Tribunal refused permission to appeal, prompting an application for judicial review. When his deportation was imminent, the Court of Sessions gave the section 11 directions to protect him from the anticipated risk of violence. The BBC, a non-party to the proceedings, applied to have those directions varied or revoked, arguing amongst other things that the directions violated its right to freedom of expression.

The Supreme Court commenced the substantive part of its judgment by stating,

> It is a general principle of our constitutional law that justice is administered by the courts in public, and is therefore open to public scrutiny. The principle is an aspect of

[58] *R (Elgizouli) v Secretary of State for the Home Department* (n 35) [193] (per Lord Carnwath).
[59] *A v BBC* (n 41).
[60] *Petition of A v Secretary of State for the Home Department* [2013] CSIH 43, 2013 SC 533.

> the rule of law in a democracy. As Toulson LJ explained in *R (Guardian News and Media Ltd) v City of Westminster Magistrates' Court* (Article 19 intervening) [2013] QB 618, para 1, society depends on the courts to act as guardians of the rule of law. Sed quis custodiet ipsos custodes? Who is to guard the guardians? In a democracy, where the exercise of public authority depends on the consent of the people governed, the answer must lie in the openness of the courts to public scrutiny.[61]

Saying that the principle of open justice was inextricably linked to the freedom of the media to report on court proceedings, the Court said one must look at the proportionality of what was proposed, striking a balance between

> the purpose of the open justice principle, the potential value of the information in question in advancing that purpose and, conversely, any risk of harm which its disclosure may cause to the maintenance of an effective judicial process or to the legitimate interests of others.[62]

The Supreme Court found against the BBC; the publication of information revealing A's identity would have subverted the basis of the Tribunal's decision to authorise his deportation, thereby frustrating years of legal proceedings. In those circumstances,

> it was plainly necessary in the interests of justice, and in order to protect the safety of a party to the proceedings, to depart from the general principle of open justice to the extent involved in the making of the orders made …[63]

C. *R (UNISON) v Lord Chancellor*

While the three cases just analysed and *Osborn v Parole Board* are important for the wider trajectory and development of common law constitutional rights, building an initial momentum which catapulted domestic rights adjudication and constitutional interpretative principles on the main stage of contemporary public law adjudication, the actual points they decided were arguably relatively unspectacular. The courts' case management powers are vast, and, effectively, the courts were, in *Guardian News* and *A v BBC*, concerned with their own procedural rules. No government department or similar public authority was affected by the two decisions. Meanwhile, the judgment in *Kennedy v Charity Commission*, albeit containing significant constitutional statements, was, in its application, relatively underwhelming. The enthusiasm for domestic rights protection died down following *Kennedy v Charity Commission*, and it was not until *UNISON v Lord Chancellor*[64] that common law constitutional rights re-entered the public law arena.[65]

[61] *A v BBC* (n 41) [23].
[62] *ibid* [41].
[63] *ibid* [75].
[64] *R (UNISON) v Lord Chancellor* (n 7).
[65] It is worth highlighting, however, that one year after *Kennedy v Charity Commission* the Supreme Court handed down its momentous decision in *R (Evans) v Attorney-General* [2015] UKSC 21, [2015]

In *UNISON v Lord Chancellor*, the Supreme Court held that fees which had been introduced by the Lord Chancellor in the exercise of his statutory powers under the Employment Tribunals and the Employment Appeal Tribunal Fees Order 2013 for bringing (and continuing) claims in employment tribunals and the Employment Appeal Tribunal were unlawful. Under the Order, claimants had to pay an issue fee as well as a hearing fee, unless they were exempted. Some claimants would qualify for a remission of the fees, and, in exceptional circumstances, the Lord Chancellor could also exercise his discretionary power to remit any fees paid.

The trade union UNISON argued that the fees violated the right of access to justice under the common law and European Union law, and that they discriminated unlawfully against women and other protected groups who typically brought 'type B' claims, which included unfair dismissal claims, equal pay claims and discrimination claims, and which attracted a fee of £1,200, comprising an issue fee of £250 and a hearing fee of £950, in the employment tribunal. At the Employment Appeal Tribunal, there was only one fee, which stood at £1,600.

Lord Reed gave the lead judgment, with which the rest of the Court agreed. He began by comparing the fees system to that employed in the County Court, noting that even the highest fees payable in the latter for small claims were well below the employment tribunals fees for type B claims. He then proceeded to set out how the remissions system worked, noting there was a two-stage test that looked, first, at an individual's (or family's) disposable capital, followed by looking at their gross monthly income. He showed that a couple of two minimum wage earners each working 40 hours per week at £7.50 per hour would not ordinarily qualify for any remission for a type A claim, but might secure a partial remission of the hearing fee for a type B claim.

The Court also highlighted two hypothetical examples which demonstrated the effect of the fees on a number of hypothetical claimants in low to middle income households, including that of

> a single mother with one child, working full-time as a secretary in a university. She has a gross income from all sources of £27,264 per annum. Her liability to any issue or hearing fee is capped under the remission scheme at £470 per fee. She therefore has to pay the full fees (£390) in order to pursue a type A claim to a hearing, and fees totalling £720 in order to pursue a type B claim. The net monthly income which she requires in order to achieve acceptable living standards for herself and her child, as assessed by the Joseph Rowntree Foundation in its report, Minimum Income Standards for the UK in 2013, is £2,273: an amount which exceeds her actual net monthly income of £2,041. On that footing, in order to pursue a claim she has to suffer a substantial shortfall from what she needs in order to provide an acceptable living standard for herself and her child.[66]

AC 1787, which, if space had permitted, would have featured in chapter two as an example of common law constitutionalist reasoning.

[66] *R (UNISON) v Lord Chancellor* (n 7) [51].

The Government had argued that it would be possible for a person in the situation described to afford the calculated fee by not spending money on anything other than what it deemed strictly necessary (excluding expenditure on clothing and personal good and services) for two months (type A claim) and three and a half months (type B claim) respectively. The Court did not accept that the Government's approach was practically feasible and, beyond that, said it could not be right that individuals had to sacrifice ordinary and reasonable expenditure to access their rights. Deciding the appeal principally on the basis of the common law, Lord Reed held that to determine the extent of the power conferred on the Lord Chancellor by section 42(1) of the Tribunals, Courts and Enforcement Act 2007,

> the court must consider not only the text of that provision, but also the constitutional principles which underlie the text, and the principles of statutory interpretation which give effect to those principles. In that regard, there are two principles which are of particular importance in this case. One is the constitutional right of access to justice ...[67]

That right, whose historical significance and present day status Lord Reed comments on in detail, was valuable to a democratic society, not just to the particular individuals involved in an employment law claim. Any hindrance to the right put in place by the executive required clear authorisation by Parliament, which was lacking in this instance; section 42 of the 2007 Act contained no words authorising the prevention of access to the relevant judicial institutions. Lord Reed said the Fees Order was ultra vires, and void *ab initio*, because there was 'a real risk that persons will effectively be prevented from having access to justice',[68] a conclusion that was no doubt in part prompted by the Government's own statistic that since the Fees Order had come into force, there had been a reduction in claims of 66–70 per cent.

III. The First Characteristic: Rights Specific Conceptualisations of Jurisdiction to Develop Domestic Rights Jurisprudence

The concept of the High Court's inherent jurisdiction is derived, 'not from any statute or rule of law, but from the very nature of the court as a superior court of law, and for this reason such jurisdiction has been called inherent'.[69] It was exercised before the jurisdiction of the superior courts was first recognised

[67] *ibid* [65].
[68] *ibid* [87].
[69] IH Jacob, 'The Inherent Jurisdiction of the Court' (1970) 23(1) *Current Legal Problems* 23 which says that the High Court's judicial review jurisdiction is derived from the inherent common law jurisdiction.

by statute, which means that Parliament, by virtue of the Senior Courts Act 1981, merely recognised such jurisdiction, instead of creating it.[70] Today, it is widely accepted that inherent jurisdiction is not something solely reserved for the senior courts, or indeed the High Court alone.[71]

The courts' inherent jurisdiction is found across a spectrum of legal areas and contexts. In *Bremer Vulkan Schiffbau und Maschinenfabrik v South India Shipping Corporation Ltd*, the House of Lords described the court's inherent jurisdiction as a 'general power to control its own procedure so as to prevent its being used to achieve injustice'.[72] From a procedural perspective, it is relatively uncontroversial that courts have an inherent jurisdiction to develop their own procedures, subject to limitations, including common law limitations. Examples include the powers to stay proceedings and strike out statements of case.[73] The courts' inherent jurisdiction is also regularly used to facilitate judicial protection, especially in the context of the judicial protection of uncapacious or vulnerable adults, where it operates as a 'safety net'.[74]

Kennedy v Charity Commission, *Guardian News* and *A v BBC* all rely to some extent on the concept of the courts' inherent jurisdiction, and they present it as what could be referred to as the respective court's *enabling power*, ie the power that enables it to recognise, develop and enforce common law constitutional rights. The clearest connection between common law constitutional rights and the concept of inherent jurisdiction is made in *A v BBC*, in which Lord Reed unequivocally, and likely unprecedentedly at Supreme Court level, establishes a link between *principles*, *constitutional status* and *inherent jurisdiction*. Specifically, he suggests that principles which are of constitutional status automatically lead to there being an inherent jurisdiction of the court. In his words,

> Since the principle of open justice is a *constitutional principle to be found in the common law*, it follows that it is for the courts to determine its ambit and its requirements, subject to any statutory provision. The courts *therefore have an inherent jurisdiction to determine how the principle should be applied*.[75]

[70] J Auburn and others, *Judicial Review: Principles and Procedure* (Oxford University Press, 2013). Already in 1886 it was recognised that 'rules … do not … deprive the Court in any way of the inherent power which every Court has to prevent the abuse of legal machinery …': *Willis v Earl of Beauchamp* (1886) 11 PD 59.

[71] County Courts Act 1984, s 76; see also *Langley v North West Water Authority* [1991] 1 WLR 697, [1991] 3 All ER 610.

[72] *Bremer Vulkan Schiffbau und Maschinenfabrik v South India Shipping Corporation Ltd* [1981] AC 909, [1981] 2 WLR 141, 976.

[73] *Reichhold Norway ASA and another v Goldman Sachs International (a firm)* [2000] 1 WLR 173 (stay of proceedings); *Summers v Fairclough Homes Ltd* [2012] UKSC 26, [2012] 1 WLR 2004 (strike out).

[74] See *A Local Authority v DL* [2012] EWCA Civ 253, [2013] Fam 1 in which the Court of Appeal confirmed that the High Court had an inherent jurisdiction to deal with the protection of vulnerable adults who fell outside the scope of the Mental Capacity Act 2005.

[75] *A v BBC* (n 41) [27] (emphasis added).

This quote is similar to the words uttered by Toulson LJ in *Guardian News*, which precedes *A v BBC*, namely,

> The *open justice principle is a constitutional principle* to be found not in a written text but in the common law. It is for the courts to determine its requirements, subject to any statutory provision. *It follows that the courts have an inherent jurisdiction to determine how the principle should be applied.*[76]

Notably, the 'constitutional status triggers inherent jurisdiction' reasoning was not recognised as the enabling power to ground common law constitutional rights in *Osborn v Parole Board*, in which Lord Reed gave the single majority judgment. There are two main possible explanations for this. First, there may have been an oversight of the importance of the court's inherent jurisdiction in *Osborn*, which seems unlikely given Lord Reed's approach in *A v BBC*. Alternatively, the actual connecting factor here is not the relationship between a constitutional right under the common law and inherent jurisdiction, but, instead, the case fell into a category that would have triggered inherent jurisdiction either way, and the 'constitutional rights element' is simply gloss. This latter explanation seems more likely also because there is a longstanding tradition by the courts to use their inherent jurisdiction to grant non-party access to certain documents to ensure open justice.[77] Thus, whether viewed through the lens of constitutional rights or not, the courts in *Guardian News* and *A v BBC*, but not *Osborn*, could have relied on their inherent jurisdiction to arrive at the conclusions they arrived at and grant the remedies they granted. In *Osborn*, there was no context or question of judicial processes; procedural fairness was simply seen as part and parcel of the common law, and conceptualised as a human right.[78]

This discrepancy signals that common law constitutional rights are not necessarily perceived by the judiciary as one uniform concept. Rather, rights are determined individually on a case by case – and area by area (of law) – basis. Thus, although we can say that all of the reasoning we encounter in these cases can be characterised as capturing and enforcing common law constitutional rights, there are significant differences in how these rights are conceptualised, including what their legal foundation is, and, relatedly, on the basis of what power judges have jurisdiction to enforce them against individuals or indeed the state.

For example, *UNISON v Lord Chancellor* is based exclusively on the rule of law.[79] Meanwhile, in *Osborn v Parole Board*, the rule of law is mentioned as one

[76] *R (Guardian News and Media Ltd) v City of Westminster Magistrates' Court* (n 38) [69] (emphasis added).

[77] See, eg, *GIO Personal Investment Services Ltd v Liverpool & London Steamship Protection and Indemnity Association Ltd* [1999] 1 WLR 984 (CA); *Church of Scientology of California v Department of Health and Social Security* [1979] 1 WLR 723 (CA). This basic understanding is also expressly endorsed in *Kennedy v Charity Commission* (n 40) [26] and [109] where the concept was extended to public bodies in the context of carrying out statutory inquiries.

[78] R *(Osborn) v Parole Board* (n 31) [57] and, indirectly, [58].

[79] *R (UNISON) v Lord Chancellor* (n 7) [66].

of the values or virtues that necessitated a hearing to take place, alongside considerations such as arriving at better decisions. Similarly, relying in part on his own Court of Appeal judgment in *Guardian News*, Lord Toulson in his judgment in *Kennedy v Charity Commission* reiterates that 'open justice is a principle at the heart of our system of justice and vital to the rule of law'.[80] In contrast, in *UNISON* it is said that the constitutional right in question itself is 'inherent in the rule of law'.[81] There are two ways of looking at this. One is to say that common law constitutional rights are in future to be considered to be based on the rule of law. The other is to suggest that this specific right of access to the courts is – according to the courts – based on the rule of law, and that future common law constitutional rights cases may entail yet another foundational basis or enabling power. The latter seems more likely given Lord Reed's context-specific elaboration on the rule of law. Specifically, he emphasises the importance of the role of the courts in upholding the rule of law, and reasons that for the courts to fulfil their function in a democracy, individuals need to be able to bring cases to the courts in the first place, the latter thus not only benefiting the respective individuals concerned but society at large.[82]

Thus, the first characteristic of this jurisprudence is that the courts have employed a context and rights specific conceptualisation and development of constitutional rights protection by the common law. Rather than there being an overarching principled approach towards the enabling power behind common law constitutional rights, the latter appear to be largely driven by their own precedential history as well as individual judicial interpretations as to what enables, or indeed requires, judges to enforce these judge-made constitutional legal values.

IV. The Second Characteristic: The Principle of Legality

Common law constitutional rights are, effectively, entrenched through the principle of legality, which is generally associated in its modern form with the decision in *R v Secretary of State for the Home Department, ex p Simms*.[83] As I said in chapter three, the substantive High Court decision[84] which followed the Supreme Court's

[80] *Kennedy v Charity Commission* (n 40) [112].
[81] *R (UNISON) v Lord Chancellor* (n 7) [66].
[82] *ibid* [69]–[72].
[83] *R v Secretary of State for the Home Department, ex p Simms* [2000] 2 AC 115 (HL), [1999] 3 WLR. 328
[84] *R (Privacy International) v Investigatory Powers Tribunal* [2021] EWHC 27 (Admin), [2021] QB 936.

judgment in *R (Privacy International) v Investigatory Powers Tribunal*[85] explained the basic idea of the principle of legality in a succinct way:

> Parliamentary sovereignty means that Parliament may legislate to override fundamental rights. However, Parliament is and must be subject to political constraints: if Parliament decides to enact legislation that is contrary to fundamental rights, it must squarely confront what it is doing and accept the political cost. That Parliament has confronted a breach of rights may be demonstrated not only in the express language of a statute but also by necessary implication. In the absence of either of those mechanisms, the courts will presume that fundamental rights are untouched …[86]

Sir Philip Sales, now a Justice of the Supreme Court, puts it more succinctly in one of his extra-judicial papers, saying,

> The 'principle of legality' is the rather strange name given by Halsbury's Laws, and then adopted by Lord Steyn in [*Simms*] to the doctrine that rights and constitutional principles recognised by the common law will not be treated as overridden by statute unless by express language or by clear and necessary implication.[87]

Linking the interpretative mechanism to parliamentary sovereignty, he also said,

> Where constitutional principles or understandings can be established, or constitutional rights have been recognised, statutory interpretation will be moulded around them. They exist as a form of presumptive constitutional order, albeit one capable of being overridden by Parliament by clear language used in a statute.[88]

This analysis paraphrases the well-known formula devised by Lord Steyn according to which

> Parliament does not legislate in a vacuum. Parliament legislates for a European liberal democracy founded on the principles and traditions of the common law. And the courts may approach legislation on this initial assumption. But this assumption only has prima facie force. It can be displaced by a clear and specific provision to the contrary.[89]

The judgments in question confirm that, through the principle of legality, common law constitutional rights are conferred qualified protection.[90] They are conceptualised as a type of 'presumption[s] which can be displaced only by clear words'.[91] Lord Toulson's judgment in *Kennedy v Charity Commission* applies the principle of

[85] *R (Privacy International) v Investigatory Powers Tribunal* [2019] UKSC 22, [2019] 2 WLR 1219.
[86] *R v Secretary of State for the Home Department, ex p Simms* (n 83) [37].
[87] P Sales, 'A Comparison of the Principle of Legality and Section 3 of the Human Rights Act 1998' (2009) 125 *LQR* 598, 600.
[88] *ibid* 601.
[89] *R v Secretary of State for the Home Department, ex p Pierson* [1998] AC 539 (HL), 587, [1997] 3 WLR 492.
[90] M Elliott, 'Constitutional Adjudication and Constitutional Politics in the United Kingdom: The Miller II Case in Legal and Political Context' (2020) 16(4) *European Constitutional Law Review* 625, 640.
[91] *R (W (A Child)) v Secretary of State for the Home Department* [2020] EWHC 1299 (Admin), [2020] 1 WLR 4420 [34].

legality without expressly referring to it when he says '... although the sovereignty of Parliament means that the responsibility of the courts for determining the scope of the open justice principle', which he treats as transferable from the courtroom context to the public inquiry context,

> may be affected by an Act of Parliament, Parliament should not be taken to have legislated so as to limit or control the way in which the court decides such a question unless the language of the statute makes it plain beyond possible doubt that this was Parliament's intention.[92]

The question, Lord Toulson says, is 'was whether the Act demonstrated unequivocally an intention to preclude the courts from determining in a particular case how the open justice principle should be applied'. His approach, which is inextricably linked with the stipulation that the common law in substance meets any substantive protection offered by article 10 ECHR, and, constitutionally, takes priority over the Convention, is presented as being more respectful towards parliamentary intention. A reading down of the absolute exemption of the legislation in question, the FOIA, is avoided under the common law approach, which, operative through the principle of legality, 'runs with the grain' of the FOIA.

Lord Reed's reasoning in *Osborn v Parole Board* does not contain any direct or indirect manifestation of the principle of legality, arguably because the decision did not, at its centre, concern public power devised by legislation. Equally, *A v BBC* mainly deals with the exceptions to the principle of open justice, and with how the latter can limit protection under article 10 ECHR. It is therefore not concerned with legality for the purposes of this section either. The other main case to be considered alongside *Kennedy v Charity Commission* and *Guardian News* is *UNISON v Lord Chancellor*, which expressly endorses the rule that 'nothing less than express words in the statute taking away the right of the King's subjects of access to the courts of justice would authorize or justify it'.[93] The approach the courts should, according to Lord Reed, take in access to justice cases is to ask themselves 'whether the impediment or hindrance in question had been clearly authorised by primary legislation'.[94] As explained above, in the absence of such express curtailment, if it was the practical effect of fees to deny absolutely the right of access to justice, they would be unlawful. One of the remarkable features of *UNISON* is the probing, realistic assessment of the evidence to determine whether the right in question had been violated, namely,

> In order for the fees to be lawful, they have to be set at a level that everyone can afford, taking into account the availability of full or partial remission. The evidence now before the court, considered realistically and as a whole, leads to the conclusion that that requirement is not met.[95]

[92] *Kennedy v Charity Commission* (n 40) [117].
[93] *Chester v Bateson* [1920] 1 KB 829 (KB) 836, cited in *R (UNISON) v Lord Chancellor* (n 7) [76].
[94] *R (UNISON) v Lord Chancellor* (n 7) [79].
[95] *ibid* [91].

Thus, the principle of legality acted as a gateway to substantive domestic constitutional rights protection. *UNISON* is, indeed, a strong principle of legality case in all but name.[96]

That said, we must be clear that the principle of legality does not inevitably lead to the enforcement of common law constitutional rights, nor can it be said that the principle of legality has in general necessarily benefitted claimants.[97] Cases such as *UNISON* make this interpretative principle appear particularly potent, however, the UK constitution being a nuanced one, examples on the other end of the spectrum can be found with relative ease. For example, in *Beghal v DPP* rights protected by the English common law were easily abrogated by the Supreme Court without there being any explicit statutory language to that effect. To reiterate, in this case the Court held that the privilege against self-incrimination, which can be conceptualised as a common law constitutional right, had been abrogated by Schedule 7 of the Terrorism Act 2000. The Justices of the Supreme Court arrived at this conclusion by applying the second part of the test devised in *Simms*, which says that in the alternative to a clear and unequivocal enactment, a right may be taken away by 'necessary implication'. In *Beghal*, the reasoning employed suggests that it may be sufficient for Parliament to have legislated in an area of public importance for a constitutional right to have been abrogated. This stands in stark contrast to the legal analysis in the cases referred to above, providing a completely different threshold for human rights protection. Parliament could have chosen to expressly limit or completely undermine the right in question. A helpful example of what this might have looked like is provided by the Theft Act 1968, which provides in section 31(1) that 'A person shall not be excused, by reason that to do so may incriminate that person … of an offence under this Act'.

What we can take from this section is that the principle of legality, despite being a strong facilitator of common law constitutional rights, also presents an opportunity for common law constitutional rights to be limited or abrogated; it is by no means necessarily rights friendly. Further, as I argue in the next chapter, though express derogation appears to carry greater weight in terms of legitimacy compared to abrogation by necessary implication, the former is still difficult to defend on normative grounds where constitutional rights are at stake.

V. The Third Characteristic: Turning to the Common Law First (but not Exclusively)

In 'an age of rights',[98] the Supreme Court's common law constitutional rights jurisprudence 'presents an opportunity to mainstream human rights into the UK's

[96] R Rawlings, 'The UNISON Case: A New High-Water Mark' (2018) 29 *Public Law Review* 190, 192.
[97] See P Craig, 'Judicial Review, Methodology and Reform' [2021] *PL* 19, 32.
[98] N Bobbio, *The Age of Rights* (Polity Press, 1996).

bloodstream and build upon the jurisprudence of the Strasbourg court to take a more developed and nuanced approach to rights protection'.[99] The judgments in question indicate a seemingly novel methodology towards human rights adjudication. The parties' approach to the respective legal question was criticised for assuming that 'because an issue falls within the ambit of a Convention guarantee, it follows that the legal analysis of the problem should begin and end with the Strasbourg case law'.[100] In *UNISON*, Lord Reed noted that,

> the issue concerning the effect of the Fees Order on access to justice was argued before the courts below on the basis of EU law, although some domestic authorities and judgments of the European Court of Human Rights were also cited. Before this court, it has been recognised that the right of access to justice is not an idea recently imported from the continent of Europe, but has long been deeply embedded in our constitutional law. The case has therefore been argued primarily on the basis of the common law right of access to justice, although arguments have also been presented on the basis of EU law and the European Convention on Human Rights.[101]

The judgment in *Guardian News* is perhaps the clearest example of a judge putting the common law, which was assessed to be 'in vigorous health and flourishing',[102] truly centre-stage. Whilst there is a survey of the status quo of ECtHR jurisprudence, this is not presented as the foundation for Toulson LJ's appreciation of the law, but rather as part of counsel's submissions.[103] His conclusions start with an unequivocal commitment to domestic law. The open justice principle 'is a constitutional principle to be found *not in a written text but in the common law*'.[104] This constitutes the firm basis of his judgment, which is marked by explicit criticism of what he identifies as an imbalance he 'regrets', namely the UK courts' frequent citing of Strasbourg decisions instead of referring to decisions of senior courts in other common law jurisdictions. Lord Neuberger MR (as he then was) and Hooper LJ do not even consider the applicability of the ECHR in their concurring judgments, making *Guardian News* the most common law-exclusive judgment of the cases discussed.

The reasoning in *Osborn v Parole Board*, *Kennedy v Charity Commission* and *A v BBC* is less independent from the ECHR. Blair sees this trio of cases as standing for the following two suggestions about the relationship between Strasbourg jurisprudence and domestic law. First, they reject the notion that Strasbourg has primacy. Second, the Convention is utilised as an inspiration.[105] To some extent, this is correct. However, the trio in fact also demonstrates a close level of interaction

[99] D Blair, 'Quis custodiet ipsos custodes? The Opportunities and Democratic Legitimacy of the Post-Osborn Human Rights Debate' (2016) 2 *Juridical Review* 83, 103.
[100] *R (Osborn) v Parole Board* (n 31) [63].
[101] *R (UNISON) v Lord Chancellor* (n 7) [64].
[102] *R (Guardian News and Media Ltd) v City of Westminster Magistrates' Court* (n 38) [88].
[103] *ibid* [41]–[53].
[104] *ibid* [69] (emphasis added).
[105] Blair (n 99) 87.

and integration between the two sources of law. *Guardian News* is exceptional in how insularly the common law is presented. By comparison, in *Osborn v Parole Board* the Supreme Court recognised that the common law duty to act fairly was influenced by the requirements of article 5, as interpreted by the ECtHR.[106] Lord Reed endorsed the view that 'the courts of the United Kingdom are able to (and should where appropriate) take account of obligations arising under the ECHR in the development of the common law'.[107] Meanwhile, in *Kennedy v Charity Commission*, Lord Mance said 'The development of common law discretions, to meet Convention requirements and subject to control by judicial review, has become a fruitful feature of United Kingdom jurisprudence' and that in certain cases 'the House of Lords and Supreme Court modelled a common law discretion to meet the needs of article 8'.[108]

Indeed, any conceptualisation of common law primacy paired with *exclusivity* is necessarily flawed. Common law constitutional rights cannot convincingly be labelled as *purely* domestic alternatives to which the ECHR is complementary. In reality, it will be hard to find a domestic constitutional right (case) that has not been influenced by Strasbourg jurisprudence. Digging a little deeper into the case law shows that, unsurprisingly, over the past few decades there has been a significant blurring between domestic law and European law in human rights adjudication. For example, in *Osborn v Parole Board* the main domestic authorities relied on to determine the requirements of procedural fairness are *R (Smith) v Parole Board for England and Wales*,[109] Byles J's citation in *Cooper v Wandsworth Board of Works*[110] of the dictum of Fortescue J in *R v Cambridge University, ex p Bentley*,[111] *R v Parole Board, ex p Bradley*,[112] and *R v Parole Board, ex p Wilson*.[113] The intertwined relationship between the English common law and European law becomes clear if we look more closely at these cases and trace them further. For example, in *R (West) v Parole Board*, the 1994 judgment of *Doody*,[114] which concerned the sentencing of a convicted murderer, was applied. Importantly, *Doody* was decided against the background of the ECtHR judgment in *Thynne v United Kingdom*,[115] after which Parliament changed the law in the UK to comply with its Convention obligations.[116] This shows that common law constitutional rights do not operate in a world of their own; often they will have been directly or indirectly influenced by

[106] *R (Osborn) v Parole Board* (n 31) [2xii].
[107] *R (Elgizouli) v Secretary of State for the Home Department* (n 35) [107], citing *R (Osborn) v Parole Board* (n 31) [57].
[108] *Kennedy v Charity Commission* (n 40) both [38].
[109] *R (Smith) v Parole Board for England and Wales* [2005] UKHL 1, [2005] 1 WLR 350.
[110] *Cooper v Wandsworth Board of Works* [1863] 143 ER 414, (1863) 14 CB NS 180 (Court of Common Pleas).
[111] *R v Cambridge University, ex p Bentley* (1724) 2 Ld Raym 1334.
[112] *R v Parole Board, ex p Bradley* [1991] 1 WLR 134 (QB).
[113] *R v Parole Board, ex p Wilson* [1992] QB 740 (CA).
[114] *R v Secretary of State for the Home Department, ex p Doody* [1994] 1 AC 531 (HL).
[115] *Thynne v United Kingdom* (1991) 13 EHRR 666.
[116] Criminal Justice Act 1991, s 34.

ECtHR judgments at some point in time. Lord Rodger suggested as much when he said that it would be wrong 'to see the rights under the European Convention as somehow forming a wholly separate stream in our law; in truth they soak through and permeate the areas of our law in which they apply'.[117]

Thus, as the late Lord Kerr put it in *Elgizouli*, 'Development of the common law is not immune from nor does it disavow external influence'.[118] In the context of common law constitutional rights or, as they are sometimes referred to, fundamental rights, the main source of influence has been the ECHR. In recognition of the close interaction between the two sources of law, the Supreme Court (and the Court of Appeal in *Guardian News*) says that, where a common law right is available, one ought to turn to that right first. In this sense, the UK Government's previously introduced Bill of Rights bill can be seen, ironically perhaps, as being more focused on European law than domestic jurisprudence at the highest level. Section 3(2)(b) of the bill states 'A court determining a question which has arisen in connection with a Convention right may have regard to the development under the common law of any right that is similar to the Convention right'. Evidently, not only is this already the case, but the Supreme Court's jurisprudence on common law constitutional rights in fact goes further than 'may', stipulating that one *ought* to turn to the common law *first*.

What is less clear is to what extent the Strasbourg component of the judgments analysed might have been more prominent had the Strasbourg case law been deemed to be more unambiguous. For example, in *Kennedy v Charity Commission*, Lord Toulson doubted that article 10 ECHR could add anything to what he found in domestic law, commenting on what he perceived to be an unsatisfactory state of the Strasbourg case law: 'What is so far lacking from the more recent Strasbourg decisions, with respect, is a consistent and clearly reasoned analysis of the "right to receive and impart information" within the meaning of article 10 …'.[119]

Does this suggest that the Convention would have applied, and that it here would have been the first port of call, if the case law had been more satisfactory? As it happens, the claim that the Strasbourg jurisprudence in question was ambiguous appeared to be ill-founded. The dissenting opinions given by Lord Carnwath and Lord Wilson on this point were subsequently validated when the Supreme Court's majority's approach in *Kennedy v Charity Commission* was rejected by the ECtHR's Grand Chamber.[120] The Court in Strasbourg held that article 10 *did* confer a right of access to information. This is a powerful reminder that under the current constitutional set-up, there is a higher instance in human rights questions that unsatisfied claimants can resort to, and which can 'correct' domestic interpretation of the ECHR. That reality, namely that the UK is bound by its obligations under the European Convention as a source of international law, was one of the

[117] *HM Advocate v Montgomery (David Shields)* (2000) JC 111 [117].
[118] *R (Elgizouli) v Secretary of State for the Home Department* (n 35) [107].
[119] *ibid* [145].
[120] *Magyar Helsinki Bizottság v Hungary* App no 18030/11 (ECtHR, 8 November 2016).

key motivating factors for the common law developing in the late 1980s and 1990s to 'keep up'. It seems that the now shelved Bill of Rights bill would – had it been passed – have risked a return to a system where, because of an inferior domestic rights protection framework, successful challenges before the ECtHR would have risen to unsustainable levels.

The way in which the interaction between the two sources of law is conceptualised in the case law entails some other problematic tendencies. For example, in *Osborn v Parole Board*, Lord Reed says that action falling short of satisfying the common law duty of fairness automatically leads to the consequential failure of the equivalent principles or rights under the ECHR[121] before stating that,

> in order to comply with common law standards of procedural fairness, the board should hold an oral hearing … whenever fairness to the prisoner requires such a hearing …. By doing so the board would also fulfil its duty under section 6(1) of the Human Rights Act 1998 to act compatibly with article 5(4) of the European Convention for the Protection of Human Rights and Fundamental Freedoms, in circumstances where that article is engaged.[122]

This approach is not without risk. For instance, one can quite easily imagine a situation where the common law, even if it works in favour of the right-bearer, provides a lower standard than the Convention, and would therefore potentially not offer the same level of protection. Assuming compatibility risks not being aware of any potential discrepancies, which in turn prevents the courts from rectifying them. The Supreme Court has held that the Convention 'may be expected, at least generally even if not always, to reflect and to find their homologue in the common or domestic statute law'.[123] Of course, 'in time a synthesis may … emerge'.[124] However, assuming compliance bears the risk of the common law under-delivering and the UK being in breach of binding international human rights standards. Where *primacy* is equated with *sufficiency*, a court – by not engaging with the Strasbourg jurisprudence at all – is at risk of violating its own obligation under the HRA, which explicitly mandates that it screen domestic law for Convention compatibility.[125] Arguably, this risk is significantly higher, and in some instances only present, where the outcome of a case is not beneficial to the individual seeking to rely on a common law constitutional right, ie where no violation is established.

In summary, we can see from this section that common law constitutional rights jurisprudence suggests that one ought to turn to the common law first rather than going immediately to the Convention. This renewed emphasis on domestic constitutional rights protection has, in some cases, led to pleadings now reflecting

[121] R *(Osborn) v Parole Board* (n 31) [113].
[122] *ibid* [2].
[123] *Kennedy v Charity Commission* (n 40) [46].
[124] *ibid* [46].
[125] Human Rights Act 1998, s 6(3).

a new hierarchy. For instance, in *Xavier v The Governor of HMP Whitemoor & Another*, the claimant, who was serving an indeterminate sentence and complained about the prison's treatment of his confidential legal correspondence, brought four grounds of challenge, namely

> (1) that the defendants failed to apply their own policies; (2) breach of the claimant's common law constitutional right to unimpeded access to his lawyers; (3) violations of Article 6 and/or 8 of the European Convention on Human Rights ('the ECHR') and (4) unlawful insufficiency in the defendants' published policies and/or systemic failure to ensure compliance with the requirements of Article 6 and/or Article 8.[126]

Litigants also appear to have been emboldened by the emphasis on the strength of the common law, including the claim made by the Supreme Court in obiter dicta that in extreme circumstances a common law right might trump primary legislation, a notion stemming from *Moohan v Lord Advocate*,[127] in which the Supreme Court held that there was, at common law, no right to vote. For example, in *Shindler and another v Chancellor of the Duchy of Lancaster and another*, counsel for Mr Shindler unsuccessfully submitted that the Court ought to make a declaration that the legislation in question, the European Union Referendum Act 2015, was unconstitutional due to a conflict with the fundamental constitutional right to vote.[128] More recent cases also show a continuing link between the two sources of law in the sense that the protection offered by the ECHR, or the lack of protection, has direct implications on how far the common law can develop. Thus, in *R (Elgizouli) v Secretary of State for the Home Department* the Supreme Court clearly stated that the Court's reasoning in *Osborn v Parole Board* and *Kennedy v Charity Commission* 'support[s] the development of the common law in line with the European Convention, but not beyond as here proposed'.[129]

VI. The Fourth Characteristic: A Fluid Notion of Precedent and the Influence of Non-Legal Sources

Where do common law constitutional rights come from? Where do they originate? In the cases analysed, references to precedent or legal principles from older authorities are notably sparse. Apart from *UNISON v Lord Chancellor*, which relies heavily on relatively recent precedents, the cases analysed mention only a handful of other cases spanning several centuries. Generally, a strong emphasis is placed on

[126] *Xavier v The Governor of HMP Whitemoor & Another* [2021] EWHC 3060 (Admin), [2022] ACD 3 [2].

[127] *Moohan v Lord Advocate* (n 49) [25] (per Lord Hodge).

[128] *Shindler and another v Chancellor of the Duchy of Lancaster and another* [2016] EWCA Civ 469, [2017] QB 226 [48]–[49].

[129] *R (Elgizouli) v Secretary of State for the Home Department* (n 35) [192]–[193] (quote taken from [193])(per Lord Carnwath).

the notion that common law constitutional rights have been around for a long time. One might term this approach 'legitimacy through longevity'. For example, in *A v BBC*, Lord Reed identified the roots of the constitutional principle of open justice as being ancient enough to have been covered by 'the constitutional legislation enacted following the accession of William and Mary' in the Court of Session Act 1693.[130] The case law is then traced very sporadically to outline the development of the right in question to its most recent judicial citation.

The precedential foundation of a common law constitutional right may be very weak indeed. This is demonstrated formidably by the repeated references to *Scott v Scott*,[131] on which all judgments analysed (other than *Osborn v Parole Board* and *UNISON v Lord Chancellor*, which do not deal with the right to open justice) rely to a varying degree. *Scott v Scott* suggests that the principle of open justice requires the judicial process to be open to the public, unless there are strong countervailing reasons. Toulson LJ begins his judgment in *Guardian News* by referring to Lord Shaw's speech in *Scott v Scott* where he said, quoting Jeremy Bentham, that 'publicity is the very soul of justice'.[132] Only where publicity potentially jeopardises the entire case, or where compelling, exceptional factors such as 'wardship and lunacy' are present can the principle of open justice be departed from.

Scott v Scott is generally regarded as a constitutionally important judgment. In 2016, in the Supreme Court judgment of *R (C) v Secretary of State for Justice*, Lady Hale said *Scott v Scott* was still the leading case reflecting a long-standing common law principle.[133] To this day, the case is regularly applied,[134] considered[135] and followed.[136] A few points can be made about the reliance on *Scott v Scott* in the three judgments analysed. First, the factual situation in *Scott v Scott* differed significantly from the judgments analysed, showing the fluidity of precedents in common law constitutional rights jurisprudence. *Scott v Scott* concerned the unlawful distribution or leaking of transcripts from marriage annulment proceedings by one of the parties to the proceedings. Meanwhile, *A v BBC*, *Guardian News* and *Kennedy v Charity Commission* relate to inquiries into concerns of public interest through the media. Lord Carnwath was apprehensive about this disconnect in his dissenting opinion in *Kennedy v Charity Commission*. He reasoned that,

> there is nothing in the Guardian News case, or any other existing authority to support the view that common law principles relating to disclosure of documents in the courts can be transferred directly to inquiries. It must depend on the statutory or other legal framework within which the particular inquiry is established.[137]

[130] *A v BBC* (n 41) [24].
[131] *Scott v Scott* [1913] AC 417 (HL).
[132] *ibid* [477].
[133] *R (C) v Secretary of State for Justice* [2016] UKSC 2, [2016] AC 1081 [16], [17].
[134] See, eg, *XXX v Camden LBC* [2020] EWCA Civ 1468, [2020] 4 WLR 165.
[135] See, eg, *JK v Revenue and Customs Commissioners* [2019] UKFTT 411 (TC), [2019] SFTD 1094.
[136] See, eg, *C v Secretary of State for Justice* [2016] UKSC 2, [2016] 1 WLR 444.
[137] *Kennedy v Charity Commission* (n 40) [241].

Another example of scepticism towards a flexible notion of precedent is evident in Lord Wilson's dissenting opinion in the same case, which suggested that what was said in *Guardian News* about the principle in the context of litigation could not simply be extended to public bodies such as the Charity Commission.[138] He further noted that this comparison disclosed a basic fallacy as the foundation of the *Guardian News* decision lay in the strong constitutional principle that courts sit in public. Accordingly, it was

> no surprise that the starting point of Toulson LJ's judgment is a quotation from the great case of *Scott v Scott* [1913] AC 417, in which that principle was set in stone. It is not a large step from that principle to hold that papers supplied to the judge for the purpose of an open hearing should in principle be made available to the public, absent good reasons to the contrary. For statutory inquiries, such as those conducted by the Charity Commission, there is no such underlying principle that they should sit in public. The essential foundation that is needed for application of the *Guardian News* approach is wholly absent.[139]

Those concerns, however, were not shared by the majority, which took a more liberal approach to the notion of precedent, focusing on the essence of the principle in question, rather than placing it in its context. Overall, the cases analysed endorse reliance on a broad principle that may undermine the importance of the legal framework and factual patterns in which it applies, which is how human rights law more broadly speaking is often conceptualised.

It is also worth highlighting that Lord Reed in *Osborn v Parole Board* relies, indirectly, on non-legal sources to explain the purpose of the common law protection offered to prisoners. Identifying three values to justify the requirement for an oral hearing in substance, he first notes that procedurally fair decision-making 'is liable to result in better decisions, by ensuring that the decision-maker receives all relevant information and that it is properly tested'.[140] However, it is the second value we are particularly interested in for present purposes. In offering a hearing, Lord Reed says, one may avoid a 'sense of injustice which the person who is the subject of the decision will otherwise feel'.[141] This is linked to the concept of respect and dignity, which Lord Reed develops by citing Jeremy Waldon, who has said,

> Applying a norm to a human individual is not like deciding what to do about a rabid animal or a dilapidated house. It involves paying attention to a point of view and respecting the personality of the entity one is dealing with. As such it embodies a crucial dignitarian idea – respecting the dignity of those to whom the norms are applied as beings capable of explaining themselves.[142]

[138] *ibid* [236]–[238].
[139] *ibid* 455 [240].
[140] *R (Osborn) v Parole Board* (n 31) [67].
[141] *ibid* [68].
[142] *ibid*, citing J Waldon, 'How Law Protects Dignity" [2012] *CLJ* 200, 210.

The reliance on academic writings is then supported by references to religious text in previous judgments. Thus, Lord Reed continues,

> This point can be illustrated by Byles J's citation in *Cooper v Wandsworth Board of Works* (1863) 14 CB (NS) 180, 195 of a dictum of Fortescue J in *Dr Bentley's Case (R v Chancellor of Cambridge, Ex p Bentley* (1748) 2 Ld Raym 1334):
>
> 'The laws of God and man both give the party an opportunity to make his defence, if he has any. I remember to have heard it observed by a very learned man, upon such an occasion, that even God himself did not pass sentence upon Adam before he was called upon to make his defence.'[143]

The link between what are understood to be religious teachings and constitutional rights is evident in the following paragraph, in which Lord Reed adds that Byles J had in *Cooper v Wandsworth Board of Works* observed that the language used by Fortescue J in *Dr Betley's Case* 'is somewhat quaint, but … *has been the law from that time to the present*'.[144] The expression 'from that time' is important. We must recognise, a point I discuss more extensively in chapter five, that every common law constitutional right must have an ultimate, original foundation. What I mean by this is that, despite the common law's insistence on historical legal foundations, every legal principle must have been mentioned and recognised for the very first time at some point. The existence of a line of cases which endorse a legal value that has previously been enforced should not make us blind to the fact that, originally, the foundation of that legal value was more likely than not based on the opinion of a particular judge, or a bench of judges. That opinion may have been influenced by literature, philosophy, religion and other factors, including arguably one's understanding of values and public opinion at the time. This is exemplified by *Scott v Scott*, which has no reference to any other relevant case law. Rather, what we find is that *Scott v Scott* is infused with judicial statements that blend the personal with the legal, embodied by the statement made by the Earl of Halsbury, 'I am of opinion that every Court of justice is open to every subject of the King'.[145]

To repeat, there must always be a case – such as *Scott v Scott* – in which a common law constitutional right was first relied upon, a case in which no other cases could be used to provide 'historical validation' or legitimacy. Accordingly, in such cases, the sole foundation would have been logic, normative moral considerations and the like. If this is considered acceptable as the foundation for principles and rights enforced today, logically there is nothing that prevents new rights from being recognised and enforced as well. However, realistically, as I discuss in chapter five, the common law's reliance on the past is bound to hamper the recognition of rights for which no precedent can be found. Indeed, the historical tracing of common law constitutional rights shows that the foundation of common law constitutional rights is normative, meaning the initial recognition of

[143] *ibid* [69].
[144] *ibid*, citing *Cooper v Wandsworth Board of Works* (n 110) 420 (emphasis added).
[145] *Scott v Scott* (n 131) 442 (per Lord Earl of Halsbury).

a constitutional right is based on considerations of personal and political morality. However, a right's subsequent *maintenance* and *development* through judicial endorsement turns them into legal tradition. The notion of legal tradition, embodied through the system of precedent, frames and legitimises the use of common law constitutional rights today; substantive normative elaborations are secondary.

Kennedy v Charity Commission shows how fragile common law constitutional rights protection can be in a system that is not built on a strong, explicit domestic human rights tradition. Its majority opinions are somewhat confused and incomplete, unveiling uncertainty as to the basic elements and the strength of the common law constitutional right in question. As Lord Wilson notes in his highly persuasive dissent,

> the scheme identified by the majority for disclosure by the commission outside the FOIA is profoundly unsatisfactory. With respect, it can scarcely be described as a scheme at all and there is certainly no example of its prior operation or other recognition of its existence ... Although the majority of my colleagues reject Mr Kennedy's assertion that he has rights under article 10 which are engaged by his request for disclosure by the Commission, they proceed to suggest that his entitlement to disclosure otherwise than under the FOIA would be likely to be as extensive as any entitlement under article 10 (Lord Mance, paras 45, 50, 56, 92 and 101(iv)). The suggested scheme otherwise than under the FOIA is so vague and generalised that I regard the determination thereunder of any request for disclosure as impossible to predict.[146]

Thus, this judgment shows how fragile domestic rights protection can be where there is no clear precedent and where more established concepts are borrowed or cross-applied.

What then do we make of a case in which no precedent can be found, but the value in question has been recognised rather more intangibly in domestic jurisprudence? That question was answered, to some extent, in *R (Elgizouli) v Secretary of State for the Home Department and another*,[147] which was mentioned in the discussion of the second characteristic. *Elgizouli* raised the question whether it was lawful for the Secretary of State for the Home Department to provide evidence to the United States that could facilitate the imposition of the death penalty. The request for the evidence in question had been made under a 1994 treaty on mutual legal assistance in criminal matters. The US Government was conducting an investigation into terrorist activities committed by individuals with a connection to the UK who were suspected of having been involved in the murders of US citizens in Syria. The US request was for materials gathered by UK police as part of a domestic investigation of the individuals concerned. The Home Secretary shared the requested information without getting certain assurances from his US colleagues following their persistent unwillingness to provide the latter. Specifically, he had, in line with long-standing UK policy, sought assurances that the individuals would

[146] *Kennedy v Charity Commission* (n 40) [198]–[199].

[147] *R (Elgizouli) v Secretary of State for the Home Department* (n 35).

not be subject to the death penalty. It was expressly admitted that 'there was a serious risk that Mr El Sheikh … would, if prosecuted and convicted, face execution as a direct result of UK assistance'.[148]

The claimant, the mother of one of the individuals concerned, argued there was a common law principle that the UK will not give mutual legal assistance where there is a risk that this would lead to the imposition of the death penalty. The prerogative power exercised by the Secretary of State, she argued, needed to be exercised in accordance with that principle. She purported that the death penalty offended against the 'evolving requirements of humanity enshrined in the common law', was contrary to article 10 of the Bill of Rights 1688 which prohibits 'the infliction of cruel and unusual punishments',[149] and that 'the facilitation of inhuman treatment' was contrary to the fundamental principles of the common law as well as the European Convention.[150]

Lord Kerr, who gave the longest of the Court's judgments, but was in the minority in finding that the Secretary of State had fallen foul of the common law, framed the claim as concerning the 'fundamental common law principle of justice'.[151] In his discussion, the Bill of Rights 1688 provided the 'backdrop'[152] to the question of whether the common law entailed the protection the claimant said it did. After discussing contemporary 'British values', he turned to external influences, to determine 'whether there should now be recognised a common law principle that the UK government will not facilitate the imposition of the death penalty'.[153] The first external source considered, which was acknowledged not to be purely external, was the jurisprudence of the ECtHR and several ratified by the UK. Lord Kerr concluded that 'The jurisprudence is … important and noteworthy as an influencer to the conclusion that the contended for common law right should be recognised'.[154] The second source is European Union law which was surveyed and thought to indicate a settled opposition to the death penalty in every circumstance. Similar to the relevance of the ECHR, Lord Kerr suggested,

> It cannot be irrelevant to the development of our common law that the UK was a member of the EU for more than 40 years. The influence that EU law in general and its hostility to the death penalty in particular has on a decision as to the current state of the common law is undeniable.[155]

The other two factors resulting – as far as Lord Kerr was concerned – in the common law having developed a constitutional right were reason/logic (it was deemed

[148] *ibid* [60].
[149] *ibid* [66].
[150] *ibid* [68].
[151] *ibid* [71].
[152] *ibid* [102].
[153] *ibid* [108].
[154] *ibid* [113].
[155] *ibid* [134].

illogical that the UK would refuse to extradite individuals for trial where a risk of the death penalty being imposed existed on the one hand, but then, on the other hand, facilitate precisely such an outcome through mutual legal assistance) and the jurisprudence of the Judicial Committee of the Privy Council. How could those sources influence domestic rights protection? Lord Kerr said,

> Law, whether enacted or developed through the common law, if it is operating as it should, must be responsive to society's contemporary needs, standards and values. It is a commonplace that these are in a state of constant change. That is an essential part of the human condition and experience. As a deeper understanding of the human psyche and the enlightenment of society increase with the onward march of education, tolerance and forbearance in relation to our fellow citizens, the law must march step-by-step with that progress. I am convinced that the adjustment to the common law which I propose reflects the contemporary standards and values of our society.[156]

Combining the above reasons, Lord Kerr concluded that it was unlawful at common law for the UK to facilitate the execution of the death penalty (against one of its citizens or others within its jurisdiction) anywhere in the world.

Lord Kerr's carefully structured approach did not find favour with the majority. There is, at common law, no constitutional right not to have one's trial in a foreign jurisdiction facilitated where there is a prospect that such a trial would lead to the death penalty being carried out. The key difference between the minority and the majority opinions was the concept of 'incrementalism'. Lord Carnwath said the power to develop the common law had to be exercised with caution.[157] Similarly, Lord Reed opined, 'the common law is subject to judicial development, but such development builds incrementally on existing principles'.[158] Highlighting the need for legal certainty, he added that 'dramatic' legal change was the prerogative of the elected branches of state. It was recognised that Lord Bingham had said in *R (Amin) v Secretary of State for the Home Department* that 'A profound respect for the sanctity of human life underpins the common law'.[159] That was reflected in the criminal law relating to homicide and the law of tort, for example. This did not, however, translate into a legally enforceable right. One also needed to take into account that Parliament had recently legislated in this field, via the Data Protection Act 2018, which was in fact the ground on which the claimant's claim succeeded. That said, given what was at stake, namely life, the courts would be required to take a more rigorous approach when reviewing the exercise of discretion.

Elgizouli shows the inherent limits to the development of new common law rights, a theme which is picked up again in chapter five.

[156] *ibid* [144].
[157] *ibid* [193].
[158] *ibid* [170].
[159] *R (Amin) v Secretary of State for the Home Department* (n 34) [30].

VII. The Fifth Characteristic: Domestic Validation Through Legal Comparativism

There is no clearly established constitutional rights framework in this jurisdiction and the courts have traditionally held back with the development of the content of common law constitutional rights. Consequently, it seems almost inevitable that the courts look to external sources which can provide both substance and legitimacy now that common law constitutional rights are being increasingly enforced. One mechanism through which this is achieved is judicial reference to, and reliance on, foreign judgments from other common law jurisdictions. As the preceding section signals, this is only possible where there is deemed to be sufficient domestic legal material to warrant the enforcement of the right in question. Relying on external sources alone could not, the jurisprudence suggests, make up for a complete lack of domestic precedent.

To start, we find ample evidence of judicial constitutional comparativism in common law constitutional rights jurisprudence.[160] For example, in *A v BBC*, Lord Reed, reasoning that the exceptions developed in *Scott v Scott* are not exhaustive and that the principle of open justice will develop in response to societal changes, suggests that this right could also be developed by

> having regard to the approach adopted in other common law countries, some of which have constitutional texts containing guarantees comparable to the Convention rights, while in others the approach adopted reflects the courts' view of the requirements of justice.[161]

A similar approach can be detected in other common law constitutional rights judgments, young[162] and old.[163] As I have written elsewhere,[164] overall, the Supreme Court's general approach to judicial comparativism in constitutional cases is commendable, as it is thorough, sufficiently flexible and humble in the sense that the nuances inherent in other legal systems are consciously engaged with. What must equally be recognised, however, is that constitutional comparativism is a mechanism that facilitates the courts bypassing the underlying

[160] Of course, the citation and use of foreign legal sources is by no means a phenomenon exclusive to constitutional cases, see, eg, E Mak, 'Comparative Law before the Supreme Courts of the UK and the Netherlands: An Empirical and Comparative Analysis' in M Andenas and D Fairgrieve (eds), *Courts and Comparative Law* (Oxford University Press, 2015). However, some argue it is more contentious in this context due to the special status attributed to constitutional law and its intimate connectedness with the social, cultural and wider legal framework of nation states, see M Tushnet, *Weak Courts, Strong Rights: Judicial Review and Social Welfare Rights Comparative Constitutional Law* (Princeton University Press, 2008).

[161] *A v BBC* (n 41) [40].

[162] See, eg, *Moohan v Lord Advocate* (n 49).

[163] See, eg, *Attorney General v Times Newspapers Ltd* [1974] AC 273 (HL).

[164] C Lienen, 'Judicial Constitutional Comparativism at the UK Supreme Court' (2019) 39(1) *Legal Studies* 166.

questions about the legitimacy and domestic foundational basis of common law constitutional rights.

In saying this, I do not mean to suggest that the engagement in judicial comparativism to help build the content of domestic rights is in any way disingenuous. I merely point out that relying on constitutional comparativism provides a 'short-cut' to legitimacy. The fact that other eminent common law courts have enforced a right is viewed as partly legitimising their domestic enforcement. However, to address concerns over legitimacy satisfactorily, the courts must engage more consciously with the aspects of political morality that lie behind constitutional rights. Constitutional comparativism contributes to these questions being left unaddressed.

Constitutional comparativism may suggest that domestic constitutional rights jurisprudence is relatively 'hollow'. The courts need to *prop up* domestic jurisprudence to provide a solid foundation for common law constitutional rights, the borrowing from other common law jurisdictions being one way of achieving this. As the cases analysed show, such references to foreign law need not necessarily be limited to judicial decisions. Notably, in *Guardian News* Toulson LJ (as he then was) cited not only foreign case law to strengthen his interpretation of the principle of open justice, but also softer forms of authority, including a report by the Law Commission of New Zealand on Access to Court Records (2006).[165] His approach, which relies heavily on foreign law, is worth citing in full. He said that his decision was based

> on the common law principle of open justice. In reaching it I am fortified by the common theme of the judgments in other common law countries to which I have referred. Collectively they are strong persuasive authority. The courts are used to citation of Strasbourg decisions in abundance, but citation of decisions of senior courts in other common law jurisdictions is now less common. I regret the imbalance. The development of the common law did not come to an end on the passing of the Human Rights Act 1998. It is in vigorous health and flourishing in many parts of the world which share a common legal tradition. This case provides a good example of the benefit which can be gained from knowledge of the development of the common law elsewhere.[166]

This can be contrasted with *UNISON v Lord Chancellor* and *Osborn v Parole Board*, neither of which make reference to judgments from other common law jurisdictions. This supports my argument that judicial constitutional comparativism operates as a sort of gap-filler and means of external validation. *UNISON* shows that the right of access to the courts is clearly considered 'established' enough to go all the way by itself. The Supreme Court could rely on precedents that point to a foundation in domestic law. In fact, it had case law at its disposal that specifically mentioned the constitutional right of access to the courts as opposed to case law that merely pointed to related rights or principles. Lord Reed was able to rely on several authoritative cases, stating that 'in English law, the right of access to the courts has

[165] *R (Guardian News and Media Ltd) v City of Westminster Magistrates' Court* (n 38) [2].
[166] *ibid* [88].

long been recognised'.[167] The Magna Carta, Edward Coke's *Institutes of the Laws of England*, Blackstone's *Commentaries on the Laws of England*, and numerous cases from the first phase of common law constitutional rights in the 1980s and 1990s were referred to.[168] Outside the framework of well-established rights, common law constitutional rights cases rely heavily on judicial comparativism.

VIII. The Sixth Characteristic: Proportionality Review

It is well known that 'Substantive review in English law has been dominated by the concept of unreasonableness'.[169] The traditional Wednesbury standard for interference is a high one, allowing judges to disturb a decision by a public body only where that decision is 'so unreasonable that no reasonable authority could ever have come to it'.[170] Proportionality review, in contrast, is a legal construct that operates as a methodological tool to assess the lawfulness of public action via a 'sequence of three enquiries – suitability, necessity, and fair balance'.[171] In *Bank Mellat v Her Majesty's Treasury (No 2)*, Lord Sumption restated that this is captured in four stages, which require one to determine

> (i) whether [a measure's] objective is sufficiently important to justify the limitation of a fundamental right; (ii) whether [a measure] is rationally connected to the objective; (iii) whether a less intrusive measure could have been used; and (iv) whether, having regard to these matters and to the severity of the consequences, a fair balance has been struck between the rights of the individual and the interests of the community.[172]

As Sayer and Murray have noted, in general, 'the initial stages (centred on the rationality of a public authority's decision-making) are swiftly dispatched, and the balancing exercise has become the dominant element since the House of Lords' *Huang* decision'.[173] Opinion has differed as to whether proportionality should exist as a separate, or indeed the only ground of review in cases not concerned with EU law or human rights protected by the ECHR. Williams has encapsulated the academic debate comprehensively, and I will not repeat the argument here.[174]

[167] *R (UNISON) v Lord Chancellor* (n 7) [74].

[168] Such as *Bremer Vulkan Schiffbau und Maschinenfabrik v South India Shipping Corporation Ltd* (n 72), *Raymond v Honey* [1983] 1 AC 1 (HL) and *R v Secretary of State for the Home Department, ex p Leech (No 2)* [1994] QB 198, [1993] 3 WLR 1125.

[169] Lord Woolf and others, *De Smith's Judicial Review*, 8th edn (Sweet & Maxwell, 2021) Ch 11 – 'Substantive Review and Justification' 11-012.

[170] *Associated Provincial Picture Houses Ltd v Wednesbury Corporation* [1948] 1 KB 223, 229–30.

[171] M Teo, 'Proportionality as Epistemic Independence' [2022] *PL* 245, 245.

[172] *Bank Mellat v Her Majesty's Treasury (No 2)* [2013] UKSC 39, [2014] AC 700 [20].

[173] T Sayer and CRG Murray, 'A Tale of Two Doctrines: Re-Evaluating Bifurcation in Substantive Review before the Supreme Court' [2021] *PL* 47, 50, citing *Huang v Secretary of State for the Home Department* [2007] UKHL 11, [2007] 2 AC 167 [19] (per Lord Bingham).

[174] R Williams, 'Structuring Substantive Review' [2017] *PL* 99. See also J Lee, 'Substantiating Substantive Review' [2018] *PL* 632; Teo (n 171); Sir P Sales, 'Rationality, Proportionality and the Development of the Law' (2013) 129 *LQR* 223.

The unification of reasonableness and proportionality review (or the replacement of the former by the latter) seemed likely when *Pham v Secretary of State for the Home Department*[175] was handed down by the Supreme Court in 2015. The question in *Pham* had been whether the Home Secretary could deprive the appellant, who was born in Vietnam, of his acquired British citizenship and deport him to Vietnam on the grounds of terrorist charges. This, it was argued, would leave him stateless as the Vietnamese Government had alleged that he was no longer considered a Vietnamese national. The Home Secretary's decision was unanimously held to be lawful. The judgments of Lords Carnwath, Mance and Reed can be interpreted as standing for a softening of the traditionally rigid distinction between domestic and supranational legal sources. Indeed, the judgment stands not for a replacement of rationality review, but rather for the conclusion that the application of the principle of proportionality would not differ in practice from the application of a context-sensitive standard of common law unreasonableness.[176]

Just a few months after *Pham*, in *R (Keyu) v Secretary of State for Foreign and Commonwealth Affairs*,[177] the Supreme Court declined the opportunity to determine definitively whether Wednesbury reasonableness should be replaced by or merged with proportionality review. The case concerned the decision by the Secretaries of State for Foreign Affairs and Defence to refuse to hold a public inquiry into the killing of 23 unarmed civilians in the village of Batang Kali in Selangor by a patrol of the Scots Guards. The appellant had argued

> that the time has come to reconsider the basis on which the courts review decisions of the executive, and in particular that the traditional Wednesbury rationality basis for challenging executive decisions should be replaced by a more structured and principled challenge based on proportionality.[178]

Lord Neuberger, with whom Lord Hughes agreed, reasoned that a panel of five judges could not determine such a constitutionally significant question. Lord Kerr, dissenting, stated that the question 'will have to be frankly addressed by this court sooner rather than later'.[179] More recent case law casts further doubt over the abandonment of the traditional standard of review. For instance, *R (Gallaher Ltd) v Competition and Markets Authority* appears to suggest that Wednesbury/unreasonableness is wide enough to accommodate within it, depending on the context, proportionality review.[180] Either way, Wednesbury review continues to be routinely applied in a wide range of public law cases, and it seems highly unlikely that it will be replaced by proportionality review, especially in the current political climate.

[175] *Pham v Secretary of State for the Home Department* [2015] UKSC 19, [2015] 1 WLR 1591.
[176] *ibid* [59] (Lord Carnwath).
[177] *R (Keyu) v Secretary of State for Foreign and Commonwealth Affairs* [2015] UKSC 69, [2016] AC 1355. See also P Daly, 'Wednesbury and Proportionality – Where are We Now?' (*Administrative Law Matters Blog*, 28 November 2016).
[178] *Keyu, ibid* [131].
[179] *ibid* [271].
[180] *R (Gallaher Ltd) v Competition and Markets Authority* [2018] UKSC 25, [2019] AC 96 [27].

Contrary to the uncertainty surrounding the standard of review in administrative law more generally,[181] we find relative uniformity when it comes to common law constitutional rights protection. I stress the word 'relative' because, in 2018, the Court of Appeal conducted a Wednesbury-type review in a common law constitutional rights case on the basis of outdated jurisprudence.[182] However, at Supreme Court level the position is clear. In fact, out of the six characteristics identified, this is the most consistent one: in the context of common law constitutional rights, proportionality review applies.

Kennedy v Charity Commission is the most relevant judgment for this characteristic. It endorses Craig's view that the underlying function of both tests is the same, namely to weigh and to balance.[183] What proportionality is said to offer is 'an element of structure … by directing attention to factors such as suitability or appropriateness, necessity and the balance or imbalance of benefits and disadvantages'.[184] Lord Mance continues that there is no reason why these factors should not be appropriate to be considered in purely domestic cases. With reference to Lord Bridge of Harwich's remarks in *R v Secretary of State for the Home Department, ex p Bugdaycay*,[185] he then reasons that the gravity of the issue determines the intensity of review in every particular case.[186]

Meanwhile, in *UNISON* proportionality review was endorsed in a clear-cut way without any reference to scholarly works.[187] We can therefore conclude that while 'it is at best uncertain to what extent the proportionality test … has become part of domestic public law',[188] in the context of common law constitutional rights the proportionality review has been endorsed at the highest level. Importantly though, and to repeat the point made in the context of the third characteristic, this endorsement falls short of suggesting that proportionality review has become an independent head of review in English law. Common law constitutional rights and rights covered by the ECHR are not entirely distinct. Their paths will generally have crossed, if only tangentially, at some moment in time. Furthermore, they are in any case referred to and relied on alongside each other, operating as alternative options in human rights adjudication. Given this close interaction between the two regimes, having two separate standards of review for the same rights protected

[181] See also *R (Youssef) v Secretary of State for Foreign and Commonwealth Affairs* [2016] UKSC 3, [2016] AC 1457 [55]–[57].

[182] *Browne v The Parole Board of England & Wales* [2018] EWCA Civ 2024 (20 September 2018, unreported).

[183] *Kennedy v Charity Commission* (n 40) [54]; P Craig, 'The Nature of Reasonableness' (2013) 66(1) *Current Legal Problems* 131. See also M Elliott, 'Common-Law Constitutionalism and Proportionality in the Supreme Court: Kennedy v The Charity Commission' (*Public Law for Everyone Blog*, 31 March 2014).

[184] *Kennedy v Charity Commission* (n 40) [54].

[185] *R v Secretary of State for the Home Department, ex p Bugdaycay* [1987] AC 514 (HL) 531.

[186] *Kennedy v Charity Commission* (n 40) [51].

[187] *R (UNISON) v Lord Chancellor* (n 7) [88]–[89].

[188] *Kennedy v Charity Commission* (n 40) [246].

by different legal sources would indeed be peculiar.[189] That said, given the fact that common law constitutional rights cannot really be described as one coherent category of legal protection, and due to the increasingly complex layers of both proportionality and of irrationality review, is cannot be said with certainty that the simple notion of proportionality review set out in the beginning of this section will indeed be applied in all cases where a constitutional right or fundamental principle of the common law forms part of the basis of a legal claim.

IX. Taking Stock

Chapters three and four have provided an in-depth analysis of the historical development and the shared characteristics of common law constitutional rights in the UK. Their findings and arguments provide the basis for this book's final chapter, which is more normative in nature. In light of the impending critical analysis, it is helpful to make one key observation. This chapter has shown that while common law constitutional rights incorporate many other public law principles and reasoning techniques, the quest to characterise them as one uniform or coherent model or concept proves, despite their likeness in nature, very challenging. As I show in the final chapter, the fragility, uncertainty and insularity that can be associated with this jurisprudential development is reflective of the wider inconsistencies and shortcomings underlying the nuanced constitution.

[189] For the opposite view, see J Goodwin, 'The Last Defence of Wednesbury' [2012] *PL* 445.

PART III

Rights under the Nuanced Constitution

5

The Shortcomings of the Nuanced Constitution: Rights Protection, Unlimited Legislative Power and the English Common Law

So far, this book has focused on portraying aspects of how constitutional law adjudication works, and what this says about the nature of our constitution. Common law constitutional rights have been a prominent feature in this analysis, as have significant public law judgments outside the sphere of common law constitutional rights. The key thesis put forward in this book is that the sum of what we find when we look at Supreme Court jurisprudence in the constitutional sphere is best described not as political constitutionalist or legal constitutionalist, but both, and that this co-existence of two opposing legal principles creates a fragile basis for the protection of constitutional rights. As Gee and Webber observe, 'Britain's constitution today embraces, perhaps in uncertain ways and to an uncertain extent, both a political model and a legal model'.[1]

I have described this combination as *nuanced*. I have argued that we can conceptualise constitutional law adjudication as a spectrum, and that judicial opinions as to the correct approach to the interpretation of legislation and to the application of constitutional concepts and principles are scattered across that spectrum. Sometimes we see divergence, in the same case and in the same judgment, and sometimes in the same case but at different judicial instances. While traditional constitutional theory suggests that there are no legal limits to Parliament's authority, judicial practice paints a more complicated and indeed convoluted picture. This stems from the fact that judges recognise and enforce substantive constitutional values – including constitutional rights – which may compromise the concept of parliamentary sovereignty in that legislative intent is either contextualised, expanded or qualified.

In this chapter, I evaluate the ramifications of the findings in chapters one to four and elaborate on the shortcomings of the nuanced constitution as far as constitutional rights protection through the common law is concerned. My critique can be prefaced by three points. The first point is that on an adjudicative level, ie in

[1] G Gee and GCN Webber, 'What is a Political Constitution?' (2010) 30(2) *OJLS 273*, 292.

judicial reasoning, there is, in many cases, no standardised understanding of how we ought to interpret public law cases where competing important legal values and principles are at play. The second point is that, on a substantive level, given the inherent strong pull towards the political constitutionalist side of the spectrum, which often operates as the lens through which a case is initially approached, the substantive constitutional values we theoretically adhere to are at constant risk of being undermined. Even if they are not undermined, they are likely to be shaped or significantly influenced by institutional rather than substantive considerations. Finally, the principled development of a comprehensive rights regime anchored in a firm foundation has been hampered by the way in which the English common law works and develops. The result is that public law adjudication, including in cases concerning constitutional rights, can be highly ambiguous, and uncertain.

I. The Uncertainties Underlying Common Law Constitutional Rights Jurisprudence: Theories, Sources and Values

Revising two of the characteristics of the nuanced constitution brought out in chapter two, our constitution is marked by significant disagreement between this jurisdiction's most senior judges as to the meaning and application of constitutional fundamentals. Judgments often entail judicial reasoning which attempts the impossible by trying to reconcile what is in essence common law constitutionalist reasoning with the orthodox Diceyan position of unlimited legislative law-making power. The result is typically logically and conceptually vulnerable judicial reasoning. The preceding chapters have shown that there is no established judicial template for combining both tenets successfully where there is a clash, both within and outside the constitutional rights context. Put differently, there is no set understanding of how much value ought to be given to common law and political constitutionalist principles and ideals. I argue that we can observe a natural tension in the case law because the two models are ultimately irreconcilable. What is the basis for this argument? First, political constitutionalism, even in its contemporary understanding, cannot accommodate reasoning that limits the elected branches' law-making ability.[2] Legal constitutionalism on the other hand is a commitment to limiting government by law, often through the protection of constitutional non-derivatives.[3] While both theories may be able to acknowledge

[2] See, eg, J Goldsworthy who in 2013 wrote that 'the constitution's most fundamental 'unwritten' doctrine … maintains that Parliament possesses sovereign law-making authority – authority that is legally (but not morally or practically) unlimited' in 'Parliamentary Sovereignty and Constitutional Change in the United Kingdom' in R Rawlings, P Layland and AL Young, *Sovereignty and the Law: Domestic, European and International Perspectives* (Oxford University Press, 2013) 50.

[3] A Sajó and R Uitz, *The Constitution of Freedom: An Introduction to Legal Constitutionalism* (Oxford University Press, 2017) 1.

and promote some form of a 'multi-layered'[4] perception of our constitutional arrangements, political constitutionalism cannot attribute to the courts a role that is not focused on the faithful enforcement of legislative intent; if it did so, its core premise would collapse. Likewise, legal constitutionalism's central tenet would be undermined if it accepted that Parliament, although constrained in some ways, remained legally unrestrained in all circumstances. Accordingly, there is bound to be tension when elements of both schools of thought are recognised to matter (something that may be done implicitly) simultaneously. Elliott describes this as

> a tension between two visions of the constitutional order. As we have seen, the first – the traditional – vision places the sovereignty of Parliament centre stage and refracts other constitutional principles, and hence the judicial role, through it. But a competing vision postulates a different dynamic: one that acknowledges fundamental constitutional principles' capacity to influence and shape one another, and that therefore gives rise to a different understanding of the judicial role – one that is informed to a greater degree by constitutional principles' potential to drive, as well as constrain, judicial intervention.[5]

The indeterminate footing of the nuanced constitution seems indefinitely torn between legal and political constitutionalism. As I argued in chapter two, the resulting lack of a principled constitutional philosophy can manifest itself in judicial attempts to rationalise substantive rule of law-based reasoning within a parliamentary sovereignty framework, which is bound to entail logical inconsistencies. Building on the observations made in chapter four, we have seen that the nuanced constitution's inherent tension, its lack of a principled approach and the resultant uncertainty impact on the judicial enforcement of common law constitutional rights. Lord Lester noted before the passing of the Human Rights Act 1998 (HRA) that

> without the benefit of a Bill of Rights or other Parliamentary code to guide them, English judges [had] the difficult task of developing coherent legal principles to protect fundamental human rights and freedoms where the common law suffers from ethical aimlessness or worse.[6]

Now that such 'guidance' is in place, the senior judiciary's engagement with the development of common law constitutional rights has intensified and, as I have argued at different points in this book, increased in authority. However, as I suggested in chapter four, the case law has not produced a uniform, properly reasoned foundation for the judicial power to *recognise* and *enforce* common law-based human rights. Moreover, the substantive values underlying the enforcement of common law constitutional rights are typically equally unestablished. By way of example, the judiciary has struggled to identify a sound justificatory basis

[4] N Bamforth and P Leyland, *Public Law in a Multi-Layered Constitution* (Hart Publishing, 2003).

[5] M Elliott, 'Judicial Power and the United Kingdom's Changing Constitution' (2017) 36(2) *University of Queensland Law Journal* 273, 275.

[6] Lord Lester, 'English Judges as Law Makers' [1993] *PL* 269, 278.

for the enforcement of non-legislative rights against the state. As I showed in chapter four, sometimes the courts invoke jurisdictional or procedural principles to legitimise the development and enforcement of common law constitutional rights. For instance, *Kennedy v Charity Commission*,[7] *R (Guardian News and Media Ltd) v City of Manchester Magistrates Court*[8] and *A v BBC*[9] all rely to some extent on the concept of inherent jurisdiction as the power that enables the courts to recognise, develop and enforce common law constitutional rights. Thus, in *A v BBC* Lord Reed said,

> Since the principle of open justice is a *constitutional principle to be found in the common law*, it follows that … the courts … *have an inherent jurisdiction to determine how the principle should be applied*.[10]

This is the sole argument justifying the judicial enforcement of constitutional rights in this particular judgment. Anything that is *part of* the English common law is for judges to determine. This reasoning is self-fulfilling and circular: a judge identifies something as part of the common law, which means that he or she is constitutionally entitled to develop it. In other words, there is a 'non-test'. No criteria are developed, and no actual justification is given which takes into account the constitutional complexities inherent, as a matter of constitutional theory, in the enforcement of non-statutory rights.

Incidentally, the reliance on the courts' inherent jurisdiction reinforces one of the facts of the nuanced constitution, namely the drawing in opposite directions on the constitutional spectrum. Thus, much like the rule of law, the concept of inherent jurisdiction can act as a vessel for the expression of a deeper political theory or substantive values, and, much like the rule of law also, its strength and reach are contested. At one end of the judicial spectrum we find the belief that the courts' inherent jurisdiction is in effect a mechanism 'to correct any injustice, however it may have arisen'.[11] There are those who suggest that the concept can be invoked on 'a regular basis and that one should *not* "conclude that the circumstances justifying its use must always be 'dire and exceptional' or 'at the very extreme end of the spectrum'"'.[12] Meanwhile, other senior judicial actors have characterised the courts' inherent jurisdiction as an anomaly in 'an age of detailed and comprehensive statutory provisions'.[13] They have also cautioned that, if the concept is not limited to exceptional circumstances, there is a high potential for it illegitimately to cut across the statutory scheme. This, then, reinforces a lesser commitment to substantive notions of justice, and a stronger allegiance to the principle of parliamentary

[7] *Kennedy v Charity Commission* [2014] UKSC 20, [2015] AC 455.

[8] *R (Guardian News and Media Ltd) v City of Westminster Magistrates' Court* [2012] EWCA Civ 420, [2013] QB 618.

[9] *A v BBC* [2014] UKSC 25, [2015] AC 588.

[10] *ibid* [27] (emphasis added).

[11] *R (Edwards) v Environment Agency* [2010] UKSC 57, [2011] 1 WLR 79 [35] (per Lord Hope).

[12] *ibid* [59] (per Lord Toulson, Lady Hale).

[13] *ibid* [81] (per Lord Sumption).

sovereignty. In other words, two of the main concepts or principles which have been identified as enablers of judicial constitutional rights protection, inherent jurisdiction and the rule of law, are themselves heavily contested.

Moving away from the enabling power to the substantive values shaping common law constitutional rights, we can see that it is not established what values judges can draw on to develop domestic rights. In the Court of Appeal's judgment in *Guardian News*, which is discussed extensively in chapter four, Toulson LJ focused on maintaining elements that he deemed fundamental to a liberal democracy. Specifically, he opined that in a democratic system public power depends on the consent of the people governed, and that there needs to be transparency of the legal process so that the guardians of the rule of law – the judiciary – can be scrutinised. While *Guardian News* can be said to be democracy-driven, we find a dignity-driven justification for the enforcement of a right in *A v Secretary of State for the Home Department.*[14] In this case, the House of Lords held that a UK court could not admit as evidence information obtained through torture overseas. The Court concluded that the common law alone, ie without regard to international law, demanded the exclusion thereof. Lord Nicholls begins his opinion by saying 'torture is not acceptable. This is a bedrock moral principle in this country. For centuries the common law has set its face against torture'.[15] Lord Hoffmann finds equally strong words when he says that 'the use of torture is dishonourable. It corrupts and degrades the state which uses it and the legal system which accepts it'.[16] It should not come as a surprise that different values underlie the two rights in question. I contrast the two to show the potential breadth of common law constitutional rights and the fact that they are not limited to a specific theme, such as rights that are quintessential to a democracy.[17] Furthermore, questions arise about the values that lie behind common law constitutional rights, including who determines, and how do we determine, what values are worthy of judicial protection.

Next, there is uncertainty around the types of sources that can shape, and indeed create, a common law constitutional right. As was shown by reference to *Scott v Scott*,[18] the mere *opinion* (in the ordinary sense of the word, not the judicial one) of one judge was sufficient to devise a constitutional right which more than a century later is held in the highest judicial esteem. Meanwhile, academic opinion has also shaped common law constitutional rights jurisprudence. Referring to the liberty

[14] *A v Secretary of State for the Home Department* [2005] UKHL 71, [2006] 2 AC 221. See also ATH Smith, 'Disavowing Torture in the House of Lords' (2006) 65(2) *CLJ* 251.

[15] *A v Secretary of State for the Home Department, ibid* [64].

[16] *ibid* [82].

[17] Note though the link Friedman has shown between the two, highlighting that the House of Lords in *A v Secretary of State for the Home Department* (n 14) was drawn by one intervening party to the concept of democracy as a reason as to why torture was unacceptable: D Friedman, 'Torture and the Common Law' (2006) 2 *European Human Rights Law Review* 180, 198–99.

[18] *Scott v Scott* [1913] AC 417 (HL).

and dignity of the individual, the House of Lords in *A v Secretary of State for the Home Department*[19] endorsed academic statements proclaiming that torture was 'repugnant to reason, justice and humanity'[20] and that the common law developed as it did due to the cruelty of the practice, the unreliability of confessions obtained through torture and the degrading of all involved in the practice. Then, we also find religious references in the case law. In *R (Osborn) v Parole Board*, Lord Reed illustrates the dignitarian point he invokes with respect to the right to be granted a hearing by invoking the Bible, saying that,

> The laws of God and man both give the party an opportunity to make his defence, if he has any. I remember to have heard it observed by a very learned man, upon such an occasion, that even God himself did not pass sentence upon Adam before he was called upon to make his defence.[21]

As I stated in the previous chapter, Lord Reed proceeds to note that the relevant reference from the eighteenth century 'has been the law from that time to the present'.[22]

Finally, there is uncertainty around what exactly makes a value legally enforceable. Here we can contrast *A v Secretary of State for the Home Department* in which Lord Bingham explicitly recognised the 'doubtful validity' of the legal sources and principles relied on in support of what was deemed a constitutional protection against torture.[23] However, this does not act as a bar to enforcing the right in question. His express recognition of this fact shows that its enforcement was warranted by moral considerations, not precedent. This can be contrasted with *R (Gallaher) v The Competition and Markets Authority*, in which the Supreme Court suggested in the context of a discussion on the grounds for judicial review that 'fairness, like equal treatment, can readily be seen as a fundamental principle of democratic society; but not necessarily one directly translatable into a justiciable rule of law ….'[24] In the context of common law constitutional rights, similar reasoning was employed in *R (Elgizouli) v Secretary of State for the Home Department*, in which the majority said that the case law merely supported 'the recognition of what might more aptly be described as a value to which the courts attach great significance when exercising their supervisory jurisdiction', not an enforceable right.[25]

[19] *A v Secretary of State for the Home Department* (n 14).

[20] *ibid* [12], citing D Jardine, *A Reading on the Use of Torture in the Criminal Law of England Previously to the Commonwealth: Delivered at New Inn Hall in Michaelmas Term* (1836) 6, 12. See Friedman (n 17), for a balanced overview of the UK's historical attitude to torture.

[21] *R (Osborn) v Parole Board* [2013] UKSC 61, [2014] AC 1115 [69], citing Byles J's citation in *Cooper v Wandsworth Board of Works* [1863] 143 ER 414 195 of a dictum of Fortescue J in *R v Cambridge University, ex p Bentley* 93 ER 698 (1724) 2 Ld Raym 1334.

[22] *R (Osborn) v Parole Board, ibid* [69].

[23] *A v Secretary of State for the Home Department* (n 14) [11].

[24] *R (Gallagher) v The Competition and Markets Authority* [2018] UKSC 25, [2019] AC 96 [31].

[25] *R (Elgizouli) v Secretary of State for the Home Department* [2020] UKSC 10, [2021] AC 937 [175] (per Lord Reed).

II. The Trump Card: Parliamentary Sovereignty and Fundamental Rights

Having looked at a range of factors inhibiting the development of coherent domestic constitutional rights jurisprudence in the previous section, in this section I focus on a major factor that may prevent the enforcement of rights which are said to be of a constitutional nature. In summary, while there is a lot of room for constitutional rights protection through value-infused interpretation under the nuanced constitution, ultimately there is an insurmountable barrier to their enforcement: express statutory wording. The latter typically trumps constitutional rights, even those of the most cherished kind.

It is part and parcel of the nuanced constitution that, given the historical development of the UK legal order, parliamentary sovereignty in many ways still provides the framework within which constitutional rights are (inadequately) protected. This is reflected in the fact that both legal scholarship and judicial analysis are often to an extent preoccupied with institutional legitimacy. The latter has framed and dominated constitutional debate, and institutional legitimacy continues to provide a barrier to the development of an effective, coherent constitutional rights system. Some leading scholarly opinions have essentially reduced the complexities of the normative considerations underlying public law adjudication to one criterion, ie parliamentary supremacy. Dicey's dominant focus on the proposition that Parliament can make and unmake any law, and that law thus promulgated cannot be questioned by any other institution has shaped the constitutional fabric of this jurisdiction significantly. It is widely accepted that it was Griffith's 1978 lecture – regarded 'as a benchmark for those who see representative and parliamentary government as important constitutional desiderata'[26] – which reinforced the Diceyan path. Warning that the law should not be a substitute for politics, Griffith argued that government by law was an unattainable idea, and that calling political claims 'rights' would see the 'waters of natural law close over our heads'.[27] His focus on the 'political' led him to say that the constitution

> is no more and no less than what happens. Everything that happens is constitutional. And if nothing happened that would be constitutional also.[28]

Kavanagh suggests that we should not read Griffith's famous statements that the constitution is 'no more and no less than what happens', and that 'everything that happens is constitutional' literally, as this would mean that it was (a) hyperbolic, (b) wrong, or (c) that there would be no constitution whatsoever.[29] She further

[26] C Harlow, 'The Political Constitution Reworked' in R Bigwood (ed), *Public Interest Litigation: New Zealand Experience in International Perspective* (LexisNexis, 2006) 190.

[27] JAG Griffith, 'The Political Constitution' (1979) 42(1) *MLR* 1, 7.

[28] *ibid* 19.

[29] A Kavanagh, 'Recasting the Political Constitution' (2019) 30(1) *King's Law Journal* 43, 49.

argues that it would be dangerous to take Griffith's statement at face value as it implies that government is able to do anything, without being subject to constitutional restraints. However, taken to its full conclusion, if one reads 'constitutional' as 'legal values that are able to contradict Parliament', this is what the political constitution represents, namely that there are no antecedent rights in the strict sense of the word, nor are there higher enforceable values. Only elected representatives can determine which values a democracy ought to embody and uphold. The logical consequence of these beliefs is that there should be 'no legal limit to the wishes of the people',[30] which is reflective of Griffith's remarks.[31]

As this book shows, there are many principles which, as a matter of legal practice, inform public law adjudication. However, as a matter of constitutional theory, those norms and principles may not amount to anything meaningful if this would go against express parliamentary intention. While political constitutionalism may recognise that there are constraints on legislative power in the loose sense, it also demands that those constraints will give way to political will as expressed through legislation. As Kavanagh says, Griffith himself thought for example that 'Parliament's law-making power is subject to *political* rather than legal limits'.[32]

Returning to the nuanced constitution, as I have suggested throughout this book, we can conceptualise the nuanced constitution as a spectrum. We can picture parliamentary sovereignty on the left end of the spectrum, and legal constitutionalism on the right (or vice versa).[33] Cases migrate between these two principled positions; in some cases, elements of the political constitution will be more prominent,[34] in others aspects of the legal constitution will dominate.[35] Conceptual difficulties arise not only because the two tenets are irreconcilable, but also because the framing of the spectrum is explicitly political constitutionalist in nature, whereas the substantive reasoning in any given case may in fact detract from it. If a right is characterised as fundamental or constitutional, the powerful

[30] KD Ewing, 'The Resilience of the Political Constitution' (2013) 14(12) *German Law Journal* 2111, 2118.

[31] Note that he argued that primary legislation is not subject to any legal limits elsewhere too, see, eg, JAG Griffith, M Ryle and MAJ Wheeler-Booth, *Parliament: Functions, Practice and Procedures* (Sweet & Maxwell, 1989) 244–45.

[32] Kavanagh (n 29) 49 (emphasis added).

[33] For a discussion on whether the political constitution should be considered as being loosely associated with the political right, see G Gee, 'The Political Constitution and the Political Right' (2019) 30 *King's Law Journal* 148.

[34] See, eg, *R (Lord Carlile of Berriew QC and others) v Secretary of State for the Home Department* [2014] UKSC 60, [2015] AC 945, but note Lord Kerr's dissenting opinion.

[35] See, eg, *R (Joint Council for the Welfare of Immigrants) v Secretary of State for the Home Department* [2019] EWHC 452 (Admin), [2019] 4 All ER 527 in which the High Court, after noting that we 'live in a fair, free and democratic society founded upon the rule of law' found that sections 20–37 of the Immigration Act 2014 (part of the Government's 'hostile environment' policy) are racially discriminatory and accordingly incompatible with articles 8 and 14 of the European Convention on Human Rights. R Ekins has branded this judgment a 'travesty': 'The High Court's Right to Rent Decision is a Travesty' (*The Spectator Blog*, 2 March 2019). The judgment was subsequently overturned on appeal: [2020] EWCA Civ 542, [2021] 1 WLR 1151.

interpretative tool of the principle of legality is triggered,[36] pulling a case closer to the legal constitutionalist end of the spectrum. However, the right in question becomes negligible if Parliament expressly permits its abrogation or the statutory scheme dictates that the right ought to be abrogated.

The principle of legality has many virtues that strengthen UK public law adjudication. In theory, it prevents politicians from abrogating rights they may have committed themselves to publicly without taking responsibility for the abrogation. Any politician or government attempting to limit rights must do so expressly and 'accept the political cost'.[37] This, it is said, reinforces accountability. Yet, we must recognise that while the principle of legality facilitates a structured engagement with legal arguments, and while it invites the protection of constitutional rights and other fundamental principles on the one hand, at the same time it also reinforces parliamentary sovereignty. As I argued in chapter four, while we may have moved on from regarding free speech and open justice as mere residual liberties, we should recognise that this does not mean common law constitutional rights are in any way 'guaranteed'. They remain, to some extent, conditional upon non-interference. What has changed – and this is indeed a significant change – is that the test has become stricter. Common law constitutional rights have become more resilient as part of an overall constitutionalisation process which aims to keep political power in check and contextualises and adds to legislative sources of law. However, the point is that ultimately there is a barrier in place. What on the face of it looks like a strong commitment to constitutional rights, ie 'one can only interfere with constitutional rights on the basis of express legal authority', is in fact a manifestation of the vulnerability of common law constitutional rights.[38]

This allows us to put Lord Reed's seemingly powerful judgment in *R (UNISON) v Lord Chancellor* into perspective.[39] Taking a similarly probing approach to the evidence presented to him by the Government as Lord Neuberger took in *R (Evans) v Her Majesty's Attorney General*,[40] Lord Reed relied partially on 'elementary economics', scrutinising a range of different sources, including tribunal statistics and hypothetical scenarios to reject the claim put forward by the Government that the tribunal fees would not have the effect of preventing access to the courts. However, one must recognise that 'Lord Reed's detailed marshalling

[36] For a formidable overview of the development of the principle of legality in various common law jurisdictions, see B Lim, 'The Normativity of the Principle of Legality' (2013) 37(2) *Melbourne University Law Review* 372.

[37] *R v Secretary of State for the Home Department, ex p Simms* [2000] 2 AC 115 (HL) 131E, [1999] 3 WLR 328.

[38] The same vulnerability is inherent in other legal principles facilitating the enforcement of common law constitutional rights. For example, the scope of the inherent jurisdiction of the senior courts is infinite, unless Parliament has expressly curtailed it, see *Re E (SA) (A Minor) (Wardship)* [1984] 1 WLR 156, [1984] 1 All ER 289.

[39] *R (UNISON) v Lord Chancellor* [2017] UKSC 51, [2017] 3 WLR 409.

[40] *R (Evans) v Her Majesty's Attorney General* [2015] UKSC 21, [2015] AC 1787.

of evidence, which grounds the Supreme Court's unanimous ruling against the Lord Chancellor,'[41] happened in a context where there was no primary statutory language to the contrary. Thus, had Parliament authorised the introduction of employment tribunal fees more explicitly, including an acknowledgment of the detrimental impact on the constitutional right of access to justice, there is little doubt Lord Reed would have considered himself bound to enforce the statutory infringement of the right of access to justice.

Thus, as Elliott astutely observes,

> the legal violability of common-law constitutional rights may, at least in some circumstances, obscure their political inviolability – or at least overstate the extent to which they are in practice vulnerable to legislative disturbance. In this way, the doctrine of common-law constitutional rights may serve to erode the distinction between political and legal forms of constitutional constraint by erecting a legal barrier to interference with rights – in the form of an explicitness requirement – that is politically, albeit not legally, insuperable.[42]

Legally, Parliament retains unlimited power to develop the law (substance) provided it expresses itself in the appropriate way (form). In cases where statutory language is ambiguous, judges sometimes attempt to 'pull off the trick of being positive law servants and natural law masters at one and the same time'.[43] In those cases, the legal constitutionalism end of the spectrum navigated by the principle of legality comes to the fore. This is one of the reasons that we can argue that parliamentary sovereignty has been qualified; one can regularly observe that the reliance on normative principles facilitates a departure from legislative intent. However, in cases where Parliament has given express authorisation for the executive to abrogate rights, the courts generally consider themselves as having no option but to accept Parliament's will.

III. The English Common Law: Simultaneous Facilitator and Impediment

A third factor contributing to the unprincipled development of common law constitutional rights is the English common law. Despite the common law's positive contribution to the development of constitutional rights and other fundamental constitutional principles, it has not 'placed substantive limitations on the legislative capacity of Parliament through the subjection of legal sovereignty to

[41] R Rawlings, 'The UNISON Case: A New High-Water Mark' (2018) 29 *Public Law Review* 190, 190.

[42] M Elliott, 'Legislative Supremacy in a Multidimensional Constitution' in M Elliott and D Feldman (eds), *The Cambridge Companion to Public Law* (Cambridge University Press, 2015) 78–79.

[43] C Gearty, *Principles of Human Rights Adjudication* (Oxford University Press, 2005) 25.

superior immutable values'.[44] Under the nuanced constitution, there are, subject to a handful of obiter dicta in some cases,[45] no immutable or minimum values.

Second, outside any discussion about institutional legitimacy, the common law is not a suitable 'spirit of the whole system of valid rules'[46] for this would ascribe to the latter inherent qualities that are simply not borne out in practice. First, the development of a principled constitutional rights framework is hampered by the common law's strong affiliation with the past. Encapsulated in the relatively recent doctrine of stare decisis,[47] we can say that a key ingredient of common law reasoning is 'tradition', as opposed to principle. As Blackstone put it, one of the basic underlying notions is that to show that something is a rule of the common law is to show that 'it hath been always the custom to observe it'.[48]

Tradition continues to play a vital role in common law adjudication today. We may not quite trace the law back to 'the Year Books, and perhaps beyond them to the customs of the Salian Franks' to 'find out the practical motive for what now best is justified by the mere fact of its acceptance and that men are accustomed to it'.[49] While the 'English common law to this day treats the coronation of Richard I as the date distinguishing time beyond from time within legal memory',[50] in practice judgments rarely go that far back.[51] Also, new ideas can be integrated into the legal system. However, the adherence to 'judicial custom' through the concept of precedent means that the common law is not 'a structured set of authoritatively posited, explicit directives, but of rules and ways implicit in a body of practices and patterns of practical thinking "handed down by tradition, use, [and] experience"'.[52] Combined with the English common law's traditional affinity for procedure,[53] remedies and questions of jurisdiction,[54] the preoccupation with 'tradition' is one factor that stifles the development of a principled, clearly reasoned constitutional rights framework.

[44] M Gordon, 'The Conceptual Foundations of Parliamentary Sovereignty: Reconsidering Jennings and Wade' [2009] *PL* 519, 521–22, referencing T Poole, 'Back to the Future? Unearthing the Theory of Common Law Constitutionalism' (2003) 23(3) *OJLS* 435, 453.

[45] See *Moohan v Lord Advocate (Advocate General for Scotland intervening)* [2014] UKSC 67, [2015] AC 901 [25] (per Lord Hodge); see also *Shindler and another v Chancellor of the Duchy of Lancaster and another* [2016] EWCA Civ 469, [2017] QB 226 [48]–[49].

[46] As implied by Allan when discussing the works of Hayek in TRS Allan, *The Sovereignty of Law: Freedom, Constitution, and Common Law* (Oxford University Press, 2013) 99.

[47] The system of precedent, under which like cases are supposed to be treated alike, is comparatively young, only cementing itself in the 19th century, see N Duxbury, *The Nature and Authority of Precedent* (Cambridge University Press, 2008) 53–57.

[48] W Blackstone, *Commentaries on the Laws of England* (Clarendon Press, 1765–69) i.17.

[49] O Wendell Holmes, 'The Path of the Law' (1897) 10 *Harvard Law Review* 457, 458.

[50] N Duxbury, 'Custom as law in English law' (2017) 76(2) *CLJ* 337, 348.

[51] But see, eg, *R v Jogee* [2016] UKSC 8, [2017] AC 387 in which the Supreme Court looked at over 500 years of case law and determined that the House of Lords had taken a wrong turn in *Chan Wing-Siu v The Queen* [1985] 1 AC 168 (UKPC).

[52] Blackstone (n 48) vol 1, 68.

[53] M Lobban, *The Common Law and English Jurisprudence, 1760–1850* (Clarendon Press, 1991) 16.

[54] HP Glenn, *On Common Laws* (Oxford University Press, 2007).

The 1868 decision in *Chorlton v Lings* is instructive.[55] The claimant, Mary Abbott, sought to challenge the contention that the Representation of the People Act 1867 excluded women from voting in parliamentary elections. Counsel had argued that women had 'a right to the franchise at common law, that nothing had taken it away from them, and that they were therefore not incapacitated from voting' which should mean that 'women are now entitled to the franchise as a common-law right'.[56] Saying that their decision had nothing to do with any 'underrating of the sex either in point of intellect or worth' (which would be 'quite inconsistent with one of the glories of our civilisation, – the respect and honour in which women are held'),[57] the Bench noted that the main obstacle to enforcing the right for women to vote was that over the past centuries not one single example could be found of (a) the assertion of such a right or (b) the exercise of such a right. This was taken as a strong presumption against its legal existence.

Of course, as *R (Elgizouli) v Secretary of State for the Home Department*[58] expressly states, it *is* possible that new rights develop incrementally. The way in which privacy law developed in this jurisdiction and the way in which tort law has been infused with rights thinking is an example of the way in which the common law has evolved under the influence of the HRA. Whereas in *Wainwright*[59] the House of Lords found that there was no general tort of 'invasion of privacy', there is now a central cause of action, known as 'misuse of private information',[60] which was developed out of the law on breach of confidence, starting with the case of *Campbell v Mirror Group Newspapers Ltd*.[61] However, developments such as these do not take away from the verdict that if we look beneath the surface, the characteristics even of the current phase of common law constitutional rights, including *UNISON*, raise doubts as to the ultimate strength and stability of the common law to uphold constitutional fundamentals. Indeed, the true picture emerging of constitutional jurisprudence is one in which both the capabilities and the record of accomplishment of the English common law are often exaggerated. The celebrated decision in *Somerset v Stewart*,[62] which I referred to in more detail in chapter two, is a key example of this phenomenon.

Moreover, the English common law is not naturally prone to providing the theoretical foundation to the effective enforcement of constitutional norms, as

[55] *Chorlton v Lings* (1868–69) LR 4 CP 374 (Court of Common Pleas).

[56] *ibid* 383.

[57] *ibid* 388 (per Willes J).

[58] *R (Elgizouli) v Secretary of State for the Home Department* (n 25).

[59] *Wainwright v Home Office* [2003] UKHL 53, [2004] 2 AC 406.

[60] *Vidal-Hall v Google Inc* [2015] EWCA Civ 311, [2016] QB 1003. Subsequently, the Supreme Court refused Google permission to appeal against this aspect of the Court of Appeal's decision.

[61] *Campbell v Mirror Group Newspapers Ltd* [2004] UKHL 22, [2004] 2 AC 457. A more recent examination of the law on privacy occurred in the Supreme Court's decision in *PJS v News Group Newspapers Ltd* [2016] UKSC 26, [2016] AC 1081 where it was said that the misuse of private information could now be taken to cover both unwanted access to private information and unwanted intrusion into an individual's privacy.

[62] *Somerset v Stewart* (1772) Lofft 1, 98 ER 499.

is claimed by Allan. For example, it was the judiciary which made itself bound by their own precedents; it took a Practice Statement in 1966 to free the Law Lords from themselves. Further, as Lord Lester has pointed out, the adoption of literal rules of interpretation was self-imposed.[63] A much more accurate description – compared to Allan's – recognises the traditional conservatism and stagnation of the common law. For instance, it took the courts over 250 years to outlaw marital rape. Allan's overestimation of the virtue and strength of the common law is mirrored by his claim that there is a 'very substantial overlap' between the European Convention on Human Rights (ECHR) and the rights protected by the English common law,[64] a claim which has often been repeated by the judiciary. Elliott provides a more accurate comparison when he suggests that,

> The differences between the regimes are such that one cannot simply stand in for the other. The normative reach of the common law traditionally was – and probably still is – more modest than that of the Convention. The rigour of the protective techniques available under the Act has not always been imitated at common law. And Convention rights … have a degree of constitutional resilience that their common-law counterparts do not … enjoy. The courts' protective commitment to … rights lying at or near the common law's normative core may confer upon those rights a degree of legal security approximating to that which is associated with Convention rights under the HRA; but the same cannot plausibly claimed of the whole range of rights (and values) acknowledged at common law.[65]

In fact, saying, as I do too, that the English common law does not offer a similar level of constitutional or human rights protection is reflective of academic consensus.[66]

IV. Where We are at: A Snapshot of the Constitutional Rights Recognised under the Nuanced Constitution

I have argued that there are various characteristics of the nuanced constitution that have led to an underdeveloped constitutional rights framework. What follows is an overview of some of the common law constitutional rights that have been recognised in said framework. Taking a closer look at these reinforces the concerns raised.

[63] Lord Lester, 'Judges and Ministers' (1996) 18(8) *London Review of Books* 10.

[64] Allan (n 46) 38.

[65] M Elliott, 'Beyond the European Convention: Human Rights and the Common Law' (2015) 68(1) *Current Legal Problems* 85, 115–16.

[66] M Elliott and K Hughes (eds), *Common Law Constitutional Rights* (Hart Publishing, 2020).

True to its nature, 'the common law does not recognize a catalogue of human rights, or of constitutional rights, as such'.[67] Indeed, as I have emphasised in this book, it would be a mistake to treat common law constitutional rights as one unified, inherently homogenous concept.[68] That being said, the courts have acknowledged and, *to different degrees and in different shapes*, protected what we can refer to and understand as common law constitutional rights in the broad sense. These can be captured in the following non-exhaustive list:

- the right of access to the court;[69]
- the right to property;[70]
- the right to privacy;[71]
- the right to self-determination;[72]
- the right to legal professional privilege;[73]
- the right to open justice;[74]
- the right to free speech/freedom of expression;[75]
- the right to a fair hearing before an unbiased court or tribunal;[76]
- the right to a fair trial/procedural fairness;[77]
- the right to procedural fairness;[78]

[67] B Dickson, *Human Rights and the United Kingdom Supreme Court* (Oxford University Press, 2013) 33.

[68] On this see also Elliot and Hughes (n 66) 7.

[69] *R (UNISON) v Lord Chancellor* (n 39); *R (Gujra) v Crown Prosecution Service* [2012] UKSC 52, [2013] 1 AC 484 [59]; *Raymond v Honey* [1983] 1 AC 1 (HL); *Chester v Bateson* [1920] 1 KB 829 (KB); *Bremer Vulkan Schiffsbau und Maschinenfabrik v South India Shipping Corpn Ltd* [1981] AC 909 (HL); *R v Lord Chancellor, ex p Witham* [1998] QB 575 (QB).

[70] *Chesterfield Propertie de Walden Estates s Plc v Secretary of State for the Environment* (1998) 76 P&CR 117, [1998] JPL 568; *Attorney-General v Blake* [2001] 1 AC 268 (HL), [2000] 3 WLR 625.

[71] *Douglas v Hello! Ltd (No 6)* [2005] EWCA Civ 595, [2006] QB 125. See also the right to privacy of the home: *Morris v Beardmore* [1981] AC 446 (HL); *PJS v News Group Newspapers Ltd* [2016] UKSC 26, [2016] AC 1081.

[72] *Montgomery v Lanarkshire Health Board* [2015] UKSC 11, [2015] AC 1430; *R v Secretary of State for the Home Department, ex p Robb* [1995] Fam 127 (Fam).

[73] *R (Prudential Plc) v Special Commissioner of Income Tax* [2013] UKSC 1, [2013] 2 AC 185.

[74] *W (Algeria) v Secretary of State for the Home Department* [2012] UKSC 8, [2012] 2 AC 115; *R (C) v Secretary of State for Justice* [2016] UKSC 2, [2016] 1 WLR 444; *R (Guardian News and Media Ltd) v City of Westminster Magistrates' Court* (n 8); *Kennedy v Charity Commission* (n 7); *A v BBC* (n 9).

[75] *R v Shayler* [2002] UKHL 11, [2003] 1 AC 247; *Rushbridger v Attorney-General* [2003] UKHL 38, [2004] 1 AC 357; *Derbyshire CC v Times Newspaper Ltd* [1993] AC 534 (HL). For an example of a constitutional rights case with horizontal dimensions, see *Rhodes v OPO* [2015] UKSC 32, [2016] AC 219.

[76] *Al Rawi v Security Service* [2011] UKSC 34, [2012] 1 AC 531; *R (Sky Broadcasting Ltd) v Central Criminal Court* [2011] EWHC 3451 (Admin), [2011] EWHC 3451; *A v Her Majesty's Treasury* [2008] EWHC 869 (Admin), [2008] 3 All ER 361; *R v Gough* [1993] AC 646 (HL).

[77] *Al Rawi v Security Service, ibid*; *Jude v Her Majesty's Advocate* [2011] UKSC 55, 2012 SLT 75.

[78] *R (Barclay and another) v Secretary of State for Justice and the Lord Chancellor and others* [2014] UKSC 54, [2015] AC 276; *R (Bourgass and another) v Secretary of State for Justice* [2015] UKSC 54, [2016] AC 384; *R (Osborn) v Parole Board* (n 21).

- the right of a British citizen to come to and remain within the jurisdiction;[79]
- the right against arbitrary detention/ right to liberty;[80]
- the right not to be tortured;[81]
- the privilege against self-incrimination;[82]
- the right to non-discrimination;[83]
- the right to life;[84] and
- the right to vote.[85]

This selection appears to show that there is a wide range of rights touching upon various aspects of an individual's interests. This would suggest it is inaccurate to say that common law constitutional rights are predominantly about political participation[86] or that they are exclusively process rights. That said, it is apparent, from this list as well as the case law, that process rights are particularly well protected. Indeed, rights cases such as *R (Osborn) v Parole Board*[87] and *R (UNISON) v Lord Chancellor*[88] have set remarkable precedents for the respective rights they protect: the right of access to the courts and the right to procedural fairness. Both have had significant implications at the policy level,[89] and it will take skilled parliamentary draftsmen to devise a statutory formula that could successfully limit either of these rights. Process rights have historically enjoyed wide judicial acceptance, and the ability of the courts to resort to prominent authorities bolsters the authority of these rights. This reinforces the importance of historical adherence to a right, which I alluded to above.

Indeed, the importance of historical recognition is once again centre-stage if we contrast the right of procedural fairness and the right of access to justice

[79] *R (Halligen) v Secretary of State for the Home Department* [2012] UKSC 20, [2012] 1 WLR 1604 [31]; *In the matter of D (A Child)* [2017] EWCA Civ 1695, [2018] PTSR 1791.

[80] *In Re S-C (Mental patient: habeas corpus)* [1996] QB 599 (CA) 603; *R v SSHD* [2007] EWCA Civ 1363 (22 November 2007, unreported); *R (Kambadzi) v Secretary of State for the Home Department* [2011] UKSC 23, [2011] 1 WLR 1299; *R (Mighty) v Secretary of State for the Home Department* [2011] UKSC 12, [2012] 1 AC 245; *B v Secretary of State for Justice* [2011] EWCA Civ 1608, [2012] 1 WLR 2043; *R (Conway) v Secretary of State for Justice* [2018] EWCA Civ 1431, [2020] QB 1.

[81] *A v Secretary of State for the Home Department* (n 14) [11]–[12]; *R (Mohamed) v Secretary of State for Foreign and Commonwealth Affairs (No 1)* [2008] EWHC 2048 (Admin), [2009] 1 WLR 2579; *R (Youssef) v Secretary of State for Foreign and Commonwealth Affairs* [2016] UKSC 3, [2016] AC 1457.

[82] *Beghal v DPP* [2015] UKSC 49, [2016] AC 88.

[83] Older authorities include *Kruse v Johnson* [1898] 2 QB 91 (QB).

[84] *R (Amin) v Secretary of State for the Home Department* [2003] UKHL 51, [2004] 1 AC 653.

[85] *Moohan v Lord Advocate* (n 45), *Watkins v Secretary of State for the Home Department* [2006] UKHL 17, [2006] 2 AC 395.

[86] As suggested in KD Ewing and C Gearty, *The Struggle for Civil Liberties: Political Freedom and the Rule of Law in Britain, 1914–1945* (Oxford University Press, 2000).

[87] *R (Osborn) v Parole Board* (n 21).

[88] *R (UNISON) v Lord Chancellor* (n 39).

[89] See, eg, Parole Board for England and Wales 'Annual Report and Accounts 2016/17', 24, which states that 'there has been a dramatic move away from paper-based panels to oral hearings over the last decade; and this accelerated following the Osborn judgment'.

with, for instance, the more 'modern' right to non-discrimination and the right to equality, or equal treatment, a right that is firmly established (but with sometimes highly dubious application) in both the European and the international context. Domestically, however, the development of anti-discrimination law and the right to equality in the employment context was for a long time stifled 'in part by concerns that discrimination law posed a risk to individual autonomy, and in particular to the extensive freedom historically enjoyed by employers and service providers under the common law to conduct their business as they see fit'.[90] According to O'Cinneide, one of the 'drag factors' contributing to the slow development of domestic anti-discrimination law was that 'non-discrimination was not acknowledged to be a core common law value' fuelling 'an underlying perception that discrimination law represented a useful but alien transplant into the stable ecosystem of UK law, whose growth had to be contained and limited'.[91]

Arguably, things have, to some degree, progressed. The common law has moved on from Lord Denning's opinion that differential treatment of men and women in the workplace 'is not discrimination' but rather a manifestation of 'the courtesy and chivalry which we have been taught to believe is right conduct in our society'.[92] However, 'the exact status, scope and substance' of the common law principle of equality still remains unclear.[93] This is, for example, reflected in the review mechanism employed to protect it. Thus, as O'Cinneide explains further, 'while other foundational rights and principles such as access to justice are treated as free-standing common law norms',[94] equality is kept confined to irrationality review. No doubt, the development of equality rights today is further hampered by the fact that there is a relatively comprehensive statutory system in place which individuals can, in principle, rely on both in the context of their private dealings, and in the context of public law. Thus, the Equality Act 2010 provides a degree of legal protection against direct, indirect and other forms of discrimination and lack of equal opportunity. Whilst this is in principle a positive development, the point for the purposes of our discussion is that for as long as the Equality Act remains in place, it is highly unlikely that the court will develop any significant complementary common law protections. In turn, should the Equality Act be abolished or replaced by a system with a lower level of statutory protection, the common law will be unable to fill the gap, or to replace any substantive values lost altogether.

In short, rights with a stronger claim to domestic roots, are typically better protected compared to more 'contemporary' rights. Indeed, there is an inherent

[90] C O'Cinneide, 'Values, Rights and Brexit – Lessons to be Learnt from the Slow Evolution of United Kingdom Discrimination Law' (2017) 30 *Australian Journal of Labour Law* 1, 5. Note that O'Cinneide says such reserved attitudes were not confined to the judiciary.

[91] *ibid* 6.

[92] *Peake v Automotive Products Ltd* [1978] QB 233 (CA) 238.

[93] O'Cinneide (n 90) 8 citing Scott Baker J's opinion *in Association of British Civilian Internees Far East Region v Secretary of State for Defence* [2002] EWHC 2119 (Admin), [2002] CLY 46 [53]–[54].

[94] C O'Cinneide, 'A Core Common Law Principle, or "Mere" Rationality?' in Elliott and Hughes (n 66) 190.

bias in the common law, subject to exceptions,[95] to historical continuity.[96] This in turn prejudices the development of fully-fledged common law constitutional rights of the more 'modern' kind, some of which, such as equality, are arguably indispensable in a liberal democracy.

Going back to the list, some rights that are commonly protected in international treaties or domestic constitutions are noticeably absent. For instance, I have been unable to detect any authorities suggesting that the common law recognises a right to freedom of religion and/or conscience.[97] Additionally, the scope of many of these rights and indeed the actual practical legal force beyond their high level recognition is unclear. For example, in *R (Amin) v Secretary of State for the Home Department* the House of Lords stated that 'a profound respect for the sanctity of human life underpins the common law'.[98] However, in *R (BA) v Secretary of State for Health*[99] the Administrative Court held that the common law right to life did not include a right to receive medical treatment. As Mavronicola concludes after a thorough investigation of the common law's guarantee to bodily integrity, in which she comments on a gap between 'mythology and reality',

> Today, while the right to life has been given the label of common law constitutional right by some, it is unclear to what extent this rhetoric is reflected in judicial practice, what content we can convincingly ascribe to this right, and what its demands are in particular situations.[100]

R (Elgizouli) v Secretary of State for the Home Department strongly reinforces this point. As as Lord Carnwath states in this judgment,

> the death penalty as such has never attracted the attention of the common law. It is notable that the developments of the law have come relatively recently, from Parliament or the European Court of Human Rights, rather than the domestic courts. It was not until 1965 that the death penalty was abolished for murder (Murder (Abolition of Death Penalty) Act 1965); abolition of the penalty for the remaining offences had to wait until the Crime and Disorder Act 1998.[101]

In fact, it is Lord Reed's judgment in *Elgizouli* which, on the basis of the right to life, makes an important observation about lists of rights, including in leading

[95] See P Giliker, 'A Common Law Tort of Privacy? The Challenges of Developing a Human Rights Tort' (2015) 27 *Singapore Academy of Law Journal* 761 which analyses the developments following *Wainwright v Home Office* (n 59) and *Campbell v Mirror Group Newspapers Ltd* (n 61).

[96] Elliot and Hughes (n 66) use the phrase 'an elite subset of common law rights', 16.

[97] See, eg, *Lee v Ashers Baking Co Ltd and others* [2018] UKSC 49, [2018] 3 WLR 1294, which reviewed the case law in this area extensively. See also K Monaghan, 'Religious Freedom and Equal Treatment: A United Kingdom Perspective' (2014) 22(2) *Journal of Law and Policy* 673.

[98] *R (Amin) v Secretary of State for the Home Department* (n 84) [30].

[99] *R (BA) v Secretary of State for Health* [2017] EWHC 2815 (Admin), [2018] 4 WLR 2.

[100] N Mavronicola, 'The Mythology and the Reality of Common Law Constitutional Rights to Bodily Integrity' in Elliott and Hughes (n 66) 31.

[101] *R (Elgizouli) v Secretary of State for the Home Department* (n 25) [194]. Other rights which have expressly been said not to exist include the right to assisted suicide, see *Conway* (n 80) [181].

practitioners' books, suggesting that there is a difference between a value inherent in the common law and a right:

> In that regard, it is relevant to consider the idea of a right to life, which is included among the common law constitutional rights listed in De Smith's Judicial Review, 8th ed (2018), para 11–054, and has been discussed in a number of authorities. Those authorities do not vouch the existence of a right in the sense in which that term is used in the law of obligations, and the idea that there might be a right of that character is absent from leading cases concerned with questions of life and death, such as *Airedale NHS Trust v Bland* [1993] AC 789, *R v Cambridge Health Authority, Ex p B* [1995] 1 WLR 898, *In re A (Children) (Conjoined Twins: Surgical Separation)* [2001] Fam 147 and *R (Nicklinson) v Ministry of Justice (CNK Alliance Ltd intervening)* [2015] AC 657. Nevertheless, the authorities support the recognition of what might more aptly be described as a value to which the courts attach great significance when exercising their supervisory jurisdiction.[102]

Likewise, *Elgizouli* makes it clear that the right not to be subjected to torture is in fact much more limited in scope and application than the terminology suggests. In reality, this right amounts to no more than the guarantee that evidence obtained by torture will not be admissible in court proceedings.[103] Again per Lord Carnwath,

> So far as concerns Lord Carswell's comments in the A case, he was speaking in the context of an issue as to the admissibility of evidence obtained by torture, against a background in which 'from its very earliest days the common law of England set its face firmly against the use of torture' (per Lord Bingham of Cornhill at para 11, citing authorities dating from the 15th century). As Lord Carswell acknowledged, other members of the House had accepted the view that the common law 'as it stands' would forbid the reception in evidence of any statement obtained by the use of torture.[104]

Yet other rights exist only in a very basic form, and thus would feature on this list, but in practice their content is too restricted or underdeveloped in the face of statutory occupation of the field to grant the relief sought by the individual in a particular case. To illustrate this phenomenon, the UK Supreme Court judgment in *Moohan v Lord Advocate*[105] is instructive. The case concerned applications for judicial review of the Scottish Independence Referendum Act 2013, a Scottish Act of Parliament. The appellants, two convicted criminals in detention, sought to establish their right to vote in the Scottish Independence Referendum in September 2014. Counsel for the appellants had sought to establish that the blanket disenfranchisement of convicted prisoners in relation to the independence referendum was ultra vires based on alternative submissions including A3P1 of the ECHR, EU Law, the International Covenant on Civil and Political Rights, and, crucially, 'the basic democratic principles of the common law constitution,

[102] *R (Elgizouli) v Secretary of State for the Home Department, ibid* [175].
[103] On this point see also Mavronicola (n 100) 32.
[104] *R (Elgizouli) v Secretary of State for the Home Department* (n 25) [193].
[105] *Moohan v Lord Advocate* (n 45).

namely the principle of universal suffrage and the concomitant fundamental right to vote'.[106] Whilst Lord Hodge had no difficulty in recognising the right to vote as a basic or constitutional right, referring to the decision in *Watkins v Secretary of State for the Home Department*,[107] he did not think that 'the common law has been developed so as to recognise a right of universal and equal suffrage from which any derogation must be provided for by law and must be proportionate'.[108] Meanwhile, Lady Hale pointed out that 'it makes no more sense to say that sentenced prisoners have a common law right to vote than it makes to say that women have a common law right to vote, which is clearly absurd'.[109]

Additionally, looking at the wider constitutional context facilitating the recognition and enforcement of common law constitutional rights, some examples from the above list show that rights may, in any event, be abrogated under the wider limb of the principle of legality. I have already discussed aspects of the Supreme Court's decision in *Beghal v DPP*[110] in chapter four, noting that the case is a prime example of institutional legitimacy concerns taking precedence over the substantive development of rights. To reiterate, the Court emphasised that Parliament could abrogate the privilege against self-incrimination expressly or *by implication*, and the case shows how low the threshold that might trigger the weaker component of the principle of legality can be. *Beghal* is no exception. The privilege had previously been increasingly subjected to implied abrogation 'since otherwise the obvious purpose of the statute would be stultified'.[111]

Cumulatively, these cases suggest that while some judgments contain an explicit recognition that the common law protects some basic human rights,[112] and while the above compilation of rights may at first glance strike us as inspiring, we must not forget that being able to identify these rights does not amount to an effective constitutional rights system. Common law constitutional rights have developed in a haphazard way, only certain groups of rights are relatively well established, they remain in most cases firmly in the shadow of the ECHR and, in any case, all of them are vulnerable to express statutory language.

What can we take away from this section? I suggest that one of the key points is that while the common law is indeed evolving, in practice, the well-known statement by Matthews J in *Hurtado v California* that it is 'the characteristic principle of the common law to draw its inspiration from every fountain of justice' and that 'we are not to assume that the sources of its supply have been exhausted [but that] On the contrary, we should expect that the new and various experiences of our own

[106] *ibid* [5].
[107] *ibid* [33], referring to *Watkins v Secretary of State for the Home Department* (n 85).
[108] *ibid* [34].
[109] *ibid* [56].
[110] *Beghal v DPP* (n 82).
[111] *Bishopsgate Investment Management Ltd v Maxwell* [1993] Ch 1 (CA) [17].
[112] *Montgomery v Lanarkshire Health Board* [2015] UKSC 11, [2015] AC 1430 [43] (per Lord Kerr and Lord Reed); see also [80].

situation and system will mould and shape it into new and not less useful forms',[113] does not normally 'create' new rights in practice. Once we take a step back from the powerful rhetoric, we can see that the potential for new common law rights or new dimensions of existing common law rights to be judicially recognised is relatively limited. We also established that the rights that *are* recognised, in judgments or the leading practitioner's book, may indeed be more limited (on this point see also Hughes' sobering analysis of the 'right to privacy')[114] and more constitutionally vulnerable than might appear from their designation. What this leaves us with is the impression that we talk the talk but, on closer analysis, evidently do not (or cannot) walk the walk.

V. The Constitutional Legacy of *UNISON* and *Privacy International*

The UK constitution has been characterised as being 'in the process of being legalized, such that law increasingly encroaches upon, and perhaps diminishes, legislative authority'.[115] The seminal decisions in *R (UNISON) v Lord Chancellor*[116] and *R (Privacy International) v Investigatory Powers Tribunal*[117] offer convincing support for this contention. However, as I showed in chapter two, they have not changed the nature of the UK constitution to the extent that it should now be referred to as a legal or common law constitution. It remains a constitution that is nuanced in nature, and that continues to be strongly influenced by political constitutionalist thinking. Not even the strong obiter dicta in *UNISON* and *Privacy International* change this analysis. In this section, I argue that the same can be said for constitutional rights protection. Neither of the two cases advanced the jurisprudence in a transformative way.

To begin, it is certainly the case that one cannot stress enough how vital Lord Reed's judgment in *UNISON* was as a general reminder of the constitutional role of the courts,[118] the impact it will have on individuals seeking legal redress for employment related disputes,[119] and how much of a milestone the judgment is for common law constitutional rights jurisprudence. Indeed, as I have written

[113] *Hurtado v California* (1884) 110 US 516, 531.
[114] K Hughes, 'A Common Law Constitutional Right to Privacy – Waiting for Godot?' in Elliott and Hughes (n 66).
[115] Elliott (n 42) 75.
[116] *R (UNISON) v Lord Chancellor* (n 39).
[117] *R (Privacy International) v Investigatory Powers Tribunal* [2019] UKSC 22, [2019] 2 WLR 1219.
[118] M Elliott, 'The Rule of Law and Access to Justice: Some Home Truths' (2018) 77(1) *CLJ* 5, 5–6.
[119] According to government figures, annually about 14,000 claimants did not commence proceedings due to the fees, see 'Review of Introduction of Fees in the Employment Tribunal: Consultation on Proposals for Reform' (January 2017), Annex F, and, as I state in chapter four, there was a drastic increase in claims following the handing down of the judgment.

elsewhere, the judgment in *UNISON* goes further than previous common law constitutional rights cases. For example,

> In contrast to *Osborn*, it not only puts the common law *centre-stage* by making it the starting point of the legal analysis but also implies, in the context of this right at least, the *sufficiency* of the common law … Furthermore, in contrast to *A v BBC*, this judgment is more consistent as both the law and the application of the law to the facts is common law based rather than ECHR or EU law based … Finally, citing *R v Secretary of State for the Home Department, ex p Leech* [1994] QB 198 and *R (Daly) v Secretary of State for the Home Department* [2001] UKHL 26, Lord Reed says that 'even where primary legislation authorises the imposition of an intrusion on the right of access to justice, it is presumed to be subject to an implied limitation', thereby bolstering the *authority of the common law* and the *discretion of the courts* in the face of *explicit* statutory human rights abrogation … This last point is closely connected to the court's commitment to a rich notion of the rule of law.[120]

Therefore, as Ford noted, 'for once the extravagant acclamations [following a judgment] were not hyperbolical'.[121] The judgment's rich legal analysis features many aspects that have far-reaching implications for our understanding of the UK constitution, and which warrant separate academic attention. One of these is the Supreme Court's explicit endorsement of 'rights language'. Another one is the endorsement of statements on rights and justice put forward by both Edward Coke and William Blackstone whose views on jurisprudence were anchored in natural law theory, which regards adjudication as the altering of positive law through judgments with the intention to honour the law's purpose.[122] A third is that the legal analysis in this case is 'intimately bound up with its assessment of the normative value of the right of access to justice'.[123]

However, *UNISON* must be viewed within its context. First, the case concerned the right of access to justice/the courts, a right so well established that there was no difficulty locating precedent supportive of the legal outcome in this instance. As I noted above, there are many other constitutional rights we would expect to find in a liberal democracy, such as a robust version of the right to vote, that are much less historically recognised, and that will – due to how the common law works – therefore less likely be employed with the same strength, if at all. Second, we must not lose sight of the fact that the constitutional right in question is in essence a 'process of justice' right. It concerns the role of the courts as much as it concerns individuals. Much of the substance of this right and other rights falling into this category relates to the separation of powers and the sound administration

[120] C Lienen, 'Unison v Lord Chancellor: The Things that Landmark Constitutional Cases are Made of' (*UCL Constitution Unit Blog*, 28 July 2017).

[121] M Ford, 'Employment Tribunal Fees and the Rule of Law: *R (Unison) v Lord Chancellor* in the Supreme Court' (2018) 47(1) *Industrial Law Journal* 1, 2.

[122] On this dimension of the common law, see A Beever, 'The Declaratory Theory of Law' (2013) 33(3) *OJLS* 421.

[123] Elliott (n 118) f7.

of the state. As such, the courts have a special interest in them, and given the UK constitution's focus on the state's institutional organisation, judgments enforcing these rights will be viewed with softer criticism.[124]

These observations have implications for our assessment of *UNISON*'s interpretation of the rule of law. While *UNISON* showcases a substantive notion of the rule of law, it is equally compatible with the rule of law's 'thin' conceptualisation. The right of access to justice merely demands that 'courts should be accessible',[125] which is an obvious prerequisite for any kind of law enforcement, including enforcement of substantively unjust or undemocratic laws. In this sense the right of access to justice *potentially* enables the enforcement of constitutional rights. *UNISON* protects a vital fundamental right in an unprecedentedly strong way. However, the right in question – access to justice – represents the very minimum of what we can expect of a liberal democracy, namely for law to be *enforceable*.

Thus, while *UNISON* may indeed be 'an exemplar of common law constitutionalism',[126] it is also compatible with a more limited reading, particularly in light of my aforementioned point regarding the absence of clear statutory wording. While it may pull the constitution closer to one end of the spectrum, it has not, given the rich complexities of UK public law and the divergent opinions of senior judges on these intricacies, changed the nature of the constitution altogether. Subsequent cases sitting on the opposite side of the spectrum, two of which were analysed in chapter two, support this suggestion. Finally, linking this discussion to the previous section, we must also recognise the inherent limitations which attach even to the most established of all common law rights. It would be wholly unrealistic, for example, to suggest that the right of access to court would assist litigants who are unable to afford legal representation.[127]

The same broader conclusion can be drawn about the more recent judgment in *Privacy International*. As I stated in chapter two, in what in part reads very much like an endorsement of common law constitutionalism, Lord Carnwath's opinion suggests that it is ultimately for the courts, not the legislature, to determine the limits set by the rule of law. Like *UNISON*, this judgment is a landmark constitutional law case. However, here so as well, we must not overestimate its implications. Specifically, *Privacy International* is unlikely to lead to a more principled, rigorous protection of constitutional rights or engender a fundamental change in the nature of the UK constitution.

I want to focus in particular on one argument in making this point. Lord Carnwath remarked that the judiciary could refuse to give binding legal effect to

[124] Although see Sir S Laws, 'Second-Guessing Policy Choices: The Rule of Law after the Supreme Court's UNISON Judgment' (*Policy Exchange*, 15 March 2018).

[125] J Raz, *The Authority of Law: Essays on Law and Morality* (Oxford University Press 1979) 217.

[126] A Bogg, 'The Common Law Constitution at Work: *R (on the application of UNISON) v Lord Chancellor*' (2018) 81(3) *MLR* 509, 513.

[127] On this see also S Wheatle, 'Access to Justice: From Judicial Empowerment to Public Empowerment' in Elliott and Hughes (n 66) 65.

a statute in one specific scenario, namely Parliament wholly excluding judicial review or abolishing the ordinary role of the courts. However, first, no majority was established for this contention; Lord Lloyd-Jones in his concurring judgment did not engage with this second, hypothetical issue. Second, the judgment protects an aspect of constitutional/institutional design that is so basic it ought to be considered a prerequisite that enables the protection of other constitutional rights. Third, the judgment does not guarantee that substantive rights independent of the 'administration of justice' will be recognised or enforced, in the face of contradicting primary or secondary legislation, or outside of that context. The abolition of judicial review would be the end of democracy as we know it. Accordingly, the suggestion that a court might not recognise the legally binding effect of such an attempt does not equate to a robust system in which the protection of constitutional rights can be guaranteed.

Putting it succinctly, *UNISON* and *Privacy International* protect one of many rights that are essential in a democracy. The right of access to the courts, which both judgments addressed albeit from different angles, is a necessary condition for a liberal democracy. However, the recognition of this right is not a sufficient condition. Furthermore, while both judgments give a boost to the legal constitutionalist end of the nuanced constitution's spectrum, they do not change the nature of the UK constitution more broadly. The latter will continue to be characterised by complex qualities, which often pull in opposite directions.

VI. Where Does this Leave Us? Rights Protection, Unlimited Legislative Power and the Question of Legitimacy

Guided by an absolutist conceptual starting point originating in the nineteenth century, the UK's constitution has traditionally treated legality as synonymous with legislative intent. Against this background, constitutional law has largely been framed as an incessant power struggle between Parliament and the executive on the one hand, and the judiciary on the other.[128] Issues of substance, such as the content of constitutional rights, have played second fiddle as a result, both in the case law and in academic writings. This does not mean that substance is merely of marginal concern in contemporary public law adjudication. Indeed, as the growing importance of common law constitutional rights show, there is increasingly a strong parallel emphasis on the law's substantive qualities. However, against the background of a firmly embedded conceptual framework that focuses on Parliament's unlimited law-making power even in the face of fundamental rights, this growing engagement with substantive values – enabled and sustained

[128] See Lord Sumption's remarks in The Reith Lectures (2019) as the latest example of this.

by both European and domestic developments – has been unduly limited and largely unprincipled.

Within the framework of the nuanced constitution we find that common law constitutional rights are inherently vulnerable. No matter how normatively essential a right, its importance for the UK's political-legal order typically gives way to legal precedent and/or the statutory context, subject to certain qualifications. This means that despite the judiciary's express recognition that certain common law rights are 'important',[129] 'fundamental',[130] 'basic',[131] 'near to … absolute',[132] and 'inherent … to democratic civilised society',[133] it is far from certain that an appropriate remedy will vindicate the breach of a constitutional right. Indeed, as I explained, certain fundamental rights may not be recognised in the first place due to the historical trajectory of the English common law. Therefore, though it is true that 'the common law has powerful resources on which to draw',[134] under the realities of the nuanced constitution those resources are inherently vulnerable and, largely, unprincipled. In summary, this chapter argued that the nuanced constitution's jurisprudential approach towards common law constitutional rights protection is, despite positive features, unsatisfactory. In light of the limitations outlined, we cannot have sufficient 'faith in the moral vitality … of the common law method'.[135] The common law is arguably not 'an inherently moral mode of decision-making' that embodies the fundamental values of a democratic society.[136]

VII. The Way Forward

How, if at all, could the shortcomings I have established be addressed? This is a difficult question to answer which requires further, more in-depth thought. The focus of this book has been on analysing the current state of common law constitutional rights under the realities of the UK's uncodified constitution. In other words, I have set out to show how we can best conceptualise what we find in the case law, not how it should be. What follows, by way of parting thoughts, is a high level discussion that picks up on some of the facets I have highlighted.

[129] *R v Secretary of State for the Home Department, ex p Saleem* [2001] 1 WLR 443, [2000] 4 All ER 814, 828 (per Lady Hale).

[130] *R v Secretary of State for the Home Department, ex p Simms* (n 37) [131]–[132] (per Lord Hoffmann).

[131] *Her Majesty's Treasury v Mohammed Jabar Ahmed* [2010] UKSC 1, [2010] 2 AC 697 [183] (per Lord Rodger, with whom Lady Hale agreed).

[132] *R v Lord Chancellor, ex p Witham* (n 69) (per Laws J).

[133] *R (Daly) v Secretary of State for the Home Department* [2001] UKHL 26, [2001] 2 AC 532 [30] (per Lord Cooke).

[134] TRS Allan, 'The Constitutional Foundations of Judicial Review: Conceptual Conundrum or Interpretative Inquiry?' (2002) 61(1) *CLJ* 87, 96.

[135] Poole (n 44) 435, 454.

[136] *ibid* 442–43, 445.

One of the obvious barriers to devising a more coherent, principled system of constitutional rights protection is the principle of parliamentary sovereignty. Put simply, the development of rights is significantly limited by the prominent (and indeed often dominant) factor of institutional deference. The rationale for institutional deference in the human rights arena is succinctly summarised by Bellamy, a key political constitutionalist:

> Political constitutionalists contend that a democratic political system, involving regular elections for the legislature and executive between competing parties on the basis of one person, one vote and majority rule, offers the most legitimate and effective mechanism for constraining governments so they rule in the interests of the governed, including by ensuring they protect and promote rights. Two arguments underlie this claim. First, that rights are matters of reasonable disagreement and, secondly, that the most appropriate way to show citizens equal respect and concern in resolving these disagreements is via a democratic system that treats their different views and interests impartially and equitably by giving them an equal influence in any collective decision, including those concerning rights.[137]

Put simply, the underlying idea is 'that disputes over constitutional rules (including and especially human rights) are, and should be, resolved by political debates in political arenas'.[138]

Without providing a detailed analysis of this claim, which would go beyond the scope of this book, we can see that the values generally proposed to legitimise and indeed necessitate parliamentary sovereignty fall short of what they promise or, rather, do not achieve what they are assumed to achieve. The main point to be made here is that the theoretical description of the democratic process outlined above is in reality far more, for want of a better word, *nuanced*, and indeed less causal in nature than the quote suggests. First, there is the obvious paradox that individuals are supposedly 'self-governing' whilst at the same time submitting themselves to majority will. One cannot circumvent this paradox by reasoning that the process of legislating is 'law by the people for the people', ie that legislative output is simply the aggregation of the citizens' preferences. In the UK context in particular, there is an initial barrier to equating law with the will of the people: the first-past-the-post electoral system. Besides forcing voters into difficult tactical voting dilemmas, first-past-the-post produces significant inequities and distortions. This is apparent from the 2015 General Election in which the UK Independence Party won one seat despite securing almost four million votes, whereas the Scottish National Party won 56 seats despite fewer than one and a half million votes cast in their favour. Further, '331 of 650 MPs were elected on under 50% of the vote, and 191

[137] R Bellamy, 'The Democratic Legitimacy of International Human Rights Conventions: Political Constitutionalism and the European Convention on Human Rights' (2014) 25(4) *European Journal of International Law* 1019, 1024.

[138] CC Murphy, 'Human Rights Advocacy after AB and the Supreme Court's "Conservative Approach"' (2021) 5 *European Human Rights Law Review* 465, 466.

with less than 30% of the electorate',[139] and 'votes for the two largest parties came to just 67.3% combined. 36.9% of the electorate voted for the Conservatives, the party subsequently forming the government, and 30.4% voted for Labour'.[140] These disproportionalities are not exceptional but rather 'a long-standing feature of the British electoral system'.[141]

Then there is the issue of low voter participation. In the 2017 General Election, for example, voter turnout was at 68.8 per cent, up from 66.2 per cent in 2015.[142] This means that even if votes translated directly into law and policy outcomes, and we ignored the above distortion of electoral preferences produced by the first-past-the-post system, law and policy would only ever represent a maximum of about a three quarter share of the population's preferences. However, especially when thinking about constitutional rights protection, it is important to recognise that 'just as there would be a risk that individuals would make biased and self-interested decisions on matters of principle if entrusted with such decisions, so there is a risk that elected representatives would do the same'.[143] This risk is exacerbated under the party whip system.[144]

One can also question to what extent the 'preferences' that do materialise through the election process can be said to equal meaningful will formation. As Kaye shows, political ignorance in the UK is at a high level.[145] He cites a recent survey by King's College London and the Royal Statistical Society, which found that 29 per cent of the population believe that the UK spends more on Jobseeker's Allowance than it does on pensions (we spend 15 times more on pensions), 26 per cent of the population believe that foreign aid is among the three highest public bills (when it actually made up 1.1 per cent of the UK's expenditure), and that, on average, the population believes that immigrants make up 31 per cent of the UK population (the official figure is 13 per cent).[146]

These findings pose further challenges for political constitutionalism, chiefly as far as equality and autonomy are concerned. The implications of uninformed voters go beyond 'bad' voting choices: 'ignorant voters may also be more easily misled or manipulated by rhetorically impressive but factually unsound claims' or

[139] J Garland and C Terry, 'The 2015 General Election – A System in Crisis' (*Electoral Reform Society*, 1 June 2015), available at www.electoral-reform.org.uk/a-system-in-crisis/.

[140] *ibid* 8.

[141] A Renwick, 'The Chances of Electoral Reform Revisited' (*Politics at Reading Blog*, 8 May 2015).

[142] The Electoral Commission, 'Turnout – UK Parliament General Elections – 1922–2017', available at www.electoralcommission.org.uk/media/1167.

[143] S Lakin, 'The Moral Reading of the British Constitution' (PhD Thesis, UCL, 2009) 139.

[144] Although see A Tomkins, 'What's Left of the Political Constitution' (2013) 14(12) *German Law Journal* 2275, 2277.

[145] S Kaye, 'On the Complex Relationship between Political Ignorance and Democracy' (*LSE British Policy and Politics Blog*, 16 March 2015).

[146] King's College London, Ipsos MORI and Royal Statistical Society, 'Perils of Perception Topline Results Fieldwork: 14th-18th June 2013', available at www.ipsos.com/sites/default/files/migrations/en-uk/files/Assets/Docs/Polls/ipsos-mori-rss-kings-perils-of-perception-topline.pdf.

conspiracy theories, 'or fall into patterns where they accept overly dichotomous or extremely simplified versions of reality'.[147] Why, one can therefore ask by way of example, 'should fundamental decisions – say, over the best political party for the management of immigration – be entrusted to a public that is generally mistaken about the fundamental facts of immigration and demography in the UK?'[148]

Then there is the link between voter preference and governmental output. The governing party's pre-election position on rights is a helpful example. The 2019 Conservatives' Manifesto stated, 'In our first year we will set up a Constitution, Democracy & Rights Commission that will examine [constitutional] issues in depth, and come up with proposals to restore trust in our institutions and in how our democracy operates.'[149] This has not occurred. Instead, the Government set up an independent Human Rights Act review, which received hundreds of submissions, and produced a list of key recommendations which involved a number of discreet changes, including amending section 2 of the HRA to reflect the judgments in *Osborn v Parole Board* and *Kennedy v Charity Commission*, but then went ahead and *ignored* the panel's findings and published a bill to replace the HRA instead. How could one, in that scenario, even if one ignored all of the above compromising factors, sensibly say that the changes to our human rights system that may well have been passed by Parliament would have been sanctioned by voters through the election process?

In enumerating these, what one might call, compromising facts about the democratic process, one may conclude that, on closer scrutiny, the political constitution's suggestion that constitutional rights protection ought to be dictated by 'majority will' is not in fact as inevitable a conclusion as one might initially think. That proposition is lent further support by the fact that 'one of the most fundamental of all rights … that of ordinary people to participate, on equal terms, in the political decision-making that affects their lives as much as anyone else's',[150] has been shown not to be protected domestically. As Sandro astutely observes commenting on *O (A) v Secretary of State for the Home Department*, which I discussed in detail in chapter two,

> it is baffling that certain rights like freedom of speech are afforded special protection by the common law precisely because of their link with the democratic nature of our society (*R v Secretary of State for the Home Department*, Ex p Brind [1991] 1 AC 696), while the right to the very status upon which the exercise of political rights is conditional – and thus the realisation of the principle of political equality – is not.[151]

[147] Kaye (n 145).

[148] *ibid.*

[149] Conservative Party Manifesto 2019, 48.

[150] J Goldsworthy, *The Sovereignty of Parliament: History and Philosophy* (Oxford University Press, 2001) 263.

[151] P Sandro, 'A Political Constitution, but for Whom? Citizenship Fees, Legality, and the Limits of Doctrine' (*UK Constitutional Law Association Blog*, 23 February 2022).

O (A) shows that even individuals who were born in the UK, and whose lives are just as impacted by policy and law-making as the lives of citizens, may be altogether disenfranchised and excluded from voting depending on their financial circumstances, thereby putting 'law by the people for the people' in perspective. Other factors such as the 'concentrated media, access by wealthy elites, … majoritarian bias and misinformation'[152] further distort the ideal of equality under the political constitution.

Finally, we ought to ask ourselves whether we can be comfortable with a system which purports that electoral accountability can justify any substantive outcome, and in which the fundamental tenets of our constitutional law can be amended, replaced or simply abolished if a simple parliamentarian majority says so. The political constitution is based on the naive premise that the worst will not happen. However, it may be worth asking whether a democratic legal order should leave the protection of constitutional rights to chance.

There is no better time to think in some detail about these fundamental questions than the present. At the time of writing, political and legal developments in the UK suggest that the trajectory is one that gradually moves the UK away from a system based on accountable government, as well as taking an apparently increasingly cavalier attitude towards international law. This being the case, together with the recent domestic plans to significantly lower this jurisdiction's statutory human and constitutional rights protection, the time might have come to consider more seriously how constitutional rights can be more securely entrenched. One way that this could theoretically be achieved is if UK courts took a more robust approach to the protection of common law constitutional rights, including by giving less weight to what Parliament has said about a matter in question. One of the ways in which a more structured conversation around rights could, hypothetically, take place is by exploring to what extent, from a purely normative perspective, adherence to parliamentary sovereignty is warranted in the field of constitutional rights. In light of the UK's constitutional tradition, we should not expect any seismic shifts in this regard. Yes, some obiter dicta, including those in *Moohan v Lord Advocate*,[153] suggest that legislative intent might be disregarded in the most extreme circumstances. However, it is not clear what threshold would have to be crossed for this to occur, and, in any event, this would not offer any improvement for constitutional rights protection in the round.

Alternatively, seeing as the argument presented in this book claims that the English common law is, by its nature, not an apt vehicle for the development

[152] J King, 'Three Wrong Turns in Lord Sumption's Conception of Law and Democracy' in R Ekins, P Yowell and NW Barber (eds), *Lord Sumption and the Limits of the Law* (Hart Publishing, 2016) 143, 148.

[153] *Moohan v Lord Advocate* (n 45).

of a comprehensive, resilient system of constitutional rights protection, one might want to explore whether the time is ripe for a written constitution. It remains the case that there is in the UK at present 'no live proposal'[154] to have a codified constitution. I agree with Payne that part of the problem is that we currently have an 'obscure constitution that depends upon the judiciary to piece together'.[155] This is inherent in constitutional rights protection, too. Thus, one advantage that would be gained from a codification process is that the replacing of common law constitutional rights with codified constitutional rights would likely increase their 'definitional certainty'.[156] Even if there remains a 'level of vagueness that persists in the definition of each right guaranteed in a Bill of Rights, courts can be more sure-footed by reliance on both the wording of the rights provisions and the context of the overall instrument'.[157] More broadly,

> a written constitution would be an opportunity to design an integrated and coherent body of constitutional law drawing on over 200 years of constitution-making from across the globe and the common law world assisted by comparative constitutional scholarship and the practical experience of governments and law-makers.[158]

Accordingly, the codification option carries heavy theoretical force. However, we must acknowledge that this is an option that is just that: theoretical. In any event, even if the UK did adopt a capital-C constitution, it would be uncertain what rights would feature in such a document, and, particularly given the UK's traditional constitutional philosophy, whether effective constitutional review mechanisms would be incorporated.

Perhaps the most realistic development is the gradual adaptation of the English common law towards a more principled approach that develops constitutional rights comprehensively. However, as I have stipulated throughout this book, this would go against the grain of the English common law, a legal system that has, in various forms, existed for centuries. Amongst other things, this shift would necessitate a partial departure from incrementalism, a transition from the focus on institutional legitimacy to a focus on political morality as part of the engagement with substantive values, and less deferential attitudes towards the elected branches of state, all of which are well-established facets of the constitution. In light of some of the most recent Supreme Court judgments, including those discussed in chapter two, while perhaps more realistic than the first two

[154] J Gardner, 'Can There Be a Written Constitution?' in L Green and B Leiter (eds), *Oxford Studies in Philosophy of Law: Volume 1* (Oxford University Press, 2011) 163.

[155] S Payne, 'The Supreme Court and the Miller Case: More Reasons Why the UK Needs a Written Constitution' (2018) 107(4) *The Round Table: The Commonwealth Journal of International Affairs* 441, 442.

[156] R Masterman and SS Wheatle, 'Unity, Disunity and Vacuity: Constitutional Adjudication and the Common Law', in M Elliot, JN Varuhas and SW Stark (eds), *The Unity of Public Law? Doctrinal, Theoretical and Comparative Perspectives* (Hart Publishing, 2015) 128.

[157] *ibid* 128.

[158] Payne (n 155) 450.

options, it seems unlikely that common law constitutional rights protection will be significantly strengthened in the near future.

Given the barriers to meaningful, comprehensive change, it appears that the most effective thing one can do is to counter the popular narrative that common law constitutional rights are well-established, sufficient, or indeed comparable to the level of protection offered by the HRA.

BIBLIOGRAPHY

Books

A Kavanagh, *Constitutional Review under the UK Human Rights Act* (Cambridge University Press, 2009)
A Legg, *The Margin of Appreciation in International Human Rights Law: Deference and Proportionality* (Oxford University Press, 2012)
A Sajó and R Uitz, *The Constitution of Freedom: An Introduction to Legal Constitutionalism* (Oxford University Press, 2017)
AC Hutchinson, *Evolution and the Common Law* (Cambridge University Press, 2005)
AL Young, *Parliamentary Sovereignty and the Human Rights Act* (Hart Publishing, 2009)
AR Mowbray, *The Development of Positive Obligations under the European Convention on Human Rights by the European Court of Human Rights* (Hart Publishing, 2004)
AV Dicey, Introduction to the Study of the Law of the Constitution, 8th edn (Palgrave MacMillan, 1915)
——, *England's Case against Home Rule* (Murray, 1886)
AX Fellmeth, *Paradigms of International Human Rights Law* (Oxford University Press, 2016)
B Dickson, *Human Rights and the United Kingdom Supreme Court* (Oxford University Press, 2013)
C Gearty, *Principles of Human Rights Adjudication* (Oxford University Press, 2005)
C Harlow and R Rawlings, *Law and Administration*, 3rd edn (Cambridge University Press, 2009)
——, *Pressure through Law* (Routledge, 1992)
C Palley, 'The United Kingdom and Human Rights' (42nd series, The Hamlyn Lectures, Sweet & Maxwell 1991)
D Feldman, *Civil Liberties and Human Rights in England and Wales*, 2nd edn (Oxford University Press, 2002)
D Greenberg, *Craies on Legislation*, 12th edn (Sweet & Maxwell, 2020)
E Bjorge, *Domestic Application of the ECHR: Courts as Faithful Trustees* (Oxford University Press, 2015)
F Klug, *Values for a Godless Age: The Story of the United Kingdom's New Bill of Rights* (Penguin, 2000)
F von Hayek, *The Constitution of Liberty: The Definite Edition* (Routledge, 2013)
H Patrick Glenn, *On Common Laws* (Oxford University Press, 2007)
H Potter, *Law, Liberty and the Constitution: A Brief History of the Common Law* (Boydell Press, 2015)
H Shue, *Basic Rights* (Princeton University Press, 1980)
HLA Hart, *Essays on Bentham: Jurisprudence and Political Philosophy* (Oxford University Press, 1982)
J Auburn, J Moffett and A Sharland, *Judicial Review: Principles and Procedure* (Oxford University Press, 2013)
J Beatson and others, *Human Rights: Judicial Protection in the United Kingdom* (Sweet & Maxwell, 2008)
J Goldsworthy (ed), *Parliamentary Sovereignty: Contemporary Debates* (Cambridge, Cambridge University Press, 2010)
——, *The Sovereignty of Parliament: History and Philosophy* (Oxford University Press, 2001)
J Raz, *The Authority of Law: Essays on Law and Morality* (Oxford University Press, 1979)
JAG Griffith, M Ryle and MAJ Wheeler-Booth, *Parliament: Functions, Practice and Procedures* (Sweet & Maxwell, 1989)
JW Tubbs, *The Common Law Mind: Medieval and Early Modern Conceptions* (Johns Hopkins University Press, 2000)

JWF Allison, *The English Historical Constitution: Continuity, Change and European Effects* (Cambridge University Press 2007)

KD Ewing and CA Gearty, *The Struggle for Civil Liberties: Political Freedom and the Rule of Law in Britain, 1914–1945* (Oxford University Press, 2000)

Lady Arden, *Human Rights and European Law: Building New Legal Orders* (Oxford University Press, 2015)

Lord Scarman, 'English Law – The New Dimension' (26th series, The Hamlyn Lectures, Stevens & Sons Ltd, 1974)

Lord Woolf et al, *De Smith's Judicial Review*, 8th edn (Sweet & Maxwell, 2018)

M Allen and B Thompson, *Cases and Materials on Constitutional and Administrative Law*, 10th edn (Oxford University Press, 2011)

M Elliott and K Hughes, *Common Law Constitutional Rights* (Hart Publishing, 2020)

M Lobban, *The Common Law and English Jurisprudence, 1760–1850* (Clarendon Press, 1991)

M Tushnet, *Weak Courts, Strong Rights: Judicial Review and Social Welfare Rights Comparative Constitutional Law* (Princeton University Press, 2008)

MD Walters, *AV Dicey and the Common Law Constitutional Tradition: A Legal Turn of Mind* (Cambridge University Press, 2020)

N Bamforth and P Leyland (eds), *Public Law in a Multi-Layered Constitution* (Hart Publishing, 2003)

N Bobbio, *The Age of Rights* (Polity Press, 1996)

N Duxbury, *The Nature and Authority of Precedent* (Cambridge University Press, 2008)

R Cruft, SM Liao and M Renzo (eds), *Philosophical Foundations of Human Rights* (Oxford University Press, 2015)

R Dworkin, *Law's Empire* (Fontana Press, 1986)

——, *Taking Rights Seriously* (Duckworth, 1977)

R Gordon, *EU Law in Judicial Review* (Oxford University Press, 2014)

R Pound, *Interpretations of Legal History* (Cambridge University Press, 1967)

R Singh, *The Future of Human Rights in the United Kingdom: Essays on Law and Practice* (Hart Publishing, 1997)

R Stevens, *Torts and Rights* (Oxford University Press, 2007)

RC Van Caenegem, *The Birth of the English Common Law* (Cambridge University Press, 1988)

S Fredman, *Human Rights Transformed: Positive Rights and Positive Duties* (Oxford University Press, 2008)

S Wheatle, *Principled Reasoning in Human Rights Adjudication* (Hart Publishing 2017)

T Hickman, *Public Law after the Human Rights Act* (Hart Publishing, 2010)

TRS Allan, *The Sovereignty of Law: Freedom, Constitution, and Common Law* (Oxford University Press, 2013)

——, *Law, Liberty, and Justice: The Legal Foundations of British Constitutionalism* (Oxford University Press, 1993)

V Bogdanor, *The New British Constitution* (Hart Publishing, 2009)

W Blackstone, *Commentaries on the Laws of England* (Clarendon Press, 1765–69)

WI Jennings, *The Law and the Constitution*, 5th edn (London University Press, 1959)

Book Chapters

A Le Sueur, 'From Appellate Committee to Supreme Court: A Narrative' in L Blom-Cooper, B Dickson and Gavin Drewry (eds), *The Judicial House of Lords, 1876–2009* (Oxford University Press, 2009)

A Mavronicola, 'The Mythology and the Reality of Common Law Constitutional Rights to Bodily Integrity' in M Elliott and K Hughes, *Common Law Constitutional Rights* (Hart Publishing, 2020)

A Tomkins and P Scott, 'Introduction' in A Tomkins and P Scott (eds), *Entick v Carrington 250 Years of the Rule of Law* (Hart Publishing, 2015)

AL Young, 'Fundamental Common Law Rights and Legislation' in M Elliott and K Hughes (eds), *Common Law Constitutional Rights* (Hart Publishing, 2020)

C Forsyth, '"Blasphemy against basics": Doctrine, Conceptual Reasoning and Certain Decisions of the UK Supreme Court' in J Bell and others, *Public Law Adjudication in Common Law Systems: Process and Substance* (Hart Publishing, 2016)

C Gearty, 'Beyond the Human Rights Act' in T Campbell, KD Ewing, and A Tomkins (eds), *The Legal Protection of Human Rights: Sceptical Essays* (Oxford University Press, 2011)

C Harlow, 'The Political Constitution Reworked' in R Bigwood (ed), *Public Interest Litigation: New Zealand Experience in International Perspective* (LexisNexis, 2006)

C O'Cinneide, 'A Core Common Law Principle, or "Mere" Rationality?' in M Elliott and K Hughes (eds) *Common Law Constitutional Rights* (Hart Publishing, 2020)

D Baranger, 'Law, Liberty and Entick v Carrington' in A Tomkins and P Scott (eds), *Entick v Carrington 250 Years of the Rule of Law* (Hart Publishing, 2015)

D Feldman, 'Anisminic Ltd v Foreign Compensation Commission [1968]: In Perspective' in S Juss and M Sunkin (eds), *Landmark Cases in Public Law* (Hart Publishing, 2017)

E Mak, 'Comparative Law before the Supreme Courts of the UK and the Netherlands: An Empirical and Comparative Analysis' in M Andenas and D Fairgrieve (eds), *Courts and Comparative Law* (Oxford University Press, 2015)

J Gardner, 'Can There Be a Written Constitution?' in L Green and B Leiter (eds), *Oxford Studies in Philosophy of Law: Volume 1* (Oxford University Press, 2011)

J Goldsworthy, 'Parliamentary Sovereignty and Constitutional Change in the United Kingdom' in R Rawlings, P Layland and AL Young, *Sovereignty and the Law: Domestic, European and International Perspectives* (Oxford University Press, 2013)

J King 'Three Wrong Turns in Lord Sumption's Conception of Law and Democracy' in R Ekins, P Yowell and NW Barber (eds), *Lord Sumption and the Limits of the Law* (Hart Publishing, 2016)

J McBride, 'Proportionality and the European Convention on Human Rights' in E Ellis (ed), *The Principle of Proportionality in the Laws of Europe* (Oxford University Press, 1999)

J McEldowney, 'The Factortame Litigation: Sovereignty in Question' in S Juss and M Sunkin (eds), *Landmark Cases in Public Law* (Hart Publishing, 2017)

K Hughes, 'A Common Law Constitutional Right to Privacy – Waiting for Godot?' in M Elliott and K Hughes (eds), *Common Law Constitutional Rights* (Hart Publishing, 2020)

M Elliott, 'The Fundamentality of Rights at Common Law' in M Elliott and K Hughes (eds), *Common Law Constitutional Rights* (Hart Publishing, 2020)

——, 'Legislative Supremacy in a Multidimensional Constitution' in M Elliott and D Feldman (eds), *The Cambridge Companion to Public Law* (Cambridge University, Press, 2015)

N Mavronicola, 'The Mythology and the Reality of Common Law Constitutional Rights to Bodily Integrity' in M Elliott and K Hughes (eds), *Common Law Constitutional Rights* (Hart Publishing, 2020)

N Walker, 'Sovereignty Frames and Sovereignty Claims' in R Rawlings, P Layland and AL Young, *Sovereignty and the Law: Domestic, European and International Perspectives* (Oxford University Press, 2013)

R Masterman and SS Wheatle, 'Unity, Disunity and Vacuity: Constitutional Adjudication and the Common Law' in M Elliot, JN Varuhas and SW Stark (eds), *The Unity of Public Law? Doctrinal, Theoretical and Comparative Perspectives* (Hart Publishing, 2015)

S Wheatle, 'Access to Justice: From Judicial Empowerment to Public Empowerment' in M Elliott and K Hughes (eds), *Common Law Constitutional Rights* (Hart Publishing, 2020)

T Allan, 'Constitutional Rights to Property' in M Elliott and K Hughes (eds), *Common Law Constitutional Rights* (Hart Publishing, 2020)

Journal Articles and Case Notes

A Beever, 'The Declaratory Theory of Law' (2013) 33(3) *OJLS* 421

A Bogg, 'The Common Law Constitution at Work: R (on the application of UNISON) v Lord Chancellor' (2018) 81(3) *MLR* 509

A Greene, 'Parliamentary Sovereignty and the Locus of Constituent Power in the United Kingdom' (2020) 18(4) *International Journal of Constitutional Law* 1166
A Jackman, 'Judging a Judge: A Reappraisal of Lord Mansfield and Somerset's Case' (2018) 39(2) *The Journal of Legal History* 140
A Kavanagh, 'The Role of Parliamentary Intention in Adjudication under the Human Rights Act 1998' (2006) 26(1) *OJLS* 179
——, 'Recasting the Political Constitution' (2019) 30(1) *King's Law Journal* 43
A Latham-Gambi, 'Political Constitutionalism and Legal Constitutionalism – an Imaginary Opposition?' (2020) 40(4) *OJLS* 737
A Lester, 'Citizenship and the Constitution' (2008) 79(3) *The Political Quarterly* 388
A McHarg, 'The Supreme Court's Prorogation Judgment: Guardian of the Constitution or Architect of the Constitution?' (2020) 24(1) *Edinburgh Law Review* 88
——, 'Reforming the United Kingdom Constitution: Law, Convention, Soft Law' (2008) 71 *MLR* 853
A Perry, 'The Crown's Administrative Powers' (2015) 131 *LQR* 652
A Psygkas, 'The United Kingdom's Statutory Constitution' (2020) 40(3) *OJLS* 449
A Tomkins, 'What's Left of the Political Constitution' (2013) 14(12) *German Law Journal* 2275
A Tucker, 'Parliamentary Sovereignty and the Ingenuity of the Human Rights Act' (2012) 3(1) *Jurisprudence* 307
——, 'Uncertainty in the Rule of Recognition and in the Doctrine of Parliamentary Sovereignty' (2011) 31(1) *OJLS* 61
ATH Smith, 'Disavowing Torture in the House of Lords' (2006) 65(2) *CLJ*
B Lim, 'The Normativity of the Principle of Legality' (2013) 37(2) *Melbourne University Law Review* 372
B Pillans, 'Another Serving of Alphabet Soup: A v British Broadcasting Corporation (Scotland)' (2014) 19(4) *Communications Law* 130
B Shiner and T Chowdhury, 'Ministry of Defence Impunity: the Overseas Operations (Service Personnel and Veterans) Act 2021 [2022] *PL* 289
BC Jones, 'Judicial Review and Embarrassment' [2022] *PL* 179
BJ Ong, 'The Ouster of Parliamentary Sovereignty?' [2020] *PL* 41
C Lienen, 'Judicial Constitutional Comparativism at the UK Supreme Court' (2019) 39(1) *Legal Studies* 166
C O'Cinneide, 'Values, Rights and Brexit – Lessons to be Learnt from the Slow Evolution of United Kingdom Discrimination Law' (2017) 30 *Australian Journal of Labour Law* 1
CC Murphy, 'Human Rights Advocacy after AB and the Supreme Court's Conservative Approach' (2021) 5 *European Human Rights Law Review* 465
CJS Knight, 'A Framework for Fettering' (2009) 14(1) *Judicial Review* 73
D Bailey, 'Bridging the Gap: Legislative Drafting Practice and Statutory Interpretation' [2020] *PL* 220
D Blair, 'Quis custodiet ipsos custodes? The Opportunities and Democratic Legitimacy of the Post-Osborn Human Rights Debate' (2016) 2 *Juridical Review* 83
D Feldman, 'Error of Law and Flawed Administrative Acts' (2014) 73(2) *CLJ* 275
D Friedman, 'A Common Law of Human Rights: History, Humanity and Dignity' (2016) *European Human Rights Law Review* 378
——, 'Torture and the Common Law' (2006) 2 *European Human Rights Law Review* 180
D Meagher, 'The Common Law Principle of Legality in an Age of Rights' (2011) 35(2) *Melbourne University Law Review* 449
D Oliver, 'Is the Ultra Vires Rules the Basis of Judicial Review?' [1987] *PL* 543
E Barendt, 'Libel and Freedom of Speech in English Law' [1993] *PL* 449
E Bates, 'Analysing the Prisoner Voting Saga and the British Challenge to Strasbourg' (2014) 14(3) *Human Rights Law Review* 503
E Bjorge, 'Legislation Purporting to Oust the High Court's Jurisdiction: Privacy International' (2020) 136 *LQR* 12
——, 'Common Law Rights: Balancing Domestic and International Exigencies' (2016) 75(2) *CLJ* 220
——, 'Fundamental Rights at English (and European?) Common Law' (2015) 131 *LQR* 192

E C Ip, 'The Institutional Foundations of Supreme Court Power in Britain's Representative Democracy' (2013) 49(3) *Representation: Journal of Representative Democracy* 281
E Wicks, 'The Supreme Court Judgment in Nicklinson: One Step Forward on Assisted Dying; Two Steps Back on Human Rights' (2015) 23(1) *MLR* 144
F Ahmed and A Perry, 'Constitutional Statutes' (2017) 37(2) *OJLS* 461, 461
G Gee, 'The Political Constitution and the Political Right' (2019) 30 *King's Law Journal* 148
G Gee and GCN Webber, 'What is a Political Constitution?' (2010) 30(2) *OJLS* 273
G Marston, 'The United Kingdom's Part in the Preparation of the European Convention on Human Rights, 1950' (1993) 42(4) *International and Comparative Law Quarterly* 796
G Phillipson and A Williams, 'Horizontal Effect and the Constitutional Constraint' (2011) 74(6) *MLR* 878
G Van Cleve, '"Somerset's Case" and Its Antecedents in Imperial Perspective' (2006) 24(3) *Law and History Review* 601
H Hooper, 'Justice For One Side Alone? R. (on the application of Begum) v Special Immigration Appeals Commission' [2022] *PL* 1
H Wong and M Law, 'Powers to Search, Question and Detain under Schedule 7 of the Terrorism Act 2000: Beghal v Director of Public Prosecutions' (2015) 5 *European Human Rights Law Review* 512
HJ Cook, 'Against Common Right and Reason: The College of Physicians versus Dr. Thomas Bonham' (1985) 29(4) *The American Journal of Legal History* 301
I Williams, 'Dr Bonham's Case and "Void" Statutes' (2006) 27(2) *The Journal of Legal History* 111
IH Jacob, 'The Inherent Jurisdiction of the Court' (1970) 23(1) *Current Legal Problems* 23
JAG Griffith, 'The Political Constitution' (1979) 42(1) *MLR* 1
J Buckley Dyer, 'After the Revolution: Somerset and the Antislavery Tradition in Anglo-American Constitutional Development' (2009) 71(4) *The Journal of Politics* 1422
J Goodwin, 'The Last Defence of Wednesbury' [2012] *PL* 445
J Hasnas, 'Toward a Theory of Empirical Natural Rights' (2005) 22(1) *Social Philosophy and Policy* 111
J Jowell, 'Beyond the Rule of Law: Towards Constitutional Judicial Review' [2000] *PL* 671
——, 'Restraining the State: Politics, Principle and Judicial Review' (1997) 50(1) *Current Legal Problems* 189
J Krikler, 'The Zong and the Lord Chief Justice' (2007) 64(1) *History Workshop Journal* 29
J Lee, 'Substantiating Substantive Review' [2018] *PL* 632
J McGarry and S Spence, 'Constitutional Statutes – Roots and Recognition' (2020) 41(3) *Statute Law Review* 378
J Rogers, 'Beghal v DPP: Some Unresolved Issues' (2016) 1 *Archbold Review* 4
J Straw and P Boateng, 'Bringing Rights Home: Labour's Plans to Incorporate the European Convention on Human Rights into UK Law' (1997) 1 *European Human Rights Law Review* 71
J Varuhas, 'Conceptualising the Principle(s) of Legality' (2018) 29(3) *Public Law Review* 196
J Waldon, 'How Law Protects Dignity' [2012] *CLJ* 200
JEK Murkens, 'Democracy as the Legitimating Condition in the UK Constitution' (2018) 38(1) *Legal Studies* 42
——, 'Judicious Review: The Constitutional Practice of the UK Supreme Court' (2018) 77(2) *CLJ* 349
JNE Varuhas, 'The Reformation of English Administrative Law? "Rights", Rhetoric and Reality' (2013) 72(2) *CLJ* 369
K Monaghan, 'Religious Freedom and Equal Treatment: A United Kingdom Perspective' (2014) 22(2) *Journal of Law and Policy* 673
KD Ewing, 'The Resilience of the Political Constitution' (2013) 14(12) *German Law Journal* 2111
L Clements and J Young, 'Human Rights: Changing the Culture' (1999) 26(1) *Journal of Law and Society* 1
Lady Hale, 'The Changing Legal Landscape' (2019) 19(4) *Legal Information Management* 217
Lord Bingham, 'The European Convention on Human Rights: Time to Incorporate' (1993) 109 *LQR* 390
Lord Browne-Wilkinson, 'The Infiltration of a Bill of Rights' [1992] *PL* 397

Lord Irvine, 'Constitutional Reform and a Bill of Rights' (1997) 5 *European Human Rights Law Review* 483
——, 'Judges and Decision-Makers: The Theory and Practice of Wednesbury Review' [1996] *PL* 59
Lord Lester, 'U.K. Acceptance of the Strasbourg Jurisdiction: What Really Went on in Whitehall in 1965' [1998] *PL* 237
——, 'Judges and Ministers' (1996) 18(8) *London Review of Books* 10
——, 'English Judges as Law Makers' [1993] *PL* 269
Lord Steyn, 'The Weakest and Least Dangerous Department of Government' [1997] *PL* 84
M Demetriou, 'Using Human Rights through EC Law' [1999] *European Human Rights Law Review* 484
M Elliott, 'Constitutional Adjudication and Constitutional Politics in the United Kingdom: The Miller II Case in Legal and Political Context' (2020) 16(4) *European Constitutional Law Review* 625
——, 'The Rule of Law and Access to Justice: Some Home Truths' (2018) 77(1) *CLJ* 5
——, 'Judicial Power and the United Kingdom's Changing Constitution' (2017) 36(2) *University of Queensland Law Journal* 273
——, 'Beyond the European Convention: Human Rights and the Common Law' (2015) 68 (1) *Current Legal Problems* 85
——, 'Constitutional Legislation, European Union Law and the Nature of the United Kingdom's Contemporary Constitution' (2014) 10(3) *European Constitutional Law Review* 379
M Ford, 'Employment Tribunal Fees and the Rule of Law: R (Unison) v Lord Chancellor in the Supreme Court' (2018) 47(1) *Industrial Law Journal* 1
M Gordon, 'The Conceptual Foundations of Parliamentary Sovereignty: Reconsidering Jennings and Wade' [2009] *PL* 519
M Klatt, 'Positive Obligations under the European Convention on Human Rights' (2011) 71 *Zeitschrift für ausländisches öffentliches Recht und Völkerrecht (ZaöRV)* 691
M Liao and A Etinson, 'Political and Naturalist Conceptions of Human Rights: A False Polemic?' (2012) 9(3) *Journal of Moral Philosophy* 327
M Radley, 'Wightman: A Marbury v Madison Moment?' (2021) 42(7) *European Competition Law Review* 407
M Sunkin and AP Le Sueur, 'Can Government Control Judicial Review?' (1991) 44 *Current Legal Problems* 161
M Teo, 'Proportionality as Epistemic Independence' [2022] *PL* 245
N Duxbury, 'Custom as Law in English Law' (2017) 76(2) *CLJ* 337
N Grief, 'The Domestic Impact of the European Convention on Human Rights as Mediated through Community Law' [1991] *PL* 555
NW Barber, 'The Afterlife of Parliamentary Sovereignty' (2011) 9(1) *International Journal of Constitutional Law* 144
——, 'Sovereignty Re-Examined: The Courts, Parliament & Statutes' (2000) 20(1) *OJLS* 131
OW Holmes, 'The Path of the Law' (1897) 10 *Harvard Law Review* 457
P Craig, 'Judicial Review, Methodology and Reform' [2021] *PL* 19
——, 'Constitutionalising Constitutional Law: HS2' [2014] *PL* 373
——, 'Ultra Vires and the Foundations of Judicial Review' (1998) *CLJ* 63
——, 'What Should Public Lawyers do? A Reply' (1992) 12(4) *OJLS* 564
P Giliker, 'A Common Law Tort of Privacy? The Challenges of Developing a Human Rights Tort' (2015) 27 *Singapore Academy of Law Journal* 761
P Sales, 'A Comparison of the Principle of Legality and Section 3 of the Human Rights Act 1998' (2009) 125 *LQR* 598
PF Scott, 'Ouster Clauses and National Security: Judicial Review of the Investigatory Powers Tribunal' [2017] *PL* 355
R Bellamy, 'The Democratic Legitimacy of International Human Rights Conventions: Political Constitutionalism and the European Convention on Human Rights' (2014) 25(4) *European Journal of International Law* 1019
R Berger, 'Doctor Bonham's Case: Statutory Construction or Constitutional Theory?' (1969) 117(4) *University of Pennsylvania Law Review* 521

R Cooke, 'The Road Ahead for the Common Law' (2004) 53(2) *International and Comparative Law Quarterly* 273
R Earle, 'A New Right to Information: Kennedy v Charity Commission' (2014) 25(6) *Entertainment Law Review* 214
R Masterman and JEK Murkens, 'Skirting Supremacy and Subordination: The Constitutional Authority of the United Kingdom Supreme Court' [2013] *PL* 800
R Masterman and S Wheatle, 'A Common Law Resurgence in Rights Protection?' [2015] *European Human Rights Law Review* 57
R Rawlings, 'The UNISON Case: A New High-Water Mark' (2018) 29(3) *Public Law Review* 190
R Williams, 'Structuring Substantive Review' [2017] *PL* 99
RA Edwards, 'Bonham's Case: The Ghost in the Constitutional Machine' (1996) 11(1) *The Denning Law Journal* 74
RB Taylor, 'The Contested Constitution: An Analysis of the Competing Models of British Constitutionalism' [2018] *PL* 500
RH Helmholz, 'Bonham's Case, Judicial Review, and the Law of Nature' (2009) 1(1) *Journal of Legal Analysis* 325
S Brown, ' Habeas Corpus – A New Chapter' [2000] *PL* 31
S Foster, 'The Rule of Law in Modern Times: Not a Priti Sight' (2021) 26(2) *Coventry Law Journal* 1
——, 'Back to You: Judicial Deference, Parliament and the Right to Die' (2019) 24(2) *Coventry Law Journal* 105
S James, 'The Political and Administrative Consequences of Judicial Review' (1996) 74 *Public Administration* 613
S Martin, 'Deference, "Fairness" and Accountability in the National Security Context' (2021) 80(2) *CLJ* 209
——, 'Declaratory Misgivings: Assisted Suicide in a post-Nicklinson Context' [2018] *PL* 209
S Payne, 'The Supreme Court and the Miller Case: More Reasons Why the UK Needs a Written Constitution' (2018) 107(4) T*he Round Table: The Commonwealth Journal of International Affairs* 441
S Sedley, 'A Bill of Rights for Britain' [1997] *European Human Rights Law Review* 458
——, 'Human Rights: A Twenty First Century Agenda' [1995] *PL* 386
S Stephenson, 'The Supreme Court's Renewed Interest in Autochthonous Constitutionalism' [2015] *PL* 394
S Wilson Stark, 'Facing Facts: Judicial Approaches to Section 4 of the Human Rights Act 1998' (2017) 133 *LQR* 631
SE Thorne, 'Dr Bonham's Case' (1938) 54 *LQR* 543
Sir J Laws, 'Is the High Court the Guardian of Fundamental Constitutional Rights?' [1993] *PL* 59
Sir P Sales, 'Rationality, Proportionality and the Development of the Law' (2013) 129 *LQR* 223
Sir P Sales, 'Rights and Fundamental Rights in English Law' (2016) 75(1) *CLJ* 86
T Endicott, 'Making Constitutional Principles into Laws' (2020) 136 *LQR* 175
T Hickman, 'The Investigatory Powers Tribunal: A Law unto Itself?' [2018] *PL* 584
T Poole, 'The Reformation of English Administrative Law' (2009) 68(1) *CLJ* 142
——, 'Back to the Future? Unearthing the Theory of Common Law Constitutionalism' (2003) 23(3) *OJLS* 435
T Sayer and CRG Murray, 'A Tale of Two Doctrines: Re-Evaluating Bifurcation in Substantive Review before the Supreme Court' [2021] *PL* 47
TRS Allan, 'Law, Democracy, and Constitutionalism: Reflections on Evans v Attorney General' (2016) 75(1) *CLJ* 38
——, 'The Constitutional Foundations of Judicial Review: Conceptual Conundrum or Interpretative Inquiry?' (2002) 61(1) *CLJ* 87
——, 'Dworkin and Dicey: The Rule of Law as Integrity' (1988) 8(2) *OJLS* 266
——, 'Legislative Supremacy and the Rule of Law: Democracy and Constitutionalism' (1985) 44(1) *CLJ* 111

TT Arvind and L Stirton, 'The Curious Origins of Judicial Review' (2017) 133 *LQR* 91

W Wade, 'Sovereignty: Revolution or Evolution' (1996) 112 *LQR* 568

WM Wiecek, 'Somerset: Lord Mansfield and the Legitimacy of Slavery in the Anglo-American World' (1974) 42 *University of Chicago Law Review* 86

Blogs and Online Articles

A Renwick, 'The Chances of Electoral Reform Revisited' (*Politics at Reading Blog*, 8 May 2015)

A Richardson, 'The Legality of Home Office Fees' (*UK Constitutional Law Association Blog*, 26 May 2021)

A Tucker, 'Parliamentary Intention, Anisminic, and the Privacy International Case (Part One)' (*UK Constitutional Law Association Blog*, 18 December 2018)

A Young, 'Human Rights Act Review: Whose Rights Are They Anyway?' (*Constitutional Law Matter Blog*, 9 February 2022)

C Forsyth, 'Privacy International Symposium – Ouster Clauses and Sovereignty' (*Administrative Law in the Common Law World Blog*, 21 November 2018)

C Gearty, 'In the Shallow End – Conor Gearty on the UK Supreme Court' (*London Review of Books*, 27 January 2022)

——, 'The Supreme Court Judges are Oiling the Democratic Machine, Not Telling it What to Produce' (*LSE Brexit Blog*, 25 September 2019)

C Lienen, 'Unison v Lord Chancellor: The Things that Landmark Constitutional Cases Are Made Of' (*UCL Constitution Unit Blog*, 28 July 2017)

DE Edlin, 'Judges and Unjust Laws: Common Law Constitutionalism and the Foundations of Judicial Review' (*University of Michigan Press*, 2008)

Electoral Reform Society, 'A System in Crisis' (1 June 2015) www.electoral-reform.org.uk/a-system-in-crisis/

I McDonald, 'Dominic Grieve and the Human Rights Act, St Hugh's College, Oxford – 13 November 2015' (*OxHRH Blog*, 24 November 2015)

J Garland and C Terry, 'The 2015 General Election: A Voting System in Crisis' (*Electoral Reform Society*, 26 July 2015) 8 www.electoral-reform.org.uk/wp-content/uploads/2017/06/2015-UK-General-Election.pdf

J Goldsworthy – 'Losing Faith in Democracy: Why Judicial Supremacy is Rising and What to do About it (*Judicial Power Project*, 9 March 2015)

J Metzer, 'Anisminic 2.0' (*UK Human Rights Blog*, 15 May 2019)

J Rozenberg, 'Judges Would Regret Human Rights Act Repeal, warns Lady Hale' *The Guardian* (14 March 2013)

M Elliott, 'The UK's (New) Bill of Rights' (*Public Law for Everyone Blog*, 22 June 2022)

——, 'A New Approach to Constitutional Adjudication? Miller II in the Supreme Court' (*Public Law for Everyone Blog*, 24 September 2019)

——, 'Common-Law Constitutionalism and Proportionality in the Supreme Court: Kennedy v The Charity Commission' (*Public Law for Everyone Blog*, 31 March 2014)

——, '1000 Words, Parliamentary Sovereignty' (*Public Law for Everyone Blog*, 15 October 2014)

N McWha, 'Coke in Dr Bonham's Case: His Meaning Revisited' (*University of Southern Queensland School of Law and Justice Blog*, 5 August 2021)

P Daly, 'Of Clarity and Context: R (Privacy International) v Investigatory Powers Tribunal [2019] UKSC 22' (*Administrative Law Matters*, 15 May 2019)

——, 'Three Aspects of Anisminic' (*Admin Law Blog*, 27 November 2018)

——, 'Wednesbury and Proportionality – Where are We Now?' (*Administrative Law Matters Blog*, 28 November 2016)

P Sandro, 'A Political Constitution, but for Whom? Citizenship Fees, Legality, and the Limits of Doctrine' (*UK Constitutional Law Association Blog*, 23 February 2022)

R Ekins, 'The Significance of the Supreme Court's Begum Judgment' (*Policy Exchange Blog*, 3 March 2021)

——, 'The High Court's Right to Rent Decision is a Travesty' (*The Spectator Blog*, 2 March 2019)
S Kaye, 'On the Complex Relationship between Political Ignorance and Democracy' (*LSE British Policy and Politics Blog*, 16 March 2015)
Sir S Laws, 'Second-Guessing Policy Choices The rule of law after the Supreme Court's UNISON judgment' (*Policy Exchange*, 15 March 2018)
T Poole, 'Understanding What Makes "Miller & Cherry" the Most Significant Judicial Statement on the Constitution in Over 200 Years' (*Prospect Magazine*, 25 September 2019)

Speeches

D Jardine, 'A Reading on the Use of Torture in the Criminal Law of England Previously to the Commonwealth: Delivered at New Inn Hall in Michaelmas Term' (1836)
Lady Hale, 'The Supreme Court: Guardian of the Constitution?' (Sultan Azlan Shah Lecture 2016, Kuala Lumpur, 9 November 2016)
——, 'UK Constitutionalism on the March?' (Constitutional and Administrative Law Bar Association Conference, 12 July 2014)
Lord Neuberger, 'Reflections on Significant Moments in the Role of the Judiciary' (Personal Support Unit Fundraising Breakfast, 16 March 2017)
——, 'The Role of Judges in Human Rights Jurisprudence: A Comparison of the Australian and UK Experience' (Supreme Court of Victoria, August 2014)
Lord Toulson, 'Fundamental Rights and the Common Law' (Keynote address given at the Fundamental Rights Conference: A Public Law Perspective, LSE, 10 October 2015)
S Braverman, 'Judicial Review Trends and Forecasts 2021: Accountability and the Constitution' (Public Law Project Conference, 19 October 2021)

Miscellaneous

Bill 117-EN 2019-21, March 2020, Explanatory Notes, Policy Background
Conservative Party Manifesto 2019
Council of Europe, European Court of Human Rights, Forty Years of Activity (1998)
Government's Response to the Judicial review Reform Consultation (CP 477, July 2021)
HM Government Transparency Report: Disruptive Powers 2018/19 (March 2020)
House of Commons Library Research Briefing, 'Employment tribunals after R (Unison) v Lord Chancellor' (5 November 2018)
International Criminal Court, Final Report, 9 December 2020 www.icc-cpi.int/itemsDocuments/201209-otp-final-report-iraq-uk-eng.pdf
JUSTICE, 'The Human Rights Bill: Briefing for the Second Reading in the House of Commons' (16 February 1998)
King's College London, Ipsos MORI and Royal Statistical Society, 'Perils of Perception Topline Results Fieldwork: 14th-18th June 2013' www.ipsos.com/sites/default/files/migrations/en-uk/files/Assets/Docs/Polls/ipsos-mori-rss-kings-perils-of-perception-topline.pdf
Labour Party's Green Paper, 'The Governance of Britain' CM 7170 (2007)
Leif Wenar, 'Negative and Positive Rights' (2015) The Stanford Encyclopaedia of Philosophy https://plato.stanford.edu/entries/rights/
Lords Select Committee, 'Report of the Select Committee on a Bill of Rights' (HL 176, 1978)
Ministry of Justice, 'Plan to Reform Human Rights Act' (Press Release, 14 December 2021)
——, 'Open Consultation, Human Rights Act Reform: A Modern Bill of Rights – Consultation', Foreword www.gov.uk/government/consultations/human-rights-act-reform-a-modern-bill-of-rights/human-rights-act-reform-a-modern-bill-of-rights-consultation
Parole Board for England and Wales, 'Annual Report and Accounts 2016/17'
Police, Crime, Sentencing and Courts Bill, '2021 Briefing for Peers – Bar Council Summary'
Protecting Human Rights in the UK: The Conservatives' Proposals for Changing Britain's Human Rights Laws

R Ekins and G Gee, 'Submission to the Joint Committee on Human Rights, 20 Years of the Human Rights Act' (Policy Exchange, 18 September 2018)
Review of Introduction of Fees in the Employment Tribunal: Consultation on Proposals for Reform (January 2017), Annex F
Rights Brought Home: The Human Rights Bill (Cm 3782, 1997)
S Lakin, 'The Moral Reading of the British Constitution' (PhD Thesis, UCL 2009)
The Constitution Unit (UCL) tracker: www.ucl.ac.uk/constitution-unit/research/parliament/changing-role-house-lords/government-defeats-house-lords
The Electoral Commission, 'Turnout – UK Parliament General Elections: 1922–2017' www.electoralcommission.org.uk/media/1167
The Independent Human Rights Act Review (December 2021)
UK Parliament, House of Lords written answer, HL1770, 19 October 2017

INDEX

A

Access to the court
- common law constitutional right 176
- *R (UNISON) v Lord Chancellor*
  - application of the reasoning in *UNISON* 37
  - breaking new ground 95
  - enforcement of rights through principle of legality 141–2
  - impact on parliamentary sovereignty 38
  - importance 34–6
  - key judgment in development of rights protection 118
  - leading case on the characteristics of rights 134–6
  - no established conceptual basis for courts' jurisdiction 138–9
  - proportionality review 158–9
  - redefinition of relationship between common law and ECHR 143
  - reliance in later case 84
- *R v Lord Chancellor, ex p Witham* 105–6
- rule of law 139

Accountability
- electoral accountability which can justify any substantive outcome 190
- features evidenced in *Begum* judgments 87
- key features of UK constitution 4–5
- on par with parliamentary sovereignty 90
- prerogative powers 73
- *R (Miller) v The Prime Minister* 67

Arbitrary detention *see* **Right to liberty**

B

Brexit
- effect of Withdrawal Agreement 4
- impact on human rights changes 120
- parliamentary sovereignty 30
- a time of significant constitutional change 1

C

Common law constitutional rights
- absence of uniform or coherent model 159
- barriers to devising a better system of constitutional rights protection
  - current relevance 190–2
  - electoral accountability can justify any substantive outcome 190
  - low voter participation 188
  - parliamentary sovereignty 187–8
  - voter preference 188–90
- contemporary rights protection
  - interaction between international and domestic law protection 117
  - key judgments 117–18
  - re-emergence of common law 119–21
  - significance of HRA changes 116–17
- development of modern rights protection – phase one
  - cases stressing comparative strength and sufficiency of the common law 105–7
  - enabling and contributing factors 107–12
  - overview of key points 14
- development of modern rights protection – phase two
  - co-existence between domestic and international law 112
  - continuing importance of common law 113–14
  - overview of key points 14
  - reasons for dominance of HRA 114–16
  - shift towards the HRA 112–13
- evolution of *Privacy International* judgments 69–70
- factors contributing to the unprincipled development of rights
  - English common law 172–5
  - overview of key points 16–17
  - reliance on the courts' inherent jurisdiction 166–7
  - uncertainty about enforceability 168
  - uncertainty around the types of sources 167–8
  - uncertainty of substantive values 167

freestanding source of law 7–8
history of rights protection
  cautionary note 97
  Dr Bonham's Case 102–4
  Entick v Carrington 98–100
  importance of rights decisions 95–6
  overview of key points 14
  Somerset v Stewart 100–2
human rights compared 8
importance of *R (UNISON) v Lord Chancellor* 34–7
inherent vulnerability 186
judge-made constitutional statutes 39
key questions 10
leading cases on the characteristics of rights
  Kennedy v Charity Commission and A v BBC 132–4
  overview of key points 129–31
  R (Guardian News) v City of Westminster Magistrates' Court 131
  R (UNISON) v Lord Chancellor 134–6
major factors that may prevent the enforcement of constitutional rights
  overview of key points 17
  parliamentary sovereignty 169–71
  principle of legality 171
  the common law 172–175
manifestation and driver of the nuanced constitution 9
nature and characteristics of rights
  historical approach of English common law 123
  inbuilt fragility 126
  independent source of law with heightened legal status 124–6
  positive and negative dimensions 126–9
  residual freedom approach 123–5
  six leading cases 129–36
protection of constitutionally important values 8
rights recognised under nuanced constitution
  abrogation by principle of legality 181
  human rights 181
  importance of historical recognition 177–8
  non-exhaustive list 176–7
  noticeable absences and restrictions 179–80
  overview of key points 17
  potential for new developments 181–2
  rights existing in basic form only 180–1
  rights with a stronger claim to domestic roots, 178–9
  uncertainty of common law principle of equality 178
shortcomings of nuanced constitution
  conflict between legal and political constitutionalism 165–6
  meaning and application of constitutional fundamentals 164–5
  overview of key points 16–17
six key characteristics
  broad conceptualisation of precedent 147–53
  enforcement of rights through principle of legality 139–42
  no established conceptual basis for courts' jurisdiction 136–9
  overview of key points 15
  proportionality review 156–9
  redefinition of relationship between common law and ECHR 142–7
  reliance on judicial reasoning from other jurisdictions 154–6
terminology 9
Comparativism 185–6
Constitution *see* **UK constitution**
Constitutional comparativism 185–6
Constitutional rights *see* **Common law constitutional rights**
Constitutional statutes
  HRA 114
  why UK constitution is not political 39–42
Constitutionalism
  three theories 5–6
  impact of Britain's EU membership 23–4
  key questions 10
  reconfiguration through expansion of executive power 3
  role of parliamentary sovereignty 23
  two competing forms
    legal constitutionalism 22
    Lord Steyn's explanation 21–2
    political constitutionalism 22

D

Deference *see* **Judicial deference**
Dr Bonham's Case 102–4

E

Entick v Carrington 98–100

EU law

development of modern rights protection 111

impact of Britain's EU membership on political constitutionalism 23–4

impact on constitutional change 1

impact on parliamentary sovereignty 48–50

European Convention on Human Rights 1950 *see* **Human rights**

Executive

accountability for prerogative powers 73

expansion of executive power 3

failure of courts to endorse parliamentary sovereignty as supreme constitutional principle 30–3

judicial deference

R (Begum) v Special Immigration Appeals Commission 74–81

signal sent by *Nicklinson* 44

reconfiguration of public law principles 2–3

theoretical perspectives 5–6

traditional constitutional struggle 185–6

why UK constitution is not a common law constitution 42–7

F

Fair trial/procedural fairness

common law constitutional right 176

limits of a common law right 41

R (Begum) v Special Immigration Appeals Commission

complexity of three appeals 74

Court of Appeal decision 76–7

facts of the case 74–5

political constitutionalist features 87–9

Supreme Court decision 77, 78–80

Free speech/freedom of expression

common law constitutional right 176

enforcement of rights through principle of legality 141

Kennedy v Charity Commission and A v BBC 132–4

not a quintessentially British right 123–4

rule of law 171

Fundamental rights *see* **Common law constitutional rights**

G

Government *see* **Executive**

H

Human rights

common law constitutional rights compared 8

contemporary rights protection

continuing uncertainty around HRA 120

re-emergence of common law 119–21

significance of HRA changes 116–17

development of modern rights protection – phase one

cases stressing comparative strength and sufficiency of the common law 105–7

enabling and contributing factors 110–12

development of modern rights protection – phase two

co-existence between domestic and international law 112

continuing importance of common law 113–14

reasons for dominance of HRA 114–16

shift towards the HRA 112–13

effect of parliamentary sovereignty 23

enforcement of rights through principle of legality 141

history of rights protection

leveraging by politicians 97

underlying ambivalence 97–8

immaturity and uncertainty embedded into system 90

impact of EU law 49–50

importance of judicial review 27

leading cases 27–8

leading cases on the characteristics of rights 129–31

positive and negative dimensions 126–7

proposals to replace HRA with Bill of Rights 1–2

recognition under nuanced constitution 181

redefinition of relationship between common law and ECHR 142–7

shift away from the political constitution 24–5

why UK constitution is not a common law constitution 43–4, 46

I

Institutional legitimacy
contemporary rights protection 122
Dr Bonham's Case 104
factors contributing to the unprincipled development of rights 173
R (Begum) v Special Immigration Appeals Commission 87, 89
R (Miller) v The Prime Minister 65–6
R (Nicklinson) v Ministry of Justice 43–44

International law *see also* **Human rights**
development of modern rights protection
co-existence between domestic and international law 112
interaction between international and domestic law protection 117
executive accountability to Parliament 73
potential impact of Brexit Withdrawal Agreement 4
shift away from the political constitution 24

J

Judicial deference
R (Begum) v Special Immigration Appeals Commission
complexity of three appeals 74
Court of Appeal decision 76–7
facts of the case 74–5
political constitutionalist features 87–9
Supreme Court decision 77–81
signal sent by *Nicklinson* 72–3

Judicial review
Dr Bonham's Case 103
how public power and individual rights are shaped 26–7
importance of *R (UNISON) v Lord Chancellor* 34–7
influence of proportionality principle 49
leading cases 27–8
ouster clauses
constitutional significance 56
exclusionary effect 4
R (Begum) v Special Immigration Appeals Commission see ***R (Begum) v Special Immigration Appeals Commission***
R (Miller) v The Prime Minister see ***R (Miller) v The Prime Minister***
R (O (A Child)) v Secretary of State for the Home Department see ***R (O (A Child)) v Secretary of State for the Home Department***
R (Privacy International) v Investigatory Powers Tribunal see ***R (Privacy International) v Investigatory Powers Tribunal***

Judiciary
failure to endorse parliamentary sovereignty as supreme constitutional principle 30–3
recognition of the concept of constitutional statutes 39–42
theoretical perspectives 5–6
traditional constitutional struggle 185–6
why UK constitution is not a common law constitution 42–7

K

Kennedy v Charity Commission and A v BBC
enforcement of rights through principle of legality 140–1
leading case on the characteristics of rights 132–4
no established conceptual basis for courts' jurisdiction 137–8
proportionality review 158
redefinition of relationship between common law and ECHR 143, 145

L

Legal comparativism 154–6, 185–6

Legal constitutionalism
competing forms of constitutionalism 22
R (Privacy International) 55–63
Miller v Prime Minister 63–9
shortcomings of nuanced constitution 165–6
the common law constitutionalist side of the spectrum 69–73
why UK constitution is not a common law constitution 42–7

Legal professional privilege 176

Legality principle *see* **Rule of law**

Legislature *see* **Parliament**

Legitimacy *see* **Institutional legitimacy**

Liberty *see* **Right to liberty**

Life *see* **Right to life**

N

Non-discrimination *see* **Right to non-discrimination**

Nuanced constitution
case studies
common themes 69–73
overview of key points 54–5

R (Begum) v Special Immigration Appeals Commission 74–81
R (Miller) v The Prime Minister 63–9
R (O (A Child)) v Secretary of State for the Home Department 81–6
R (Privacy International) v Investigatory Powers Tribunal 55–63
conceptualisation 6–7
factors contributing to the unprincipled development of rights
English common law 172–5
overview of key points 16–17
reliance on the courts' inherent jurisdiction 166–7
uncertainty about enforceability 168
uncertainty around the types of sources 167–8
uncertainty regarding substantive values 167
features evidenced in *Begum* judgments 87–9
features evidenced in *Miller* judgments 72–3
features evidenced in *Privacy International* judgments
common law constitutional rights 69–70
legal constitutionalism within parliamentary sovereignty framework 70–2
features evidenced in *R (O (A Child)) R (O (A Child)) v Secretary of State for the Home Department* 90–1
inadequacy of current theories 6–7
inbuilt fragility of common law constitutional rights 126
inherent vulnerability 186
introduction to underlying concept
as an alternative reading of UK's constitutional dynamics 25–8
inherent contestability of UK constitution 21
law can be viewed as operating on a spectrum 47–8
why UK constitution is not a common law constitution 42–7
why UK constitution not political 29–42
key thesis put forward 163
link to common law constitutional rights 9
overview of key points
case studies 12–13
introduction to underlying concept 11
shortcomings of rights protection 16–17
reasons behind qualification of parliamentary sovereignty
English common law approaches 50–3
EU law 48–50
rights recognised under nuanced constitution
abrogation by principle of legality 181
human rights 181
importance of historical recognition 177–8
non-exhaustive list 176–7
noticeable absences and restrictions 179–80
overview of key points 17
potential for new developments 181–2
rights existing in basic form only 180–1
rights with a stronger claim to domestic roots, 178–9
uncertainty of common law principle of equality 178
sum of the dynamics 5
underdeveloped rights framework
conflict between legal and political constitutionalism 165–6
meaning and application of constitutional fundamentals 164–5

O

Open justice principle
absence of guarantees 171
common law constitutional right 176
constitutional comparativism 154–5
constitutional principle 117–18
freestanding source of law 8
historical basis 49
inherent jurisdiction of courts 166
Kennedy v Charity Commission and A v BBC
enforcement of rights through principle of legality 140–1
leading case on the characteristics of rights 132–4
no established conceptual basis for courts' jurisdiction 137–8
proportionality review 158
redefinition of relationship between common law and ECHR 143, 145
leading cases on the characteristics of rights
Kennedy v Charity Commission and A v BBC 132–4, 137–43
R (Guardian News) v City of Westminster Magistrates' Court 131, 138–9

'legitimacy through longevity' 148
leading case on the characteristics of rights 131
no established conceptual basis for courts' jurisdiction 137–8
redefinition of relationship between common law and ECHR 143
reliance on judicial reasoning from other jurisdictions 155
Scott v Scott 148–9

Ouster clauses
constitutional significance 55–6
exclusion of judicial review 4
R (Privacy International) v Investigatory Powers Tribunal
authority relied on – *Anisminic* 56–7
constitutional significance 55–6
Court of Appeal judgment 59–60
Divisional Court judgment 58–9
facts of the case 57–8
questions before Supreme Court 60–3

P

Parliament
ability of House of Commons to outvote House of Lords 5
accountability 4–5
executive accountability for prerogative powers 73
failure of courts to endorse parliamentary sovereignty as supreme constitutional principle 30–3
parliamentary sovereignty *see* **Parliamentary sovereignty**
recently adopted measures with constitutional implications 3–4
reconfiguration of public law principles 2–3
theoretical perspectives 5–6
traditional constitutional struggle 185–6
why UK constitution is not a common law constitution 42–7

Parliamentary sovereignty
barrier to devising a better system of constitutional rights protection 187–8
factor that may prevent the enforcement of constitutional rights
failure of courts to endorse it as supreme constitutional principle 30–3
features evidenced in *Privacy International* judgments 70–2
hierarchy of law 23
history of rights protection 98–100
impact of constitutional statutes 41
inadequacy of current theories 5–6, 6–7
key questions 10
R (Miller) v The Prime Minister 65, 67
R (Privacy International) v Investigatory Powers Tribunal 56
reasons behind its gradual qualification
English common law approaches 50–3
EU law 48–50
relationship with rule of law 33–4

Political constitutionalism
competing forms of constitutionalism 22
features evidenced in *Begum* judgments and *R (O (A Child)) v Secretary of State for the Home Department* 87–91
impact of Britain's EU membership 23–4
shifts caused by devolution and international law 24–5
shortcomings of nuanced constitution 165–6
why UK constitution is not a common law constitution 46
why UK constitution is not political
failure to endorse parliamentary sovereignty 30–3
highly nuanced system of interpretation of public law 33–9
overview of key points 29
recognition of the concept of constitutional statutes 39–42

Positive obligations
ECHR 49–50, 127
HRA 2
nature and characteristics of rights 126–9
oral hearings 15

Precedent
adherence to 'judicial custom' 173
contemporary rights protection 119
history of rights protection
Dr Bonham's Case 102–4
Entick v Carrington 98–100
Somerset v Stewart 100–2
key characteristic of rights 147–53
nothing more than normative claims 122, 185–6
political constitutionalism 87–91

Prerogative powers
executive accountability 73
mutual legal assistance 152
need for legal certainty 153
R (Miller) v The Prime Minister
constitutional significance 63
facts of the case 64

High Court's judgment 65
Scottish proceedings 64–5
Supreme Court judgment 21, 65–9
residual common law powers 63

Privacy
common law constitutional right 176
constitutional vulnerability 183
right protected by the ECHR 133
shortcomings of nuanced constitution 174

Privilege against self-incrimination
abrogation by Terrorism Act 2000 142, 188
restrictive interpretative approach 45
right protected by the ECHR 44
right recognised under nuanced constitution 177

Proportionality review
development of modern rights protection 115–16
impact of EU law 49
importance 27
Kennedy v Charity Commission and A v BBC 158
key characteristic of rights 156–9
leading cases on the characteristics of rights
Kennedy v Charity Commission and A v BBC 132
overview of key points 129–31
R (UNISON) v Lord Chancellor 158–9

Public law 7
basic tenets of jurisprudence 7
historical approach of English common law 123
impact of EU law 49
importance of judicial review 27
importance of *R (UNISON) v Lord Chancellor* 34–7
key questions 10
reconfiguration of public law principles 2–3
relationship between rule of law and parliamentary sovereignty 33–4
typical judicial approach 6
why UK constitution is not a common law constitution 42–7

Public power
an alternative reading of UK's constitutional dynamics 25–8
basis of UK constitution 4
continuous reshaping 6–7
dependence on popular consent 167
history of rights protection
cause of shifting judicial attitudes 107–8
Entick v Carrington 98–100
judicial review 26
no uniformly recognised justification for the exercise of public power 69
redefined by statute and common law 38
residual freedom approach 124
traditional adherence to concept of residual freedoms 124
two leading theories 5–6

R

R (Begum) v Special Immigration Appeals Commission
complexity of three appeals 74
Court of Appeal decision 76–7
facts of the case 74–5
political constitutionalist features 87–9
Supreme Court decision
different natures of review 78–80
no effective right of appeal 77

R (Guardian News) v City of Westminster Magistrates' Court
leading case on the characteristics of rights 131
no established conceptual basis for courts' jurisdiction 137–8
redefinition of relationship between common law and ECHR 143
reliance on judicial reasoning from other jurisdictions 155

R (Miller) v The Prime Minister
constitutional significance 63
facts of the case 63
impact on parliamentary sovereignty 38
inherent contestability of UK constitution 21
Scottish proceedings 64–5
Supreme Court judgment 21
accountability 67
four key issues 65–6
legal limits of the power to prorogue 68–9
parliamentary sovereignty 67
preliminary observations 66
question of justiciability 66–7

R (O (A Child)) v Secretary of State for the Home Department
constitutional significance 81–2
Court of Appeal decision 84
facts of the case 82–3
features of nuanced constitution 90–1
High Court's judgment 83
Supreme Court judgment
need to ascertain the meaning of the words 85–6

reliance on *Unison* 84
statutory provision at stake 86
R (Privacy International) v Investigatory Powers Tribunal
authority relied on – *Anisminic* 56, 56–7
constitutional importance 55–6
constitutional legacy
endorsement of common law constitutionalism 184–5
far-reaching implications for understanding of constitution 183
protection of democratic rights 185
reminder of the constitutional role of the courts 182–3
Court of Appeal judgment 59–60
Divisional Court judgment 58–9
enforcement of rights through principle of legality 140
evolution of courts' constitutional role 52–3
link to *Entick v Carrington* 98–100
questions before Supreme Court 60–3
R (UNISON) v Lord Chancellor
application of the reasoning in UNISON 37
breaking of new ground 95
constitutional legacy
far-reaching implications for understanding of constitution 183
interpretation of the rule of law 183–4
protection of democratic rights 185
reminder of the constitutional role of the courts 182–3
enforcement of rights through principle of legality 141–2
impact on parliamentary sovereignty 38
importance 34–6
key judgment in development of rights protection 118
leading case on the characteristics of rights 134–6
no established conceptual basis for courts' jurisdiction 138–9
proportionality review 158–9
redefinition of relationship between common law and ECHR 143
reliance in later case 84
Representation
barriers to devising a better system of constitutional rights protection
electoral accountability which can justify any substantive outcome 190
low voter participation 188
voter preference 188–90
Bill of Rights bill 97
core rights for democratic participation 90
key feature of UK constitution 4–5
right to vote
comparative weakness 8
key case 118
no common law right 147
part of liberal democracy 183
prisoners' rights 180–1
referenda 41
restrictive interpretative approach 17, 90
'the principles of democracy and the rule of law' 65
women's franchise 174
Right not to be tortured
inadmissible evidence 167–8
restricted right 17, 180
right protected by the ECHR 8, 133
right recognised under nuanced constitution 177
Right to liberty
concept of a residual liberty 124
ECHR art 5 28
right recognised under nuanced constitution 177
Somerset v Stewart 101
supposed striving of the common law 47
uncertainty of sources 167–8
Right to life
right protected by the ECHR 43, 133
right recognised under nuanced constitution 177
scope 179
Right to non-discrimination
importance of historical recognition 177–8
right recognised under nuanced constitution 177
uncertainty of common law principle of equality 178
Right to property
Colonial Sugar Refining Company Ltd v Melbourne Harbour Trust Commissioners 125
common law constitutional right 176
Entick v Carrington 98–100
Right to vote
comparative weakness 8
key case 118
no common law right 147
part of liberal democracy 183
prisoners' rights 180–1

referenda 41
restrictive interpretative approach 17, 90
right recognised under nuanced constitution 177
'the principles of democracy and the rule of law' 65

Rights *see* **Common law constitutional rights; Human rights**

Royal prerogative *see* **Prerogative powers**

Rule of law
absence of principled, uniform constitutional philosophy 6–7
common law constitutional rights 139
Entick v Carrington 99
factor that may prevent the enforcement of constitutional rights 171–2
factors contributing to the unprincipled development of rights 167
importance of *R (UNISON) v Lord Chancellor* 34–7
inadequacy of current theories 5–6
key characteristic of rights enforcement 139–42
leading cases on the characteristics of rights
Kennedy v Charity Commission and A v BBC 134
overview of key points 129–31
R (O (A Child)) v Secretary of State for the Home Department
constitutional significance 81–2
Court of Appeal decision 84
facts of the case 82–3
features of nuanced constitution 90–1
High Court's judgment 83
Supreme Court judgment 84–6
R (Privacy International) v Investigatory Powers Tribunal 62
relationship with parliamentary sovereignty 33–4
residual freedom approach 125
UNISON's constitutional legacy 183–4

S

Self-determination 176

Self-incrimination *see* **Privilege against self-incrimination**

Somerset v Stewart 100–2

Statutory interpretation
development of modern rights protection
phase one 107–12
phase two 115
Dr Bonham's Case 102–4
importance of *R (UNISON) v Lord Chancellor* 34–7
Kennedy v Charity Commission and A v BBC 132
R (Begum) v Special Immigration Appeals Commission see ***R (Begum) v Special Immigration Appeals Commission***
R (Miller) v The Prime Minister see ***R (Miller) v The Prime Minister***
R (O (A Child)) v Secretary of State for the Home Department see ***R (O (A Child)) v Secretary of State for the Home Department***
R (Privacy International) v Investigatory Powers Tribunal see ***R (Privacy International) v Investigatory Powers Tribunal***
reasons behind qualification of parliamentary sovereignty
English common law approaches 50–3
EU law 48–50
why UK constitution is not a common law constitution 42
why UK constitution is not political 33–9

T

Theoretical perspectives
parliamentary sovereignty 23
UK constitution 5–6

Torture *see* **Right not to be tortured**

U

UK constitution
see also **Nuanced constitution**
absence of formal comprehensive entrenchment 4
amenability to change 4
emphasis on democratic representation and accountability 4–5
inherent contestability 21
legacy of *UNISON* and *Privacy International*
far-reaching implications for understanding of constitution 183
Privacy International's endorsement of common law constitutionalism 184–5
protection of democratic rights 185
reminder of the constitutional role of the courts 182–3
UNISON's interpretation of the rule of law 183–4

recently adopted measures with constitutional implications 3–4
struggle between Parliament executive and the judiciary 185–6
theoretical perspectives 5–6
why it is not political
failure to endorse parliamentary sovereignty 30–3
highly nuanced system of interpretation of public law 33–9
overview of key points 29
recognition of the concept of constitutional statutes 39–42

V
Voting *see* **Right to vote**